Big Data in the Arts and Humanities

and Humanities

Theory and Practice

T0270716

Data Analytics Applications

Series Editor: Jay Liebowitz

PUBLISHED

Actionable Intelligence for Healthcare
by Jay Liebowitz and Amanda Dawson
ISBN: 978-1-4987-6665-4

Analytics and Knowledge Management
by Suliman Hawamdeh and Hsia-Ching Chang
ISBN 978-1-1386-3026-0

Big Data Analytics in Cybersecurity
by Onur Savas and Julia Deng
ISBN: 978-1-4987-7212-9

**Big Data and Analytics Applications in Government:
Current Practices and Future Opportunities**
by Gregory Richards
ISBN: 978-1-4987-6434-6

Big Data in the Arts and Humanities: Theory and Practice
by Giovanni Schiuma and Daniela Carlucci
ISBN 978-1-4987-6585-5

Data Analytics Applications in Education
by Jan Vanthienen and Kristoff De Witte
ISBN: 978-1-4987-6927-3

Data Analytics Applications in Latin America and Emerging Economies
by Eduardo Rodriguez
ISBN: 978-1-4987-6276-2

Data Analytics for Smart Cities
by Amir Alavi and William G. Buttlar
ISBN 978-1-138-30877-0

Data-Driven Law: Data Analytics and the New Legal Services
by Edward J. Walters
ISBN 978-1-4987-6665-4

Intuition, Trust, and Analytics
by Jay Liebowitz, Joanna Paliszkiewicz, and Jerzy Gołuchowski
ISBN: 978-1-138-71912-5

**Research Analytics: Boosting University Productivity and Competitiveness
through Scientometrics**
by Francisco J. Cantú-Ortiz
ISBN: 978-1-4987-6126-0

**Sport Business Analytics: Using Data to Increase Revenue and
Improve Operational Efficiency**
by C. Keith Harrison and Scott Bukstein
ISBN: 978-1-4987-8542-6

Big Data in the Arts and Humanities

Theory and Practice

Edited by
Giovanni Schiuma
Daniela Carlucci

CRC Press
Taylor & Francis Group
Boca Raton London New York

CRC Press is an imprint of the
Taylor & Francis Group, an **informa** business

CRC Press
Taylor & Francis Group
6000 Broken Sound Parkway NW, Suite 300
Boca Raton, FL 33487-2742

First issued in paperback 2021

ISBN-13: 978-1-4987-6585-5 (hbk)
ISBN-13: 978-1-03-209546-2 (pbk)

Library of Congress Cataloging-in-Publication Data

Names: Schiuma, Giovanni, editor. | Carlucci, Daniela, editor.
Title: Big data in the arts and humanities : theory and practice / Giovanni Schiuma, Dr Daniela Carlucci.
Description: Boca Raton : Taylor & Francis, 2018. | Includes bibliographical references.
Identifiers: LCCN 2017053797 | ISBN 9781498765855 (hb : alk. paper)
Subjects: LCSH: Knowledge management. | Arts and technology. | Digital humanities. | Arts--Research--Methodology. | Humanities--Research--Methodology.
Classification: LCC HD30.2 .B545 2018 | DDC 658.4/038028557--dc23
LC record available at https://lccn.loc.gov/2017053797

Contents

Editors

Giovanni Schiuma is professor of innovation management at the University of Basilicata (Italy) and visiting professor of Arts Based Management at University of the Arts London. He is widely recognized as one of the world's leading experts in arts and business and has authored or coauthored more than 200 publications on a range of research topics particularly embracing strategic knowledge asset and intellectual capital management, strategic performance measurement and management, innovation systems, innovation management, and organizational development. He is an inspiring speaker and facilitator, with extensive research management expertise and excellent ability to coordinate complex projects and lead research teams. Giovanni holds a number of visiting professorships and research fellowship appointments with renowned international universities, and as a visiting lecturer, he regularly gives seminars, workshops, and master classes around the world.

Daniela Carlucci is an assistant professor at the University of Basilicata, Italy. She teaches business management, project management, and project evaluation and management. Her research interests focus mainly on knowledge assets management, performance measurement and management, decision support methods, and organizational development. She has been a visiting scholar at the Cranfield School of Management, visiting professor at the Tampere University of Technology, and visiting researcher at the University of Arts of London. She is author and coauthor of several publications, including chapters of books, articles, and research reports on a range of research topics. Her researches have been published in internationally recognized journals such as *Expert Systems with Applications, Production Planning and Control, Healthcare Management Science, Measuring Business Excellence, Knowledge Management Research and Practice*, and many others. She systematically carries out referee activities for international scientific journals. She is actively involved in relevant research and consultancy activities as researcher and has worked on research projects involving national organizations and institutions. Moreover, Daniela is systematically engaged in teaching activities in public and private institutions.

Contributors

Alexandra Albert is an ESRC (Economics and Social Research Council)-funded collaborative doctoral researcher at the University of Manchester and Lancaster University. Her PhD research examines approaches to citizen social science. She has just completed an internship with the United Nations Educational Scientific and Cultural Organization's Inclusive Policy Lab. Her research interests include participatory data initiatives, citizen science, big data, cultural metrics, cultural policy and inclusive development. Prior to her PhD, she worked as a social researcher for Arts Council England and The Work Foundation.

Kostas Arvanitis is a senior lecturer in museology at the University of Manchester. His research interests cross the fields of museology, archaeology, cultural heritage, and digital media. His recent work has focused on the emergence of a "data culture" in cultural organizations, digital media professionalization in museums, heritage activism through digital and social media, and collecting of spontaneous memorials.

Jo Berry, originally from Lancashire, has studied natural history illustration, illustration, graphic design, and printmaking. Exhibiting regularly and widely throughout the country and internationally, her work is highly regarded, with pieces in the Victoria & Albert Museum (V&A), Arts Council England (ACE) East Midland Collections, Nottingham University, and Zeiss, Munich. Her residencies include the Florence Trust Studios, London; the Natural History Museum, London; and Lakeside Arts Centre, Nottingham University. Her public art commissions include Millfield Sculpture Commission, Derbyshire Moorlands, Sheffield Galleries and Museums Trust, New Shetland Museum & Archives, and Blackpool Illuminations.

In 2005, she completed work at Loughborough University as an advanced research fellow, where she developed her interest in digital drawing and technology and created light drawings using laser cutting, computer software, material exploration, and light. Since then, she has continued to develop and explore her understanding of all these processes in the design and production of artwork, light work and animation for exhibition, commission, and for public art outputs.

Over the last six years, she has contributed to a number of art and science collaborations funded by Arts Council England and the Wellcome Trust, including "Brain Container" (2014), "Hijacking Natural Systems" (2011), and "Bridging the Gaps" (2012), an ESPRC-funded project at Loughborough University.

Her current research is an exploration of advanced imaging from a visual arts practitioner's perspective in collaboration with the Cell Signalling and Pharmacology Group and Molecular and Cellular Biology Group, University of Nottingham; the Natural History Museum, London; and the Centre for Cellular Imaging, Sahlgrenska Academy Gothenburg University, Chalmers and Malmo University.

Marilisa Biscione (https://www.researchgate.net/profile/Marilisa_Biscione; http://cnr-it.academia.edu/MarilisaBiscione) graduated with a degree in conservation of cultural heritage (archaeology) at Università degli Studi della Tuscia (Viterbo, Italy) and diploma of University Master, II level, in geotechnologies for archeology at Università degli Studi di Siena. She is a research fellow at IBAM-CNR (2011; 2012–2015) in location-based services for traceability of artistic mobile heritage, landscape archeology, and spatial analysis for the study of deserted medieval settlements in Basilicata.

She is a research technician at the Institute of Archaeological and Monumental Heritage of the Italian National Research Council (IBAM-CNR), seat of Potenza. Her work includes three main fields. The first regards the multidisciplinary research on landscape (from the archaeological point of view) through Global Information Systems (GIS), interpretation of remote sensing and geophysical prospecting, cartographic processing, historical cartography, and archival research; the second involves the use and the application of low-cost and noninvasive technologies for the monitoring and the surveillance of cultural heritage (location-based services for integrated and low-cost approach to theft and dispersion protection of artworks in high-risk context); the third is finalized to give a contribution to the knowledge, fruition, and promotion of the fortified architectural heritage through the integration of the Information and Communication (ICT) (Technologies and Applications).

Her participation in national and international research projects includes the following: ATHENA—Remote Sensing Science Center for Cultural Heritage; PRO-CULT—Advanced Methodological Approaches and Technologies for Protection and Security of Cultural Heritage; Ponte dell'Elce—research project on the Medieval and Early Modern complex in Ponte dell'Elce, Viterbo; Cancellara Cultural Heritage—a new life for the cultural heritage research through the cognitive framework update; and BasiliCastle: the digital Atlas of Castles in Basilicata (Southern Italy).

Maria Danese has been a researcher at IBAM-CNR since 2015. In 2010, she obtained her PhD in "Science and Methods Forum European Cities and Territories" at the University of Pisa. She carried out her researches at the IBAM-CNR, at the University of Basilicata, and at the National Center of Geocomputation in

Maynooth (Dublin, Ireland, directed by Stewart Fotheringham). Her research interests are focused on geographic information science applied to cultural heritage. In this field, she has published about 100 papers, many in international peer-reviewed journals.

Susanne Durst is associate professor (reader) in business administration at the School of Business at University of Skövde (Sweden) and professor of business administration at the Universidad del Pacífico (Peru). She is also the leader of the research group Knowledge and Innovation Management (KIM) at the School of Business at University of Skövde. Her research interests include small business management, small and medium enterprise (SME) business transfers, knowledge management, knowledge risk management, and corporate governance. She has been conducting several national and international research projects on company succession, corporate governance, and knowledge management in SMEs and public organizations. Her work has been recognized through different awards, including the Transeo Academic Award in 2012 and has been published in international peer-reviewed journals. Before joining the academia, she worked in different positions with private enterprises of different industries and size.

Cimeon Ellerton trained as a professional musician at Trinity College of Music and then the Guildhall School of Music and Drama, where he was awarded a master's degree (merit) in composition. As a professional musician, Cimeon founded the London Breakbeat Orchestra—recording two Live at Maida Vale sessions for BBC Radio 1 and collaborating with international DJs Swedish House Mafia.

Since then, Cimeon has applied his passion for engaging the public with high-quality arts through various development and management roles, with a focus on policy, strategy, and large-scale program management. Following seven years in arts development for local government, Cimeon joined The Audience Agency to build and manage Audience Finder—the insight sharing program—now the largest source of aggregated audience data and insight in the world.

Cimeon is also chair of Lewisham Education Arts Network—a charity championing arts education by empowering artist educators and those that work with them.

Helio Aisenberg Ferenhof holds a doctorate in production engineering from Universidade Federal de Santa Catarina (UFSC). He has a master's degree in knowledge management from UFSC, an MBA in e-business from FGV/RJ, and a bachelor's degree in computer science from UNESA. Currently, he holds a visiting professor position at After Graduation Program of Communication and Information Technology (PPGTIC) at the Federal University of Santa Catarina (UFSC) Campus Araranguá. He is also an associate member of the research group Knowledge and Innovation Management (KIM) at the School of Business at University of Skövde. His research areas include knowledge management, innovation, intellectual capital, project management, service management, product development, and computer science. Before joining academia, he worked as a system developer, system analyst, project manager, and consultant in different industries. In 2010, received a prize of innovation from Nancy-Université-INPL, "Prix d`innovation—à l'évenément international—48H pour faire émerger des idées" and has published in international peer-reviewed journals.

Abigail Gilmore is a senior lecturer in arts management and cultural policy at the University of Manchester. Her research concerns local cultural policy, management, evaluation, and participation. She is coinvestigator on the Arts and Humanities Research Council (AHRC) Connected Communities project, "Understanding Everyday Participation—Articulating Cultural Values." Recent projects include AHRC Research Network "Beyond the Campus: Higher Education and the Creative Economy" and the NESTA/Arts Council England/AHRC Digital R&D Fund for the Arts project, "Culture Metrics."

Fabrizio Terenzio Gizzi (https://www.researchgate.net/profile/Fabrizio_Gizzi) graduated with a degree in Geological Science at Università di Napoli Federico II (Naples, Italy). He is a researcher at the Institute of Archaeological and Monumental Heritage of the Italian National Research Council (IBAM-CNR), seat of Potenza. His research interests include two main fields. The first regards the analysis of natural and manmade risks affecting cultural heritage to identify suitable mitigation strategies, and the second involves the use and the application of low-cost and noninvasive technologies for the monitoring and the surveillance of cultural heritage. On these topics, he has published 110 papers in journals, conference proceedings, or book chapters.

He has been co-investigator responsible for the PRO_CULT project (Advanced Methodological Approaches and Technologies for Protection and Security of Cultural Heritage), investigator responsible for agreements between IBAM-CNR and research institutes (CNR-IGAG; CNR-IDAC; CUGRI, University of Salerno, Italy), and investigator responsible for an activity line in the framework of SMART BASILICATA Project.

With the project proposal "Past Memory, Future Cities and Societal Resilience," he was selected by the Humanities in the European Research Area—Joint Research Programme—Uses of the Past (HERA JRP UP) Board among 250 researchers all over Europe to attend the matchmaking event "Uses of the Past," Humanities in the European Research Area (held in Tallinn, Estonia, on January 2015). He has been invited to several congresses or seminars and he was co-convenor of international or national workshops or congresses. He is a member of the Editorial Board of *Disaster Advances* ISI journal, and he is reviewer of many international (ISI) journals covering the two main research fields of interest. He was among the finalists of the International Italian Heritage Award (Rome, October 2013) in the session "Safeguard of Archives and Historical Sources."

Richard A. Hawkins is Reader in History in the Faculty of Social Sciences' Department of History, Politics, and War Studies at the University of Wolverhampton, England. His research interests include teaching and learning, in particular, the use of digitized historical printed, audio, and audiovisual media in teaching. This research includes participation in a 2007–2008 British JISC (formerly the Joint Information Systems Committee)/HEA (The Higher Education Academy)-funded project involving the creation of history subject tutorials using resources from JISC *NewsFilm Online* (since relaunched as *MediaPlus* by ProQuest's Alexander Street company in partnership with JISC). A tutorial proposal for "The Holocaust and Genocide" was developed into three generative learning objects. This was followed by a an HEA teaching development grant funded 2009 project in which he introduced to a Level 5 undergraduate history module on Victorian Britain a student assessment, which requires the use of the British Library Nineteenth Century Newspapers digital database. His recent publications include *Historical Insights: Focus on Teaching: Digitised Newspapers* (2011), Coventry: History at the Higher Education Academy, and the article "Promoting the Digital Literacy of Undergraduate Historians Using Digitised Historic Newspapers" (2016), *Student Engagement in Higher Education Journal*, 1, no. 1: 1–6. Hawkins' research also includes nineteenth and twentieth century economic and business history. As the chapter in this book illustrates, this research has greatly benefitted from engagement with big data as it has evolved during the last two decades.

Andrea Hull is program associate for communications and development at the Smithsonian Provenance Research Initiative (SPRI). Since 2014, she has been working with SPRI to build its communications strategy, public programming, outreach, and grant development. She is an editor, producer, and social documentary filmmaker, which have required building partnerships and fundraising and have included projects that address cultural heritage issues. Her film and video work has been exhibited at the Museum of Modern Art, Anthology Film Archives, the Collective for the Living Cinema in New York, at INFOCOM in New Orleans, and at the Corcoran Gallery of Art in Washington, DC.

Gregory J. Jansen is a designer and systems engineer. He builds data repositories with new capabilities for computation and analysis. His systems support human rights and the public interest, through archives-based historical demography, open-access government records, and cultural preservation. He has a focus on creating traceable data curation workflows that connect new data or holdings to evidence, through open workflows and chains of provenance.

Martha King is an arts producer and action researcher based in Bristol, UK. She has programmed and produced a wide range of socially engaged, digital, and contemporary arts projects. Through her role as arts program producer at Knowle West Media Centre (KWMC), she has developed and delivered arts and research projects with citizens that explore data ethics, commons-based approaches, citizen-led codesign, and participatory sensing. As a producer, Martha has supported artists to create performances, exhibitions, installations, talks, workshops, and new commissions in a variety of contexts (from galleries to parks). Martha has also worked as theater and dance programmer at the Institute for Contemporary Interdisciplinary Art (ICIA, Bath), cofounder and director at The Parlour Showrooms, and cocurator of In the City Series. She is a coauthor of a paper entitled "A City in Common: A Framework to Foster Technology Innovation from the Bottom Up" produced for the Computer Human Interaction (CHI) 2017 Conference. She has also given public presentations about the Bristol Approach to Citizen Sensing/KWMC data projects at a range of conferences across the United Kingdom and Canada, including the ENoLL OpenLivingLab Days conference in Montreal (2016) and at NESTA, London.

Michael J. Kurtz is associate director of the Digital Curation Innovation Center in the College of Information Studies at the University of Maryland. He previously worked at the US National Archives and Records Administration for 37 years as a professional archivist, manager, and senior executive, retiring as assistant archivist in 2011. He received his doctoral degree in European History from Georgetown University in Washington, DC.

Dr. Kurtz has published extensively in the fields of American history and archival management. His works, among others, include "Archives Records and Training in the Age of Big Data" (coauthor) in *Advances in Librarianship-Re-Envisioning the MLIS: Perspectives on the Future of Library and Information Science Education*; The Enhanced "International Research Portal for Records Related to Nazi-Era Cultural Property" Project (IRP2): A Continuing Case Study (coauthor) in *Big Data in the Arts and Humanities: Theory and Practice* (forthcoming); "Archival Management and Administration," in *Encyclopedia of Library and Information Sciences* (Third Edition, 2010); *Managing Archival and Manuscript Repositories* (2004); and *America and the Return of Nazi Contraband: The Recovery of Europe's Cultural Treasures* (2006; paperback edition 2009).

Richard Marciano is a professor in the College of Information Studies at the University of Maryland and director of the Digital Curation Innovation Center. Prior to that, he conducted research at the San Diego Supercomputer Center at the University of San Diego for over a decade with an affiliation in the Division of Social Sciences in the Urban Studies and Planning program. His research interests center on digital preservation, sustainable archives, cyberinfrastructure, and big data.

He is currently the University of Maryland lead on a $10.5M 2013–2018 NSF/DIBBS implementation grant with the National Center for Supercomputing Applications at the University of Illinois/Urbana–Champaign called "Brown Dog." With partners from King's College London, the University of British Columbia, the Texas Advanced Computing Center, and the US National Archives and Records

Administration, he has launched a Computational Archival Science (CAS) initiative to explore the synergies between computational and archival thinking.

He holds degrees in avionics and electrical engineering, a master's and PhD in computer science from the University of Iowa, and conducted postdoctoral work in computational geography.

Nicola Masini is senior researcher and Responsible of Institute of Archaeological and Monumental Heritage of National Research Council of Italy, seat of Potenza. He is also professor of architectural restoration in the School of Architecture in Matera, director of the Italian Archaeogeophysics Mission in Peru, and visiting professor at RADI-Chinese Academy of Sciences in Beijing.

His scientific activity has been developing along two main lines of research: Earth observation sciences for archaeological research and noninvasive sensing technologies and sciences for architectural and archaeological heritage conservation and management.

He chaired several conferences and workshops (European Association of Remote Sensing Laboratories [EARSEL] 2008, 2013; International Conference on Computational Science and Its Applications 2011–2016), international training schools (European Space Agency [ESA] 2013, Consiglio Nazionale delle Ricerche [CNR] school in Pompeii 2016), and scientific sessions on sensing technologies for cultural heritage (European Geophysics Union [EGU] 2009–2016, SPIE 2007–2009). He directed several scientific missions in Peru (Nasca, Cahuachi, Pachacamac, and Machu Picchu), Colombia (the Walled City of Cartagena), and Italia (Pompeii) and codirected missions in China (Luoyang and Kaifeng in Henan) and Bolivia (Tiwanaku).

He has published extensively in the fields of remote sensing in archaeology, sensing technologies for cultural heritage conservation, and archaeological sciences. His works, among others, include 320 publications, among which are 80 papers and the books *The Ancient Nasca World:New Insights from Science and Archaeology* and *Sensing the Past: From Artifact to Historical Site*. He has been responsible for several national and international projects on cultural heritage management, among which are ByHeriNet, PRO_CULT, Athena, GeoMOP, and bilateral projects in China, Spain, and Colombia. He has received as best paper awards in several conferences and by several institutions, among which is the President's International Fellowship Initiative by Chinese Academy of Science in 2016.

Ian Milligan is an associate professor of history at the University of Waterloo, where he teaches in Canadian and digital history. His work explores how historians can use web archives, the large repositories of cultural information that the Internet archives and many other libraries have been collecting since 1996. In 2015, his book *The Historian's Macroscope* (coauthored with Shawn Graham and Scott Weingart) was published. Additionally, Milligan's 2014 book, *Rebel Youth: Young Workers, New Leftists, and Labour in Canada's Long Sixties*, was a finalist for the Sir John A.

Macdonald Prize in Canadian History, the annual award given to the best work of Canadian historical nonfiction. In 2016, Dr. Milligan was named the Canadian Society for Digital Humanities/Société canadienne des humanités numériques's recipient of the Outstanding Early Career Award.

Jane Milosch, founder and director of the Smithsonian Provenance Research Initiative at the Smithsonian Institution, oversees its World War II-era provenance research project and advises on international cultural heritage projects, provenance, and training programs. She previously served as Senior Program Officer for Art at the Smithsonian, where she directed pan-Institutional art programs and led new interdisciplinary initiatives and strategic planning efforts for the arts at the Smithsonian's eight art units. In 2014, Milosch was appointed to Germany's International "Schwabing Art Trove" Task Force as the US representative.

Her previous appointments include chief curator at the Renwick Gallery and curator at the Cedar Rapids Museum of Art in Iowa. She has also worked at the Detroit Institute of the Arts in the Department of 20th-Century Art, Decorative Arts, and Design; lived in Bologna, Italy, working for Johns Hopkins University-SAIS; and was a Fulbright Scholar in Munich, Germany, where she was managing editor for Prestel art books and art consultant to art museums, galleries, and other cultural institutions.

Her research interests include modern and contemporary art, craft, and design, especially the intersections of art, science, design, and new technology. Since 2017, Milosch has been Honorary Professor in the School of Culture & Creative Arts at the University of Glasgow.

Paul Moore joined the University of Ulster in 1999 and has since been active in the development of the creative arts/industries policy in the university. He was head of the School of Creative Arts and Technologies from 2008 to 2017 and has now been appointed as head of a new School of Communication and Media. He is a director of Ulster's Creative Industries Institute (CII). He was awarded a personal chair in 2009, becoming professor of creative technologies at the Magee campus, and was awarded a national teaching fellowship in 2014.

His research is focused on both the creative industries and the ways in which theory and practice can be brought together in research, training, and education. Most recently, he has been involved in various arts data research projects with national bodies such as NESTA in the UK. He has published widely in a range of journals/books, and his practice has been exhibited in a number of commissioned gallery exhibitions in London, Coventry, Belfast, Derry, Lough Neagh, and the National Gallery of Namibia.

He was the Ofcom Content Board member for Northern Ireland from 2007 to 2013. From 1995 to 2004, he was also a board member of the Northern Ireland Film and Television Commission and chaired the education committee that developed the seminal Wider Literacy policy document. In his spare time he is a freelance broadcaster with BBC Radio Ulster and has written and presented a range of documentaries for BBC national radio.

Beniamino Murgante presently is professor of spatial planning at the School of Engineering of the University of Basilicata. He presented his PhD thesis in "Sciences and methods for European cities and territory" at the Department of Civil Engineering of the University of Pisa, and he carried out other researches in Lyon at the Laboratory for Information System Engineering directed by Robert Laurini.

He is the author of more than 100 international publications in the field of technology applied to the city and the territory.

He is a member of the editorial boards of several international journals, of scientific committees of many national and international conferences, and of the scientific council of some national and international organizations.

He is the coprogram committee chair of the International Conference on Computational Science and Its Applications.

More information can be found on his personal web page: http://oldwww.unibas .it/utenti/murgante/Benny.html

Sabine Niederer is professor of visual methodologies and research director at the Amsterdam University of Applied Sciences, School of Digital Media and Creative Industries. There, she founded the Citizen Data Lab in 2014, which focuses on participatory data practices around social issues. In 2016, she obtained her PhD degree with the Digital Methods Initiative, the new media PhD program at the Department of Media Studies, University of Amsterdam, with a dissertation titled "Networked Content Analysis: The Case of Climate Change." During the spring semester of 2011, Sabine was a visiting scholar at the Annenberg School for Communication at the University of Pennsylvania, in Philadelphia, Pennsylvania. From 2004 until 2012, Sabine worked at the Institute of Network Cultures with director Geert Lovink, coordinating numerous publications (such as the *INC Reader Series* and *Network Notebooks*) and events such as Urban Screens, Video Vortex, Society of the Query, New Network Theory, and A Decade of Web Design. Sabine has been curator of new media arts since 2001, working for media arts events such as Impakt Festival and the Crypto Design Challenge, and she has taught courses in new media research at Utrecht University, Willem de Kooning Academy, University of Amsterdam, and the Amsterdam University of Applied Sciences. See also www.citizendatalab.org and www.digitalmethods.org.

Federica Perazzini has a PhD in English and American literature at University of Rome Sapienza, where she currently teaches English literature and English for fashion studies.

Awarded a Fulbright Fellowship in 2011, she was visiting researcher at Stanford University, where she joined Franco Moretti's research group at the Stanford

Literary Lab. Her main research interests involve the application of computational tools to literary problems and the pursuit of critical questions that would be unaddressable by more traditional close-reading methods. These include a variety of corpus-based researches that span from the lexical measurement of novelistic genres to cultural discourse analysis. In 2011, she took part in the first Italian Conference for Humanities Computing, discussing the future perspectives of the digital humanities in its relationship with literary studies. She continues to be active in the field with numerous conferences and publications, among them her pioneering dissertation on the synergies of computational criticism and literary history applied to the case study of the English gothic novel, published in two works titled *Nascita del Romanzo Gotico* and *Il Gotico @ Distanza* (2013). In the same year she was invited to present her works about the quantification of the gothic genre at The Penn State University ACL(x) Conference 2013.

Her latest research projects include the computational analysis of the emergence of modern subjectivity within the English eighteenth century field of cultural production and the publication of a study on the English fashion discourse intertwining cultural history and literature titled *Fashion Keywords* (2017).

Maria Rosaria Potenza is a research technician at the Institute of Archaeological and Monumental Heritage of National Research Council of Italy, seat of Potenza.

She is actively involved in many institute projects, and her research activity is focused on the following two main topics: (1) aerial photointerpretation and realization of cartography with topographic techniques and aerial and architectural photogrammetry; (2) retrieval and processing with computer techniques of ancient and modern cartographic data, as well as information coming from archival funds (state, regional, municipal, and private archives). Her work is particularly focused on retrieval, cataloging, archiving, managing, and postprocessing macroseismic data related to calamitous events and strong historical earthquakes, processed on GIS platforms.

She also supports teaching and editorial activities (from composition to publication) regarding scientific, technical and dissemination aspects.

She is author and coauthor of about 100 publications, including articles in international journals, chapters for national and international volumes, collaboration in volumes, and national and international conference papers.

Francesco Santarsiero has been a project research fellow in the Department of Mathematics Informatics and Economics of the University of Basilicata from 2016. He has a degree in economics from the University of Basilicata, and after some work experience at Spinach Ltd., a qualitative market research company based in London, in 2012, he came back to Italy to achieve, in 2015, his master's degree in Innovation Management at the University of Salerno. From 2016, he has been a member of the LICSI (Laboratorio per l'Innovazione, la Creatività e lo Sviluppo Imprenditoriale) working group, a Laboratory for Innovation, Creativity and Business Development in the Department of European and Mediterranean Cultures of the University of Basilicata. From the same year, he has been involved in the "Creative Lenses" Project, a four-year European project that seeks to make arts and cultural organizations more resilient and sustainable. From 2017, he has been working for the realization of a "Contamination Lab" at the University of Basilicata, a place where cross-fertilization and culture of entrepreneurship, sustainability, innovation, and makers are promoted. During his academic experience, he was involved in projects of applied research and precompetitive development for local companies and he attended IFKAD, an International Forum of Knowledge Asset Dynamics, several times. Here, he presented his scientific researches and published his academic papers in the proceedings of the conference. His research interests are mainly related to innovation and entrepreneurship, innovation management, entrepreneurial Universities, measurement and performance management, big data, and analytics.

Maria Sileo graduated with a degree with honors in geoenvironmental prospecting and monitoring at the University of Basilicata. From 2007 to 2015, she worked in IBAM-CNR through research fellows. In 2012, she earned a PhD degree in earth sciences, Scientific-Disciplinary Sector "Geo/09—Mining Earth resources and mineralogical-petrographic applications for the environment and for cultural heritage," at the Doctoral School of Earth Science XXIV, University of Basilicata. Since 2015, she has been a technologist at IBAM-CNR of Potenza. Until now, she has been participating in several national and international research projects such as "Bilateral Project IBAM-CNR and University of Cartagena: Technologies and Diagnostic Instruments and Conservation of Fortified Settlements of Cartagena de Indias," "ATHENA Project: Remote Sensing Science Center for Cultural Heritage" (financed by H2020-TWINN-2015 Program), "Bilateral Highly Relevant Project PGR00189: Remote Sensing Technologies Applied to the Management of Natural and Cultural Heritage Sites Located in Italy and Argentina. Risk Monitoring and Mitigation Strategies," "SMART BASILICATA Project," "Project PRO CULT—Theme: Innovative Techniques for Monitoring the Decay on Architectural and Monumental Heritage," as well as in several international missions, including "Italy–China International Mission—Archeogeophysics Surveys in the Archaeological Sites of Zhengzhou and Luoyang, Beijing, China" and ITACA International Mission, Perù, Bolivia. She is author and coauthor of several papers for international journals and chapters in the field of mineralogical–petrographic applications to cultural heritage and archaeogeophysics (https://www.researchgate.net/profile/Maria_Sileo).

Jeffrey Smith is the assistant registrar for collections information at the Freer|Sackler, the Smithsonian's museums of Asian Art. In addition to managing the collections' database and thesaurus, he is involved in the development and maintenance of numerous online scholarly catalogues and search sites and is currently preparing Freer|Sackler provenance data for its expression as linked data in a search portal for Asian provenance.

Carl Stevens is a senior officer in the Arts Council's Policy and Research team, where he leads on quality evaluation and assessment. Carl manages the Arts Council's Artistic and Quality Assessment program, which commissions independent peer assessments of the work produced and presented by National Portfolio Organisations. Carl also leads the development and implementation of the Arts Council's Quality Metrics framework, which combines standardized metrics with self, peer, and public review to provide arts and cultural organizations with feedback on their work. Carl's work aims to support the arts and cultural sector and the Arts Council to better understand people's perceptions of the quality and impact of their work and to provide useful information to inform organizations' creative and corporate decision-making. Carl has worked in a number of previous roles at Arts Council England, including planning officer and combined arts assessor. A keen musician, Carl has also worked in the voluntary music and carnival sectors both as a performer and project manager.

Roz Stewart-Hall has been working in the field of socially engaged arts practice since 1991. Her PhD was based on a program of action research, wherein young people were coresearchers. The research, which took place between 1997 and 2000, explored young people's uses of digital technology in informal spaces. Her thesis, completed in 2000, was entitled "Practicing Inclusivity with New Media: Young People, Digital Technology and Democratic Cultural Participation." The thesis described how the research led to a "process-generated" approach to evaluation. The approach and methodology that developed through the research, and which informs Roz Hall's ongoing practice, have been of interest internationally and have led to Roz's contribution to international debates around developing young-people-led approaches to evidencing the impact of arts activities in social contexts. Since completion of her PhD, Roz has worked for a wide range of arts organizations, developing and using creative approaches to evaluating and embedding ongoing reflection into practice. In her recent role as "critical friend" for the Tate-led Circuit program, Roz supported a team of young evaluators and staff to reflect on and make sense of the quality and impact of Circuit, as part of an action research process. At Knowle West Media Centre (KWMC), Roz supports the team to plan, develop, and explore creative approaches to evaluation and to ensure that reflective opportunities for all are embedded in project processes. This ensures a breadth and wealth of data and that qualitative evidence is generated from all activities and projects at KWMC.

Robert Warren is a research scientist at Myra Analytics focusing of the applications of machine learning and the semantic web to agricultural and logistics problems. He also consults with the Canadian Writing Research Collaboratory, an academic project making use of linked open data to advance literary historical analysis. Previously, he was chief data scientist at Kira Systems, a contract analysis firm and a senior research associate with the Big Data Institute at Dalhousie University in Halifax, Canada. He has held posts in industry, government, and academia both in North America and in Europe. He holds his PhD in computer science from the University of Waterloo and a bachelor's in computer engineering.

Bahram Hooshyar Yousefi is a senior lecturer at the School of Business at the University of Skövde (Sweden). Regarding his recent research activities, Bahram is mainly interested in developing a cognitive platform that supports the architectural/design process as a knowledge-based generative/creative discipline. His Dr.techn degree was granted by TU Wien under the supervision of Prof. William Alsop, and he is currently a member of the Knowledge and Innovation Management research group (KIM) in Skövde University.

Introduction

The Questioning of Arts and Humanities to Navigate Digital Abundance

One of the main features of the twenty-first century is what can be labeled as the datification of human life. Although data are not new and have accompanied society evolution, what is new in the new era is the exponential growth of data. Increasingly, organizations and institutions generate and capture a huge amount of information about their clients, suppliers, and operations, as well as the technology evolution and digital transformation are creating new smart products, devices, and machines that embed networked sensors. Therefore, big data represents the output of a world that is more and more digitized. Indeed, as digital technologies occupy a more and more central role in the working and everyday human life, individual and social realities are increasingly constructed and communicated through digital objects, which are progressively replacing and/or representing physical objects, even shaping new forms of virtual reality. From the use of social media and digital devices for communication and knowledge sharing, to the use and consumption of smart products and services, human life is progressively being digitized. The ever increasing digital transformation coupled with technology evolution and the development of computer computation is leading the shaping of a cyber society whose working mechanisms are grounded upon the production, deployment and exploitation of big data. As result, the notion of big data has nowadays penetrated the common lexicon. They can be simply considered as the generation and availability of an ever increasing volume, variety and velocity of data that are created by digital technologies and networks.

In some industries, those that can be labeled as data driven, big data is a fundamental value driver and defines the rules of competition, and companies, such as Amazon, Facebook, and Google, ground their business models on how to generate and best use big data. In other industries and sectors, there is still an attempt to understand the benefits that big data can bring and how to deploy and exploit the big data revolution. In general, the main advocacy to embrace big data is that it can enhance the decision-making of organizations. Big data, together with analytics and data mining, are acknowledged as key value drivers to improve products, to better understand consumer preferences and behaviors, to analyze market trends, to develop more effective adaptive strategies, to innovate business models and business operations, to improve organizational performance, and to design new and better products and services. In the arts and humanities, the notion of big data is still in its embryonic stage, and only in the last few years, arts and cultural organizations/institutions, artists, and humanists are starting to investigate, explore, and experiment the deployment and exploitation of big data as well as understand the possible forms of collaborations.

When applied in the arts and humanities, the notion of big data could resonate as dry and opposite with their very deep human-based nature. But in reality, data represent the expression of the organic and dynamic nature of the phenomena characterizing and distinguishing human creativity, activities, context, and means of operation. In this perspective, big data denotes the manifestation of the variety, velocity, and volume of human life. This view suggests that big data in the arts and humanities is not a dry notion, but rather a new way to understand and empower arts and cultural organizations and humanists in order to explore new and better paths of impacts and value creation. Arts and cultural institutions/organizations have traditionally experienced limited use of methods and tools to collect and use data, grounding their decision-making upon intuition and personal subjectivity. In addition, there has been a limited generation and gathering of vast amount of data in a systematic and coordinated manner mainly due to the complexity as well as the significant resource-based investments that this would have required. On the other hand, humanists have always worked with data focusing mainly on their granularity and veracity, i.e., trustfulness and truthfulness, rather than exploring and adopting approaches and tools for the creation and use a great abundance of data. As result, the arts and humanities present a general lack of "big data culture."

In the last years, there has been a growing interest in big data and in the understanding of the potentials that it can offer to the arts and humanities. The epistemological position that a growing volume of data combined with the ever increasing analytical and computational power can provide a basis for a more accurate and truthful understanding of phenomena has revealed to be attractive also for the arts and cultural sector as well as humanities for the opportunities and potentials that this can disclose. This is steadily nurturing debates about the generation of data in the arts and humanities, the importance of building a "big data culture" in the arts and cultural sector, the epistemological approaches in humanities, and the development of models and tools for the deployment and exploitation of big data to support strategic and operational decision of the arts and cultural organizations and institutions.

However, it is important to point out that part of the discourse around big data in the arts and humanities is not only about the need of arts and cultural organizations/institutions, artists, and humanists of embracing the big data revolution but also the needs of acknowledging the focal position and the need of the arts/humanities to fully disclose the potentials of big data. Indeed, the link between big data and the arts and humanities is a twofold relationship. On the one hand, the digital transformation and the big data culture will consistently impact and change the arts and humanities in many different ways, from how humanists and artists see and perform their practices to how arts and cultural institutions/organizations manage and assess their performance. On the other hand, digital transformation and big data need to give to the arts and humanities a central position in relation to their working mechanisms. Indeed, the arts and humanities play a fundamental role to support digital transformation, data mining, analytics, and big data computation in understanding the key problems as well as challenges of communities and society at large, shaping and communicating the relevant "story" that makes data actionable and significant to cope with sustainable value creation dynamics and growth.

The proficient and valuable use of big data needs the personal and organizational capacity of asking the right questions and in the right way. Big data is powerful only if it is generated, combined, or supported by the creation of strong narratives, organizationally and contextually framed. This means that the big data has to be "thick," i.e., not only quantitatively but most importantly qualitatively relevant. The arts/humanities are important in the age of digital transformation and big data because they dominate the knowledge domains of the creation and communication of narratives as well as meanings of human life. In other words, the arts and humanities are capable of embedding into big data the aesthetic human-based dimensions that ultimately make them relevant in order to identify, address, and solve key questions for sustainable societal, economic, and environment wealth creation. The arts and humanities are essential in order to make big data, analytics, data mining, and digital transformation significant for stakeholders.

This book intends to contribute to the extant debate about the relevance of big data by focusing on the meaning, assumptions, and applications of big data in the arts and humanities. We have organized the different contributions in three main sections: understanding big data in arts and humanities, digital humanities, and managing big data with and for arts and humanities.

Understanding Big Data in Arts and Humanities

The research interest in big data has been exponentially growing in the last few years. The chapter "Literature Review on Big Data: What Do We Know so far?" from Susan Durst, Helio Aisenberg Ferenhof, and Bahram Hooshyar Yousefi, provides an introductory background of the big data revolution and of the related growing research field by addressing some key insights in the current body of knowledge. The authors, on the basis of a literature review, focusing on publications included in the databases of Emerald, Scopus, and Web of Knowledge and related to business economics, international relations, social sciences, and operation research management, propose five thematic areas to map and understand big data. The identified themes are the following: application possibilities, challenges regarding big data, implications of big data, strategic renewal, big data frameworks, and miscellaneous.

The key insight emerging from the analysis of these five themes is that big data can be seen as a facilitator to improve processes and activities. In this light, big data in arts and humanities represents a fundamental value driver to transform how artists, arts/cultural organizations/institutions, and humanists operate as well as to disclose huge opportunities within and for the cultural sectors.

When we think about the most natural applications of big data, it is normal to refer to manufacturing operation forecasting, predictions regarding better ways to schedule flight times, or the analysis of consumer's trends, just to name few applications. Focusing on arts and humanities worlds, their connections to big data is less obvious. But there are several and creative contributions that the arts and humanities can make to the development of approaches to the effective use of "big data," and there are opportunities and challenges for transformative research in the arts and humanities disciplines offered by development in the capability to handle, exploit, and use very huge and complex data sets. The chapter "Toward a Data-Driven World: Challenges and Opportunities in Arts and Humanities" from Daniela Carlucci, Giovanni Schiuma, and Francesco Santarsiero introduces some key questions about the relationships between big data and arts and humanities. It points out that the field of big data in arts and humanities is still in its infancy and that in order to take advantage of new approaches to data collection and sophisticated data analytics, it is required to tackle significant challenges. For this reason, the adoption of a multidisciplinary engagement oriented toward the creation of "big data" culture in arts and humanities is essential.

The current big data revolution has echoed also in arts and humanities. As a result, there is a growing interest about the role and position of big data in the cultural and creative sector. In the chapter "Never Mind the Quality, Feel the Width: Big Data for Quality and Performance Evaluation in the Arts and Cultural Sector and the Case of Culture Metrics," the authors Abigail Gilmore, Kostas Arvanitis, and Alexandra Albert provide a reflection on the emerging rhetoric of big data in arts and humanities and address the important potential use of big data as a way both to assess the quantity and quality of arts and cultural initiatives and to get insights useful to drive decision-making within arts and cultural institutions/organizations. They highlight important issues related to the big data in the arts and cultural sector and pose their attention on two key concerns: the evaluation of the quality of arts experiences and the potentials of big data for "data-driven decision-making." These two fundamental questions are outlined in order to understand the potential value of big data for arts and humanities. On the one hand, the idea of adopting semiautomated or automated mechanisms to provide a possible answer to the understanding of the quality of art is very problematic. However, it is suggested that big data can offer new approaches, together with the development of specific tools, such as the Culture Counts discussed by Gilmore, Arvanitis, and Albert to solve this problem. On the other hand, it is expected that the characteristics and features of big data will shift the arts and cultural sector toward data-driven decision-making in order to deal with their strategic and operational challenges, such as, for example, audience management and development.

Big data has huge potentials of value creation and impact in arts and humanities. Scholars and practitioners are now gradually identifying and experimenting the possible areas of application as well as understanding the benefits that big data management can deliver. In this view, the chapter "Toward 'Big Data' in Museum Provenance" by Jeffrey Smith provides insights on the power that big data may have in the field of assisting the research of museum provenance. Smith points out that the questionable issue is not the relevance that big data can have and/ or its valuable impact, but rather the little actual data concerning the provenance of museum objects. This is the actual limitation related to the deployment of big data practices. This suggests the importance in the arts and humanities of finding and exploring ways to generate data particularly in the form of open data. For this reason, the author proposes adoption of the "linked open data" as the ideal format for museums to make sufficient provenance information available to enable large-scale harvesting, and, in particular, semantic data models such as the CIDOC-CRM that are acknowledged as a descriptive language for the translation of provenance into linked data. A key insight emerging from this chapter is the importance of shaping alliances between arts and humanities and computer science. In order to fully disclose the potentials and power of big data in the arts and humanities, it is essential to establish collaborations and building a common language between arts and cultural organizations and the semantic and computer science communities.

The rhetoric about the role of big data in arts and humanities needs to be balanced by the understanding of the role of arts and humanities for big data revolution. Indeed, the arts and humanities have a fundamental role to play in the era of big data and digital transformation. Paul Moore, in his chapter "From Big Data to Thick Data: Theory and Practice," argues that arts and humanities represent a fundamental facet of the big data analytics ecology because they are at the core of the extraction and articulation of the full meaning and value of big data insights. In this perspective, Moore points out that data, and the ways in which data are used, is a cultural problem, and he adds that all technologies are ultimately subject to the needs of the user as well as to the context in which they are applied. This suggests that the analysis of links of big data and the arts and humanities needs to take into account the ethnography standpoint, which requires a specific form of research methodology that the author labels as "data ethnography." This view provides a fundamental insight highlighting that big data in arts and humanities is not just a computational issue, a digital innovation, or data mining approach, but it represents, more crucially, a cultural imperative that involves how the data are used as a material to construct organizational cultural and contextual narratives. To make an impact, big data needs ethnographic narratives that have been particularly enriched by visual narratives in the form, for example, of organizational designed and relevant visual metaphors or infographics "which not only explain but frame the culture of the body they represent."

Digital Humanities

At the heart of big data and analytics resides the capacity of framing the right questions that will drive the identification and selection of the relevant material. The appropriate questions set up the right hypothesis that ultimately help to navigate the ever-increasing digital abundance. The importance of questioning and challenging the tools that humanists can use for their activities is the focal point of the chapter "Big Data and the Coming Historical Revolution: From Black Boxes to Models" by Ian Milligan and Robert Warren. Focusing on historians, the authors point out the need to move beyond the black-boxes approach and to learn new tools, methods, and scholarly frameworks in order to handle big data, analytics, and computing in order to perform their scholarly work. Acknowledging the digital revolution and the emergent field of digital humanities, i.e., the data consumption, processing, analytical and synthesis processes that are used by the scholar in order to perform their research, they highlight the fundamental importance of developing models of collaborations between computers scientists and humanists. In this perspective, they do not suggest that humanists should become computer scientists or, vice versa, that computer scientists should become humanists but that "different models of collaboration, publication, and communications are needed for the digital humanities owing to the complexity of the data, the volume of data, and the inherent miscommunications resulting from the increased exchange of data between scholars." Accordingly, digital humanists should be able to use "purpose-built programming languages" so that they can perform their analysis. In other words, digital humanists should see big data analytics not as one tool that can be used to get an answer but as an ecosystem of tools that needs to be fine-tuned, combined, integrated, and exploited in order to support the identification of a solution. This view expands the notion of data literacy, which, according to the authors, has to be more that primarily data visualization and manipulation, and actually it includes the development of new skills to enable humanists to collaborate with computer scientists. Therefore, the relationships between humanists and computer scientists cannot be reduced to an instrumental one, with humanists simply using tools provided by the computer scientists, assuming that their deployment will provide the solution to the investigated problems. This means that scholars should move their attention from specific tools to models by interrogating and challenging the tools that underlie their research activities.

The use of big data in humanistic research requires a cultural shift and the need to build awareness about the potentials that big data offers in order to extend traditional investigations, to fill gaps of knowledge, or to explore new research questions that the inaccessibility of information has usually hampered. For this reason, it is very important to create connections between those developing the digital humanities resources and the humanities academics who are the potential users. A particular interesting field of digital humanities is the use of big data in contemporary historical research. The chapter "The Use of Big Data in Historical Research" from Richard A. Hawkins provides good case examples of evidences of how historians can powerfully use big data to carry out their investigations. The digitization of huge amounts of historic primary sources and the vast amount of data that are currently produced offer great opportunities for historians who have had traditionally undertaken lengthy and expensive field trips to have access to information for their studies that nowadays are available with a click. In today's digital world, big data offers great opportunities and innovative ways for historical research. In order to exploit these potentials, historians need to adopt new research methodologies, using digital technology to filter, aggregate, and analyze data, and at the same time they need to be critical and rigorous by engaging with big data in order to avoid misuse.

In order to operate in the new era of big data and digital culture, it is fundamental for researchers from the arts and humanities to expand their techniques and tools to trace, analyze, and understand the mass amounts of content and network. In the chapter "Study of Network Content: Five Considerations for Digital Research in the Humanities" the author, Sabine Niederer, points out the fundamental importance for digital humanists of becoming aware of and even adaptive to the multiple and interconnected ways in which digital platforms and analytics produce content. A key insight of this contribution is the reflection that content is not neutral and evolves with the technicity of its medium. In particular, online content is increasingly networked, it has a dynamic nature, it changes over time, and its location can quickly move from the front page to archive. The acknowledgment of these features suggests the relevance of adopting a "networked content analysis" as a digital research approach. This means that digital humanists are challenged to develop a critical vocabulary, concepts, and visual languages for the mapping, interpretation, and representation of networked contents. Consequently, the value of big data in arts and humanities, and beyond, is strongly tied to the way data are networked and/or can potentially be networked.

Particularly, in literary studies, one of the implications of the big data revolution is the large accessibility and amount of digital texts. The mass availability of electronic text archives, along with the web-based accessibility of digital information, has brought to the attention of digital humanists' new questions and research opportunities. Federica Perazzini, in her chapter "The English Gothic Novel: Theories and Praxis of Computer-Based Macroanalysis in Literary Studies," stresses that this phenomenon is producing an epistemological shift from the traditional theory-driven inductive research to a new a data-driven deductive approach. In this light, the computer-based macroanalysis is proposed as a method to build new knowledge in the field of literary studies. It equals with the quantitative investigation of a large amount of digital content through the application of statistical tools and algorithms based upon computational linguistics. Therefore, the availability of thousands of texts offers the opportunity to run quantitative research investigations supported by tools and computational approaches that allow extracting value from big data. Although this opens up new research opportunities, at the same time, it poses challenges in relation to the critical understanding of the characteristics and properties of the tools that are deployed to exploit and make sense of the big data gathered and generated.

Managing Big Data with and for Arts and Humanities

The adoption and exploitation of big data can represent a key driver for the transformation of the cultural and creative industries. Cimeon Ellerton, in his chapter "Toward a Data Culture in the Cultural and Creative Industries," provides important insights about the role of big data for arts and cultural organizations. He points out that big data can help organizations to build resilience, while supporting creative risk taking, and the deployment of advanced analytics might support cultural democracy. In particular, the use of big data management can generate an important benefit for audience, technological, and organizational development. In this perspective, big data represents a powerful tool not only to support descriptive analysis but also most importantly to move cultural managerial understanding toward a potential predictive approach that could drastically improve the resilience of arts organizations. However, for this aim, it is fundamental that arts and cultural organizations adopt a strategic framework and a vision about the deployment and use of big data; otherwise, even the best audience, technological, and organizational development will have limited impact. For this reason, Ellerton stresses that cultural organizations and institutions should be working together in a coordinated way to use big data as an integral part of the audience development strategies.

One of the key issues in the arts and cultural sector is the management and the assessment of excellence. It is a quite difficult task to define excellence since it tends to be a subjective notion and vary with the art forms. Despite this, the understanding of how the arts and cultural organizations can pursue excellence in all they do is a question of primary importance. A possible answer to this question comes from the adoption of big data as a means to capture and report relevant information. The chapter "Arts Council England: Using Big Data to Understand the Quality of Arts and Cultural Work" from Steven illustrates the experience of the Arts Council England with the deployment of a digital big data platform in order to assess the quality of cultural experiences in England, by combining audiences' responses to a set of designed metrics with detailed metadata. This represents a very good example of how big data provides the arts and humanity with tools to address new and unsolved debated important questions. This chapter shows how the use of big data and digital technologies has huge potentials to support and inform how arts and cultural organizations operate and how they can address even difficult questions long debated in the sector, such as the evaluation of the intrinsic value of the arts and cultural activities. Indeed, big data plays a fundamental role in supporting data-driven decision-making in the arts and cultural sector, supporting and informing organizations/institutions to make more informed decisions, learn from each other through benchmarking systems, assess their impact and value creation dynamics, and more effectively communicate to and build relationships with stakeholders.

In order to extract value from big data, they need to be managed. In this light, data visualization provides a fundamental approach to visually represent a great amount of diverse, multilayered, structurally intricate, and complex data for different purposes ranging from data analysis and understanding to data communication and distribution. The chapter by Jo Berry, "Visualization of Scientific Image Data as Art Data," illustrates how big data visualization is an interesting field of potential and useful collaborations between artists and scientists. Indeed, the visualization of big data in arts–science collaborations can serve a twofold aim: on the one hand, it may provide the basis for artistic exploration and expression, and on the other hand, it can define a strategic managerial support for scientists to delve into big data, produced through ever more advanced technologies, and extract new meanings from them. This chapter shows how the visualization process can be deployed as a vehicle to create a "space" for new interactions and new responses. A key emerging message is that data visualizations offer new insights with high potentials for value creation. They can be used as an explorative and generative tool, leading to design decisions, or can be employed to analyze complex ideas and structures. Creating big data visualizations, it is important to bear in mind that images rely on cultural preferences to create persuasive representations; therefore, data visualizations are cultural sensitive and they need to be shaped taking into account their audience, users, and context.

A key issue related to the value of big data for arts and humanities is the "provenance" of information, i.e., the verification and safeguarding of data. The chapter "Museums, Archives, and Universities—Structuring Future Connections with Big Data" from Jane Milosch, Michael Kurtz, and Greg Jansen explores the integration of archival research data and user-contributed data as well as the cyberinfrastructure to generate new forms of analysis and research engagement. This chapter resulting from an interdisciplinary collaboration addresses the role of big data for historical research. It illustrates an interesting case study of an international research portal, launched in 2011 by 18 European and American cultural institutions in order to grant digital access to archival and museum collections documenting the theft of cultural property during the Holocaust. This case example shows how big data can be successfully incorporated into the arts and humanities. The authors discuss the interdisciplinary approach that provenance research requires to research, record, and securely share big data and point out that big data offers a great opportunity for sharing provenance data across disparate cataloguing systems by enabling access across varied disciplines.

Among the possible applications of big data in arts and humanities, there is the area of application of digital technologies and big data in the area of heritage management. This is an interesting and growing area of attention. The chapter "Mobile Technology to Contribute Operatively to the Safeguard of Cultural Heritage" from Fabrizio Terenzio Gizzi, Beniamino Murgante, Marilisa Biscione, Maria Danese, Maria Sileo, Maria Rosaria Potenza, and Nicola Masini illustrates the case example of SaveHer app, i.e., a mobile application designed for citizens and tourists with the main aim to protect monuments. The authors argue how this mobile application can be used by institutions in order to gather information to support heritage management.

The big data management process involves three main stages: data creation, data collection, and data analysis. In particular, data analysis determines how the data will be used and translated into action. In the context of "Smart City," the issue of data analysis poses questions regarding the level of engagement of a local community. The chapter "Artists, Data and Agency in Smart Cities," from Roz Stewart-Hall and Martha King, illustrates the case example of "The Bristol Approach to Citizen Sensing" and addresses the relevance of community agency. The authors argue that there is a link between social exclusion and digital exclusion and that "digital exclusion is likely to also lead to exclusion from the development of and access to online services, further extending the gap between those thriving and those struggling." An alternative way of working with big data, making sure that the people who have the experience of the issues and problems to be faced are engaged, is proposed. For this reason, it is suggested that artists and the use of arts can be deployed as a useful means to support the visualization and understanding of big data so that big data are really connected with "real-life" objects and people can understand big data and use them to make more informed choices and decisions.

Concluding, big data and digital technologies are still relatively underdeveloped within arts and humanities, despite that there is a growing interest to understand their extension and magnitude of adoption. This book, by exploring the meaning, properties, and applications of big data, intends to contribute to the development of the debate explaining and advocating the reasons and opportunities for arts and humanities to embrace the big data revolution as well as to delineate managerial implications to successfully shape a mutual beneficial partnership between arts and humanities and the big data and computational digital-based sciences. Using a metaphor, we see big data and arts and humanities as the rational and emotional mind. Only through their integration and effective intertwining is it possible to achieve excellence in shaping the best decision-making and expressing the best of human life.

Daniela Carlucci
Giovanni Schiuma

UNDERSTANDING BIG DATA IN ARTS AND HUMANITIES

1

Chapter 1

Literature Review on Big Data: What Do We Know So Far?

Susanne Durst, Helio Aisenberg Ferenhof, and Bahram Hooshyar Yousefi

Contents

Introduction

The term "big data" has been discussed often in recent years so it is high time for us to determine the current state of knowledge on big data and the benefits and challenges that its applications may bring to individuals, companies, or the society at large. We argue that such work will allow for greater dissemination of results across both academic research and practitioners. The determination of the body of knowledge will help to systematize research, whereas practitioners will get insights into the pros and cons of using big data, which in turn can provide the basis for improved use of big data or its first-time application, respectively. Based on a systematic review consisting of 87 papers, this chapter proposes a number of future research avenues that can be used to organize the study of big data. The future avenues and the determination of the current body of knowledge about big data are considered the main contributions of this chapter.

Next, we briefly discuss the term "big data." Then insights into the methodology are provided. After that, the results are presented. This is followed by a discussion about the possible future research opportunities. The chapter terminates with final remarks and conclusions.

Background

These days, one gets the impression that the term "big data" is on everyone's lips, yet what is usually missing is the provision of a definition of the term. Instead, it seems that "it is usually used under the assumption that the readers understand it at the intuitive level" (Vasarhelyi, Kogan, and Tuttle 2015, p. 381). In this chapter, we follow the definition by Gartner IT Glossary, which defines big data as high-volume, high-velocity and/or high-variety information assets that demand cost-effective, innovative forms of information processing that enable enhanced insight, decision-making, and process automation.

Method

We proceeded as follows. First, we developed a research plan that comprised the research questions of interest. This also involved the keywords and a set of inclusion and exclusion criteria. Second, we decided to use the research query (("Big data") OR ("bigdata")) and limited our search areas to business economics, international relations, social sciences, and operations research management science. Our inclusion criteria were empirical papers, peer reviewed, English language, and the databases Emerald, Scopus, and Web of Knowledge. We excluded gray literature and other languages than English. Additionally, we produced a "knowledge" matrix in a data sheet consisting of relevant criteria for establishing our understanding of big data. Next, one of us accessed the databases and searched them using combinations of the keyword set. We looked in the title, keywords, and abstract. The literature review included papers published until August 31, 2016, which returned 459 documents. Third, we imported the references to a reference manager software, established different database folders, and united them in a single folder. Fourth, each of us manually scanned the respective papers' abstracts and, if relevant, read more parts of the article to make sure that it fell within our scope of interest. This reduced the number of articles to a final number of 169 articles. Fifth, we composed the bibliographic portfolio for analysis. That means that we exported from the reference manager software information such as author(s), year, title, and name of the journal to a spreadsheet and added information such as research aim, research methods, and main findings. Sixth, the papers were divided among us and each of us coded the papers according to the criteria specified before. Seventh, the data were brought together in one spreadsheet. Then we all worked together and jointly identified themes for each individual entry. These discussion rounds led to a further reduction of the number of papers. At the end, 87 papers were included in the review. The final stage was devoted to the write-up of the findings.

Findings

General Observations

The oldest publication is from 2011. Since 2013, research activities have been intensified. Considering the short history of the study of big data, the majority of papers are conceptual ones. Additionally, what is striking is the number of papers that did not specify the research approach chosen. This can be deemed as not scientific and does not help the development of the field. To date, empirical research is based on case studies, interviews, and questionnaires. The application of mixed methods is seldom, the papers by Leeflang et al. (2014) and Gopaldas (2014) are exceptions to this.

We assigned the papers to the following themes: application possibilities, challenges regarding big data, implications of big data, strategic renewal, big data frameworks, and miscellaneous.

Application Possibilities

The application possibilities range from accounting audit system enhancements (Krahel and Titera 2015) to open innovation (Martinez and Walton 2014). The information extraction applications supported by big data platforms can provide practical advantages to businesses such as hotel and travel agencies (Dolnicar and Ring 2014; Xiang et al. 2015). The usage of big data oriented software/applications can optimize operational and organizational tasks differentiated by the types of information systems that exist in organizations (Chang, Hsu, and Wu 2015). The technical systems seem to be transformed from traditional operations of mass data capture (Chang, Kauffman, and Kwon 2014) and the associated data processing systems. New approaches are evolving along with the emergence of sensors, controllers, multimedia systems, and databases with advanced data analysis methods (Cheng and Chen 2014). At the same time, the progress in information technology (IT) has provided new platforms and opportunities regarding big data applications, and it appears that technology is the solution for big data processing (Ji and Cha 2014; Jiang et al. 2014; Jukić et al. 2015; Jun, Park, and Yeom 2014). Big data applications in the form of business intelligence and e-government and the associated mapping procedure are expected to have a considerable effect on the related knowledge landscape (Chae 2015). The increased use of business intelligence in the decision-making process of enterprises is expected to create a competitive advantage (Chang, Hsu, and Wu 2015; Dolnicar and Ring 2014). Russell and Bennett (2015) argue that the use of hard data provided by big data has the potential to make the soft stuff associated with human resources management (talent management) easier. Cook (2014) sees the big data movement as beneficial in policy research as it can facilitate richer description and more accurate prediction models. At the same time, it is also likely to create some benefits for causal and explanatory purposes. Goyal, Hancock, and Hatami (2012) regard the uncovering of growth opportunities and sales areas as possible outcomes of increased big data usage. Vinod (2013) described the role of big data, its impact on pricing and revenue management, and how it can be leveraged for competitive advantage by travel suppliers, online travel agencies, and travel agencies. Fulgoni and Lipsman (2014) illustrate how big data can improve marketing campaign effectiveness by orders of magnitude, and finally maximize performance. Finally, O'Leary (2013) shows how big data can contribute to an improved road infrastructure management.

Challenges Regarding Big Data

Alles (2015) discusses the possible scenarios regarding the application of big data by auditors. Taking a rather pessimistic view, the author expects that auditors' use of big data will likely not happen unless the failure to adopt big data is perceived by the audit profession as a serious threat. Focusing on auditing as well, Brown-Liburd, Issa, and Lombardi (2015) stress the behavioral implications related to information overload, irrelevant information, pattern recognition, and ambiguity potentially, which the authors consider as major limitations that auditors will have to overcome to fully realize the value of big data. Warren, Moffitt, and Byrnes (2015) summarize that "many organizations cannot apply big data techniques simply because the entities cannot overcome a limiting factor, such as lack of data (quantity), irrelevance or data from questionable sources (quality), or insufficient expertise in extracting information (accessibility)" (p. 404). Thus, the authors highlight issues that are not only limited to the accounting profession but also to all companies/professions in the process of assuming big data in their businesses. Vasarhelyi, Kogan, and Tuttle (2015) address the meaning of big data in the fields of accounting and auditing. In addition, the authors highlight the possible changes that big data will foster in the two domains. Based on these changes, the authors welcome an improvement of the individual's skill sets. Warren, Moffitt, and Byrnes (2015) highlight the possible positive implications of having access to different data types for the accounting profession. The authors underline the contribution to the quality and relevance of accounting information. Yoon, Hoogduin, and Zhang (2015) highlight the applicability of big data for sufficiency, reliability, and relevance considerations in the field of auditing. As critical challenges, the authors point to the issues of integration with traditional audit evidence, information transfer issues, and information privacy protection. In the field of marketing, Leeflang et al. (2014) see three big challenges for digital marketers, namely, (1) to generate and leverage deep customer insights; (2) to manage brand health and reputation in a marketing environment where social media plays an important role; (3) and to assess the effectiveness of digital marketing. Therefore, the authors draw attention to a reconsideration of both brand and reputation management in the digital age and the need for activities that address the measurement and assessment of digital marketing initiatives. Lemieux, Gormly, and Rowledge (2014) discuss the challenges regarding big data analysis and conclude that to tackle them, organizations need to have a sophisticated information governance approach in place. Talking about board of directors as one governance mechanism, Valentine and Stewart (2013) highlight the need for developing the directors' business technologies skills and understanding to reduce the potential the companies concerned are exposed to without these skills and understanding.

Implications of Big Data

Baym (2013) emphasizes that to master the availability of big data, organizations need to invest in expertise and skills as well as software and people recruitment in general. Alike, Bruns (2013) stresses the need for updating the analytical skills of scholars, whereas Einav and Levin (2014b) discuss the implications of new data sets for extant statistical methods. In another paper, Einav and Levin (2014a) conclude that big data will not substitute for common sense, economic theory, or the need for careful research designs. Indeed, these authors regard big data as a complement to them. Flick (2015) highlights the development and adaptation of qualitative inquiry to meet the digital trends. As possible downsides, Cook (2014) mentions the fear that in the domains of causation and explanation, the big data movement may contribute to a revival of the dominance of data availability and analysis over design, and even of the dominance of data over substantive theory, whereas Fulgoni (2013) shows that the pure availability of new and timely big data does not always lead to desired outcomes. Providing the case of point-of-sale scanner data, many marketers ended up increasing their trade deal, spending far beyond what they had originally anticipated. Newell and Marabelli (2015) call for action on the long-term societal effects of "datification" because, as the authors rightly stress, the implications of big data for individuals and wider society cannot be estimated at this time. Zhang, Yang, and Appelbaum (2015) conclude that intense research is needed to address issues such as data consistency, data integrity, data identification, data aggregation, and data confidentiality to increase the applicability of continuous auditing systems to big data.

Strategic Renewal

To master the age of digitalization, it is expected from organizations that they reconsider their current ways of doing business. Prescott (2014) provides an interesting account of how Nielsen Holdings reacted to changes in their industry brought about by advances in technology. Davenport (2013, 2014) emphasizes that when companies want to benefit from the new data economy, they must rethink how the analysis of data can create value for themselves and their customers. This rethinking should also involve Human Resource Management (HRM) activities such as the development and recruitment of data scientists (Davenport and Patil 2012). Decker (2014) highlights the availability of persons in the organizations who are recognizing the benefits that big data may have to offer and not just looking at the possible risks. Davenport, Barth, and Bean (2012) see a need for reconsidering the IT function, whereas Marchand and Peppard (2013), highlight the need for a different approach to big data and analytics projects compared to conventional IT projects. In the field of accounting, Bhimani and Willcocks (2014) observe a fundamental shift as the industry has started reassessing the potential of financial information change in this new context. Focusing on small and medium-sized enterprises (SMEs), Donnelly et al. (2015) underline the relevance of having more structured, formalized marketing analysis and planning approaches to better reach the marketing goals and for improved decision-making.

Big Data Frameworks

Lavalle et al. (2011) propose a framework for implementing an analytics-driven management and for rapid value creation. To address the issue of veracity, Lukoianova and Rubin (2013) developed a big data veracity index. Pousttchi and Hufenbach (2014) propose, among others, a role-based reference model for the value network of the future retail customer interface and marketing. Tirunillai and Tellis (2014) specified a unified framework for (1) extracting the latent dimensions of quality from user-generated content; (2) ascertaining the valence, labels, validity, importance, dynamics, and heterogeneity of those dimensions; and (3) using those dimensions for strategy analysis (e.g., brand positioning). Vera-Baquero et al. (2015) developed a model that represents both structural and behavioral aspects of business processes. James (2012) presents an analytical approach that addresses the new digital challenges to existing business models. Ji and Cha (2014) designed a basic-level prototype of a Hadoop-enabled cluster for SMEs. Demirkan and Delen (2013) propose a conceptual framework for decision support systems in the cloud. Dubey and Gunasekaran (2015) suggest a theoretical framework for education and training for a successful career in big data and business analytics. Erwin, Bond, and Jain (2015) propose a model for the meaningful interpretation of data that addresses the interplay between algorithms, data, and human beings. Finally, Goggins and Petakovic (2014) developed a contextual framework for measuring influence incorporating a relationship between social media technology platforms, individual goals for participation, and emergent small groups.

Miscellaneous

Due to the huge advancement experienced over the recent years in the field of Information and Communications Technology (ICT), different organizations have had to adapt to the associated challenges (Biesdorf, Court, and Willmott 2013; Brown-Liburd, Issa, and Lombardi 2015; Bryant and Raja 2014; Chang, Kauffman, and Kwon 2014), such as data analytics (Cao, Duan, and Li 2015; Chang, Kauffman, and Kwon 2014; Chen, Chiang, and Storey 2012; Cobb and Whitman 2015; Davenport 2014; Davenport, Barth, and Bean 2012; Gandomi and Haider 2014), data security (MacDonnell 2015; Mantelero 2014), IT governance (Bertot et al. 2014; Lemieux, Gormly, and Rowledge 2014; Tallon, Ramirez, and Short 2013; Valentine and Stewart 2013), and technology convergence (Bhimani and Willcocks 2014). Big data analytics as a facilitator of business decisions (Kwon, Lee, and Shin 2014; Williamson 2015) would be associated exclusively with specific methods to deal with the unstructured data to support both prospect decisions and value creation (Davenport 2014; Kwon, Lee, and Shin 2014; Lavalle et al. 2011). In accordance with unstructured sources, new technologies such as NoSQL databases (Sattar, Lorenzen, and Nallamaddi 2013), Hadoop (Ji and Cha 2014; Weihua et al. 2014), and MapReduce (Han, Xiang, and Liu 2014; Yang, Long, and Shi 2013) have been adapted to big data analytics. Issues such as the protection of personal data are affecting big data processing (Erickson and Rothberg 2013). Gretzel et al. (2015) underline that an information system should follow a concept of governance to ensure short- and long-term effectiveness.

Future Research Avenues

The findings clarify that there is a need to take a more rigorous research approach to the study of big data. At the outset, researchers need to provide transparency regarding their research methodology to demonstrate a rigorous and comprehensible research approach and process. We are convinced that the study of big data would benefit from the application of different worldviews to develop the field. Researchers should be open to the application of different forms of data collection. Given the fact that big data and its implications are still uncertain, researchers should also design studies that follow a longitudinal approach. This would help to see whether the application of big data will actually contribute improvements, and if yes, what kind of improvement. As big data application is borderless, future research may take advantage of multinational research settings.

The findings indicate a number of sectors that possibly benefit from big data; this suggests a need for supporting research and innovation projects aimed at realizing the expected potential of big data application. The challenge of manipulating, managing, storing, searching, and analyzing outsized volumes of data requires also large amounts of data related to operational activities, which must be organized and managed through integrated knowledge management approaches/systems. Also, the issue of protecting such a volume of often sensitive data should be considered in future research. Mindset development of people will need to go beyond IT people, which in turn addresses education and higher education institutes. Future research should also address the following: how to deal with the consequences of new data generation.

Final Remarks and Conclusion

Research to date on big data has been reviewed and assigned to the following themes: application possibilities, challenges regarding big data, implications of big data, strategic renewal, big data frameworks, and miscellaneous. This helps in organizing and constituting our understanding of the topic. Based on the findings, it can be concluded that big data and its usage has the potential to enhance many different areas, such as business management or knowledge management as well as sectors. It is sensible to assume that big data can and will be used as a facilitator for improved processes and activities in many areas. The application opportunities appear infinite and current practice shows that many organizations have already started big data initiatives, which have required organizations to change their business approaches. Nevertheless, it can also be concluded that our actual understanding of big data and its possible implications, in particular, are underdeveloped. Thus, we are still in a stage that sees big data through rose-tinted spectacles. This is understandable against the field's background but should change rather soon in order to position big data as a legitimate field of study.

Our results have implications for both theory and practice. From a theoretical point of view, this paper is positioned as a contribution to the current understanding of big data. Additionally, it offers suggestions for future research. From a practical point of view, the findings not only highlight the possible consequences of not applying big data but also offer insight into how to cope with the challenges of big data and what needs to be taken into consideration when thinking of possible consequences, respectively.

References

Alles, M. G. 2015. Drivers of the use and facilitators and obstacles of the evolution of big data by the audit profession. *Accounting Horizons* 29:439–449.

Baym, N. K. 2013. Data not seen: The uses and shortcomings of social media metrics. *First Monday* 18(10).

Bertot, J. C., U. Gorham, P. T. Jaeger, L. C. Sarin, and H. Choi. 2014. Big data, open government and e-government: Issues, policies and recommendations. *Information Polity* 19:5–16.

Bhimani, A., and L. Willcocks. 2014. Digitisation, 'big data' and the transformation of accounting information. *Accounting and Business Research* 44:469–490.

Biesdorf, S., D. Court, and P. Willmott. 2013. Big data: What's your plan? *McKinsey Quarterly* (2):40–51.

Brown-Liburd, H., H. Issa, and D. Lombardi. 2015. Behavioral implications of big data's impact on audit judgment and decision making and future research directions. *Accounting Horizons* 29:451–468.

Bruns, A. 2013. Faster than the speed of print: Reconciling 'big data' social media analysis and academic scholarship. *First Monday* 18(10).

Bryant, A., and U. Raja. 2014. In the realm of big data. *First Monday* 19(2).

Cao, G., Y. Duan, and G. Li. 2015. Linking business analytics to decision making effectiveness: A path model analysis. *IEEE Transactions on Engineering Management* 62:384–395.

Chae, B. 2015. Insights from hashtag #supplychain and Twitter analytics: Considering Twitter and Twitter data for supply chain practice and research. *International Journal of Production Economics* 165:247–259.

Chang, R. M., R. J. Kauffman, and Y. O. Kwon. 2014. Understanding the paradigm shift to computational social science in the presence of big data. *Decision Support Systems* 63:67–80.

Chang, Y. W., P. Y. Hsu, and Z. Y. Wu. 2015. Exploring managers' intention to use business intelligence: The role of motivations. *Behaviour and Information Technology* 34:273–285.

Chen, H., R. H. L. Chiang, and V. C. Storey. 2012. Business intelligence and analytics: From big data to big impact. *MIS Quarterly* 36:1165–1188.

Cheng, Y. C., and P. L. Chen. 2014. Global social media, local context: A case study of Chinese-language tweets about the 2012 presidential election in Taiwan. *Aslib Journal of Information Management* 66:342–356.

Cobb, W., and N. Whitman. 2015. Trending now: Using big data to examine public opinion of space policy. *Space Policy* 32:11–16.

Cook, T. D. 2014. Big data in research on social policy. *Journal of Policy Analysis and Management* 33:544–547.

Davenport, T. H. 2013. Analytics 3.0. *Harvard Business Review* 91:64–76.

Davenport, T. H. 2014. How strategists use "big data" to support internal business decisions, discovery and production. *Strategy & Leadership* 42:45–50.

Davenport, T. H., P. Barth, and R. Bean. 2012. How 'big data' is different. *MIT Sloan Management Review* 54:22–24.

Davenport, T. H., and D. J. Patil. 2012. Data scientist: The sexiest job of the 21st century. *Harvard Business Review* 90:70–76.

Decker, P. T. 2014. Presidential address: False choices, policy framing, and the promise of "big data." *Journal of Policy Analysis and Management* 33:252–262.

Demirkan, H., and D. Delen. 2013. Leveraging the capabilities of service-oriented decision support systems: Putting analytics and big data in cloud. *Decision Support Systems* 55:412–421.

Dolnicar, S., and A. Ring. 2014. Tourism marketing research: Past, present and future. *Annals of Tourism Research* 47:31–47.

Donnelly, C., G. Simmons, G. Armstrong, and A. Fearne. 2015. Digital loyalty card "big data" and small business marketing: Formal versus informal or complementary? *International Small Business Journal* 33:422–442.

Dubey, R., and A. Gunasekaran. 2015. Education and training for successful career in big data and business analytics. *Industrial and Commercial Training* 47:174–181.

Einav, L., and J. Levin. 2014a. The data revolution and economic analysis. *Innovation Policy and the Economy* 14:1–24.

Einav, L., and J. Levin. 2014b. Economics in the age of big data. *Science* 346:1–6.

Erickson, G. S., and H. N. Rothberg. 2013. A strategic approach to knowledge development and protection. *Service Industries Journal* 33:1402–1416.

Erwin, K., M. Bond, and A. Jain. 2015. Discovering the language of data: Personal pattern languages and the social construction of meaning from big data. *Interdisciplinary Science Reviews* 40:44–60.

Flick, U. 2015. Qualitative Inquiry-2.0 at 20? Developments, trends, and challenges for the politics of research. *Qualitative Inquiry* 21:599–608.

Fulgoni, G. 2013. Numbers, please: Big data: Friend or foe of digital advertising? Five ways marketers should use digital big data to their advantage. *Journal of Advertising Research* 53:372–376.

Fulgoni, G., and A. Lipsman. 2014. Numbers, please: Digital game changers: How social media will help usher in the era of mobile and multi-platform campaign-effectiveness measurement. *Journal of Advertising Research* 54:11–16.

Gandomi, A., and M. Haider. 2014. Beyond the hype: Big data concepts, methods, and analytics. *International Journal of Information Management* 35:137–144.

Goggins, S., and E. Petakovic. 2014. Connecting theory to social technology platforms: A framework for measuring influence in context. *American Behavioral Scientist* 58:1376–1392.

Gopaldas, A. 2014. Marketplace sentiments. *Journal of Consumer Research* 41:995–1014.

Goyal, M., M. Q. Hancock, and H. Hatami. 2012. Selling into micromarkets. *Harvard Business Review* 90:78–91.

Gretzel, U., M. Sigala, Z. Xiang, and C. Koo. 2015. Smart tourism: Foundations and developments. *Electronic Markets* 25:179–188.

Han, L., L. Xiang, and X. Liu. 2014. P Systems based on the MapReduce for the most value problem. *Journal of Information and Computational Science* 11:4697–4706.

James, R. 2012. Out of the box: The perils of professionalism in the digital age. *Business Information Review* 29:52–56.

Ji, Y. K., and B. R. Cha. 2014. Integration of hadoop cluster prototype and analysis/visualization for SMB. *Contemporary Engineering Sciences* 7:1087–1094.

Jiang, C., Z. Ding, J. Wang, and C. Yan. 2014. Big data resource service platform for the Internet financial industry. *Chinese Science Bulletin* 59:5051–5058.

Jukić, N., A. Sharma, S. Nestorov, and B. Jukić. 2015. Augmenting data warehouses with big data. *Information Systems Management* 32:200–209.

Jun, S.-P., D.-H. Park, and J. Yeom. 2014. The possibility of using search traffic information to explore consumer product attitudes and forecast consumer preference. *Technological Forecasting and Social Change* 86:237–253.

Krahel, J. P., and W. R. Titera. 2015. Consequences of big data and formalization on accounting and auditing standards. *Accounting Horizons* 29:409–422.

Kwon, O., N. Lee, and B. Shin. 2014. Data quality management, data usage experience and acquisition intention of big data analytics. *International Journal of Information Management* 34:387–394.

Lavalle, S., E. Lesser, R. Shockley, M. S. Hopkins, and N. Kruschwitz. 2011. Big data, analytics and the path from insights to value. *MIT Sloan Management Review* 52 (2):21–32.

Leeflang, P. S. H., P. C. Verhoef, P. Dahlstroem, and T. Freundt. 2014. Challenges and solutions for marketing in a digital era. *European Management Journal* 32:1–12.

Lemieux, V. L., B. Gormly, and L. Rowledge. 2014. Meeting Big Data challenges with visual analytics: The role of records management. *Records Management Journal* 24:122–141.

Lukoianova, T., and V. L. Rubin. 2013. Veracity roadmap: Is big data objective, truthful and credible? *Advances in Classification Research Online* 24:4–15.

MacDonnell, P. 2015. The European Union's proposed equality and data protection rules: An existential problem for insurers? *Economic Affairs* 35:225–239.

Mantelero, A. 2014. The future of consumer data protection in the E.U. Re-thinking the "notice and consent" paradigm in the new era of predictive analytics. *Computer Law and Security Review* 30:643–660.

Marchand, D. A., and J. Peppard. 2013. Why IT fumbles analytics. *Harvard Business Review* 91:104–112.

Martinez, M. G., and B. Walton. 2014. The wisdom of crowds: The potential of online communities as a tool for data analysis. *Technovation* 34:203–214.

Newell, S., and M. Marabelli. 2015. Strategic opportunities (and challenges) of algorithmic decision-making: A call for action on the long-term societal effects of 'datification'. *Journal of Strategic Information Systems* 24:3–14.

O'Leary, D. E. 2013. Exploiting big data from mobile device sensor-based apps: Challenges and benefits. *MIS Quarterly Executive* 12:179–187.

Patterson, T. 2013. Information integrity in the age of big data and complex information analytics systems. *EDPACS* 48:1–10.

Pousttchi, K., and Y. Hufenbach. 2014. Engineering the value network of the customer interface and marketing in the data-rich retail environment. *International Journal of Electronic Commerce* 18:17–41.

Prescott, M. E. 2014. Big data and competitive advantage at Nielsen. *Management Decision* 52:573–601.

Russell, C., and N. Bennett. 2015. Big data and talent management: Using hard data to make the soft stuff easy. *Business Horizons* 58:237–242.

Sattar, A., T. Lorenzen, and K. Nallamaddi. 2013. Incorporating NoSQL into a database course. *ACM Inroads* 4:50–53.

Tallon, P. P., R. V. Ramirez, and J. E. Short. 2013. The information artifact in IT governance: Toward a theory of information governance. *Journal of Management Information Systems* 30:141–177.

Tirunillai, S., and G. J. Tellis. 2014. Mining marketing meaning from online chatter: Strategic brand analysis of big data using latent Dirichlet allocation. *Journal of Marketing Research* 51:463–479.

Valentine, E. L. H., and G. Stewart. 2013. The emerging role of the board of directors in enterprise business technology governance. *International Journal of Disclosure and Governance* 10:346–362.

Vasarhelyi, M. A., A. Kogan, and B. M. Tuttle. 2015. Big data in accounting: An overview. *Accounting Horizons* 29:381–396.

Vera-Baquero, A., R. C. Palacios, V. Stantchev, and O. Molloy. 2015. Leveraging big-data for business process analytics. *Learning Organization* 22:215–228.

Vinod, B. 2013. Leveraging big data for competitive advantage in travel. *Journal of Revenue and Pricing Management* 12:96–100.

Warren, J. D., Jr., K. C. Moffitt, and P. Byrnes. 2015. How big data will change accounting. *Accounting Horizons* 29:397–407.

Weihua, M., Z. Hong, L. Qianmu, and X. Bin. 2014. Analysis of information management and scheduling technology in hadoop. *Journal of Digital Information Management* 12:133–138.

Williamson, B. 2015. Governing software: Networks, databases and algorithmic power in the digital governance of public education. *Learning, Media and Technology* 40:83–105.

Xiang, Z., Z. Schwartz, J. H. Gerdes, Jr., and M. Uysal. 2015. What can big data and text analytics tell us about hotel guest experience and satisfaction? *International Journal of Hospitality Management* 44:120–130.

Yang, Y., X. Long, and B. Shi. 2013. Spanning tree method for minimum communication costs in grouped virtual mapreduce cluster. *Journal of Digital Information Management* 11:213–219.

Yoon, K., L. Hoogduin, and L. Zhang. 2015. Big data as complementary audit evidence. *Accounting Horizons* 29:431–438.

Zhang, J., X. Yang, and D. Appelbaum. 2015. Toward effective big data analysis in continuous auditing. *Accounting Horizons* 29:469–476.

Chapter 2

Toward a Data-Driven World: Challenges and Opportunities in Arts and Humanities

Daniela Carlucci, Giovanni Schiuma,
and Francesco Santarsiero

Contents

Introduction

A huge amount of data are being generated every day, and they are being collected, searched, and shared. We are seeing the "datafication" of our world. There are several applications of datafication of our work and personal lives, e.g., datafication of social media (e.g., Twitter datafying our thoughts, Linkedin datafying our work life, Facebook datafying our friends network), datafication of personal lives (e.g., online shopping patterns, check-ins, and streaming movies), datafication of business processes (e.g., Internet of Things and artificial intelligence).

The rise of such a massive quantity of heterogeneous, structured, and unstructured data—labeled as big data—combined with the technological and digital transformation trends, is rapidly changing the whole social and economic scene.

Several private and public organizations and institutions are still evaluating whether there is value in using big data, while others have already taken the plunge and are experimenting with the benefits of the digital transformation of their products, services, and operations. According to a recent survey by Gartner, Inc. (2016), big data investments continue to rise but are showing signs of contracting. The survey revealed that 48% of companies have invested in big data in 2016, up 3% from 2015. However, those who plan to invest in big data within the next two years fell from 31% to 25% in 2016. The survey reveals that organizations typically have multiple goals for big data initiatives, such as understanding and targeting customers, enhancing the customer experience, streamlining existing processes, achieving more targeted marketing, and reducing costs. However, the understanding of the value of big data continues to remain a challenge. Further, practical challenges, including funding and return on investment and skills, continue to remain at the forefront for a number of different companies that are adopting big data.

Despite it remains still uncertain whether and how big data will bring benefits to organizations/institutions, they are more and more permeating, even if with different intensities and speeds, all the sectors of human life. Banking and securities, communication, media and entertainment, healthcare providers, education, manufacturing and natural resources government, insurance, retail and wholesale trade, transportation, energy, and utilities are different categories of industry whose players are just testing "waters" or are creating products/services that will utilize big data.

Of course, the generation and exploitation of such big data sets pose several challenges at different levels, e.g., technological, strategic, managerial, and organizational. The latest technologies, such as cloud computing and distributed systems, together with the last software, data mining, and analytics approaches can certainly help people and organizations to leverage all typologies of data and gain insights useful to overcome emergent challenges and exploit new value streams creations.

More widely exploiting big data by proper analytic techniques and tools can allow human society and behaviors to be investigated in greater detail than ever before and provide a platform that can help to extract meaning from a "data-driven world."

Certainly, crunching huge amounts of data sets is the norm of the technology industry; therefore, the use of big data seems more easily connected to information technology (IT) and IT-enabled sectors. What is interesting is to "discover" the broadness of use of big data, also at giants of the information and communications technology (ICT) sectors. Recently, Google has been ranked number one on Fortune's "best companies to work for" list. Google, through the practice of "people analytics," uses the power of data collection and analysis to improve the office environments in a way that makes the employees happier and more innovative. The company began using people analytics to evaluate the roles of managers through an initiative called "Project Oxygen." From that point on, data analysis has affected Google's decision-making at almost every level—from staff configuration to office environments decorations.

The fact is that the huge amount of data produced at different scales and in several contexts, for example, in workplaces or worldwide social networks, offers new opportunities and challenges in all fields, including those fields where emotion and human features are the main focus.

Handling data to obtain valuable insights for redesigning and improving work spaces through artefacts and interior design is just an example of how fields such as arts—where frequently big data in the collective imagination have a negative connotation—are increasingly overwhelmed by big data wave.

More generally, it is possible to state that the opportunities offered by these vast data resources are progressively engaging also human disciplines, for example, history, archaeology, law, and politics. These opportunities cover a significant range of subject areas, from the use of online gambling to the exploitation of data for more accurate political analysis (e.g., Obama's analytics-driven campaign), as well as the more efficient storage, management, and exploitation of data and information about history, music, archaeology, and so on.

Against these opportunities, certainly, the understanding about the fruitful development of big data in arts and humanities is at an embryonic stage. More research and applications are required to better value the creation and use of such "strong data-driven ecosystems" and to analyze the innovative potential of a data-driven approach across the full range of arts and humanities disciplines.

This chapter attempts to contribute to a better understanding of the potential of big data in arts and humanities.

About Big Data

The notion of big data is relatively recent. Even if, as highlighted by Ularu et al. (2012), the first reference to the term can be traced back to around 1970, it is from 2000s that the term has become more commonly used. Despite the rapid diffusion in common language, even now, the definition of big data is almost vague and evolving since it originates from different disciplinary contributions. In fact, the term "big data" itself has disputed origins (Lohr, 2013).

The *Oxford English Dictionary* defines big data as "data of a very large size, typically to the extent that its manipulation and management present significant logistical challenges." Therefore, the "big" connotation is linked not just to a certain number of terabytes but also to the interconnected nature of these data. Indeed, as underlined by Boyd and Crawford (2011), "big data is not notable because of its size, but because of its relationality to other data." Big data is "fundamentally networked" and challenges in processing are linked with its interconnected nature. A useful characterization of big data is based on the distinction of three main features as follows: the "three V's," i.e. volume, velocity, and variety. Volume refers to the quantity of data that an organization manages to collect (Ularu et al., 2012). Nowadays, the volume of data is growing exponentially as the result of the progressive digitalization of the world. An abundance of data is continually generated by machines, networks, and human interactions through social media.

Variety refers to the multiple types of data that compose big data in general (Ularu et al., 2012). In the past, there was a great focus on structured data that fits into tables or relational databases. But nowadays, most of the data are unstructured. Indeed, it is estimated that 80% of the world's data are now unstructured and therefore can't easily be put into tables (Marr, 2016). Advances in technologies are supporting the possibility and capacity of connecting, integrating, and combining different types of data (structured and unstructured), including messages, social media conversations, photos, sensor data, video, or voice recordings, by bringing them together and also by giving them a more traditional and structured format (Marr, 2016). However, in the light of the great variety of big data, it is necessary to support significant improvements in the management of data sets, in terms of software innovation and capacity building (Chen et al., 2012).

Velocity is about how fast data can be collected and then processed (Ularu et al., 2012). It deals with the speed at which data are generated (which is becoming real time with the adoption of sensors that track human life and machine activities) and the speed at which data can be transferred and moved around. The flow of data is becoming increasingly massive and continuous and the speed at which data are gathered is continuously growing. This poses some challenges for analysts who are flooded by data and information and need to find ways to handle them taking into account the limitations of processing time or capabilities. The fast progress in technology and software innovation, as well as the reduction of costs for accessing IT support, is contributing to fix these challenges.

Some scholars have pointed out a further key characteristic of big data: veracity (Marr, 2016; Ularu et al., 2012). It is about the "reliability" of data, the level of accuracy and truthfulness with which the data reflect reality. With many forms of big data, quality and accuracy are less controllable. However, it is extremely important that the data gathered are as complete and as close to the truth as possible (Kwon et al., 2014).

Finally, there is another key feature of big data to take into account, i.e., the value of big data. This represents a key debated characteristic of big data: the understanding of how to define and assess the value of big data. The availability of big data can be interesting and somehow exciting, but they become relevant only if it is possible to account its value. This is a central issue in order to motivate investments into big data management, particularly for those data initiatives that require investments and for which it is essential to understand the costs and benefits related to these initiatives.

Although the characterization of big data through the "V's" attributes is common and powerful in order to address the main properties of big data, software vendors don't describe big data by referring to "V's," but rather they prefer to focus on the intensive use of technology connected to the origin and use of these data. For example, Dijcks (2012), from Oracle, argues that big data is the derivation of value from traditional relational database-driven business decision-making, augmented with new sources of unstructured data, such as social media, network, image data, and so on. Such new sources include blogs, social media, sensor networks, image data, and other forms of data that vary in size, structure, format, and other factors.

Ward and Barker (2013), analyzing the different definitions of big data provided by experts, conclude that there are three points of similarity among the various definitions of big data: (a) size: the volume of the data sets is a critical factor; (b) complexity: the structure, behavior, and permutations of the data sets are critical factors; and (c) technologies: the tools and techniques that are used to process a sizable or complex data set are critical factors.

What is clear is that the notion of big data has a multidisciplinary connotation. In addition, significant results from big data arise when there is the right exploitation of technological knowledge and data management and computation skills as well as of social scientists' knowledge.

Riding the Big Data Wave in Arts and Humanities

Opportunities

Recently, it is becoming increasingly clear that the arts and humanities can significantly contribute to the development of approaches to the use of big data. An area of well-developed collaboration is the one of visualization and representation of big data, in which case the deployment of creative ways to translate data into meaningful, inspiring, and useful metaphors and/or representations capable of telling a "story" that are capable of engaging data users is essential (Arts and Humanities Research Council, 2014). On the other hand, it is also becoming more and more clear that there are great opportunities for research in the arts and humanities offered by the progress in the capacity to develop, exploit, and reuse very large and complex data and to link together huge and various forms of data in more and more sophisticated ways (Arts and Humanities Research Council, 2014).

Thus, several opportunities can rise from when the "diversified and original world" of arts and humanities meets the "more technological world" of big data.

A first obvious opportunity regards the easier access to data and information in digital form. In humanities, there are data "born digital," e.g., data produced through social media, and data "digitized," obtained through mass digitization process. The mass digitization process is rapidly spreading and several projects have been undertaken. An example of a mass digitization project is the online database

Delpher. "Delpher is a website providing full-text Dutch-language digitized historical newspapers, books, journals and copy sheets for radio news broadcasts. The material is provided by libraries, museums and other heritage institutions. Delpher is freely available and includes about 1 million newspapers, 180,000 books and 1.5 million journal pages" (Wikipedia, 2016). A further example of massive cultural digital objects is the millions of books scanned by Google and the ones produced by numerous other digitization initiatives (Jacquesson, 2010). And indeed, for several years, under the "tent" of "digital humanities," computer science and the humanities have been engaged in a deep conversation. Digital humanities regroup computational approaches of humanities research problems and critical reflections of the effects of digital technologies on culture and knowledge (Schreibman et al. 2008).

Moving to the wider world of arts and cultural industries, a further domain of opportunities concerns the use of big data and big data analytics to shape consumer behavior and to make better decisions about several issues such as the development of audience engagement, the nurturing of long-term relationships with stakeholders, what products/services to market, and so on. As argued by Sashi (2012), big data and big data analytics can foster audience engagement and reinforce relationships with consumers in the long-term. This is extremely important since nowadays more and more customers participate in the creation and production of products/services and desire finding their values in what they consume. Professionals in theaters, museums, and other creative and cultural organizations have recognized the advantages of nurturing long-term relationships with their customers and enhancing audience loyalty. In such a perspective, exploiting information generated by audience is strategic.

Focusing on museums, there are several recent cases showing experiences with big data and analytics. At Cooper Hewitt, Smithsonian Design Museum, for example, the launch of an innovative interactive pen brought about a deluge of generated visitor data with hundreds of thousands of visitors and millions of collected objects, prompting explorations into data warehousing and visualization to develop a deeper understanding of its visitors (Judge et al., 2017; Walter, 2016). Certainly, digital media can facilitate customers' participation and engagement and spur a wave of brand and reputation management around a cultural event or a cultural organization (Tsimonis and Dimitriadis, 2014) and the availability of vast amount of data resources can only amplify the power of digital media.

In short, big data, connectivity, digitization, and digital transformation can tremendously contribute to increase consumers' participation in creative/cultural events and to provide a cognitive platform for analyzing consumers' needs, perceptions, feelings, and wants, thus providing useful insights to reorient value propositions and managerial practices of cultural organizations. Additionally, information from big data is extremely useful also for planning and implementing effective cultural policies. In fact, the predictive power of a big data approach can help to address the needs and wants of creative and cultural consumers and to better allocate public resources.

A further way through which big data can be fruitfully exploited in the arts and cultural activities and humanities fields regards the opportunity for measuring the created economic and cultural value.

Nowadays, in creative and cultural settings, great attention is paid to the identification and use of quantifiable indicators, about, for example, audience attendance, revenues, funds and sponsors attracted, and so on. The phenomenon of digitization is enabling the collection of a huge amount of data regarding audience and performances of services provided, by making possible the generation of adequate metrics. In such a perspective, some pioneering open-access initiatives suggest that digital image metadata, using Web 2.0 tools, allow tracking and analyzing how audiences are integrating data, information, and knowledge about museum artworks (Bray, 2009).

A further domain of opportunities, closely connected to the domain previously described, concerns the creation of new types of interfaces and visualizations, for example, through digital arts that able to reconnect arts and other fields such as sciences.

Contrary to what one might think, many artists have actively engaged with big data and technology. Through big data, potentially any language such as texts, sounds, images, etc., can be codified in binary codes and handled by means of more or less sophisticated computers.

Big data offers artists great opportunities for visualizing, interpreting, and matching virtual and real life and thus generating fresh and unpredictable meanings or new approaches to play with data. These opportunities can involve designers, musicians, visual artists, and a plethora of transdisciplinary professionals who work in more traditional fields, e.g., medicine, geology, finance, and so on. Proper visualization of data can allow extracting meaning or communicating more effectively and therefore generating value for different purposes. For example, big data visualization often is used to help business users to mash up different data sources to create custom analytical views. Among others, the human genome and omics research is one of the most promising medical and health areas where big data and their accurate analysis are critical (Liang and Kelemen, 2016). Nowadays, research on the topic is attempting to demonstrate how the adaptive advanced computational analytical tools could be utilized for transforming millions of data points into predictions and diagnostics for precision medicine and personalized healthcare with better patient outcomes (Liang and Kelemen, 2016). For this purpose, high-level performance hardware and software, including visualization tools able to analyze the data from various resources, including genomic laboratory and hospital patient information systems, are under investigation.

Clearly, big data visualization is not as easy as the ones for traditional small data sets. Big data are high-volume, high-velocity, and/or high-variety data sets that require new forms of processing to enable enhanced process optimization, insight discovery, and decision-making (Fang et al., 2015). The challenges of big data lie in data capture, storage, analysis, sharing, searching, and visualization. The use of arts can help to deal with these challenges by enhancing the human visual system's ability to see patterns, trends, and correlations hidden in complex and huge data sets. Today's data visualization tools (e.g., infographics; bar charts; pie charts—better known as Camembert or Donut Chart; lines; bubbles; scatter graphs; and so on) go beyond the standard charts and graphs used in Excel and allow displaying data in a more sophisticated way. These tools seek for making visually attractive and understandable the so-called "datascapes." Arts represent a means to enrich the power of data visualization. There are experts, such as "data artists," who use arts as a new medium for enriching visualization. A data artist is a "specialist" responsible for delivering fresh insights from data in order to help an organization to meet its communication goals. He/she creates graphs, charts, infographics, and other visual tools that help people to understand complex data. *The New York Times* recently reported the case of Daniel Kohn, a painter who spent approximately a year at the Albert Einstein School of Medicine teaching geneticists how to better represent their digital data in more intuitive ways.

Digital fabrication is a further example of how a binary sequence codifying a vast amount of data can be transformed into tangible objects. This application entails valuable promises both in productive and artistic fields, e.g., creation of objects on demand or new space–time dimensions for artists to generate ideas. In short, the current explosion of digital data flows requires new ways for these data and information to be visualized. The effective storage, retrieval, management, and exploitation of these data are still an emerging field and offer work for evaluation and analysis experts as well as for artists, calling also new forms of artistic creation. In fact, nowadays, "many artists use as material for art the raw data produced by our societies, seeking innovative means of display or transforming it into a work of art" (Grugier, 2016). In doing so, they generate the so-labeled "data art," also identified as information art or informatism. As argued by Grugier (2016), "the objective of data art is to create aesthetic forms and artistic works from the digital nature of the data generated from big data (graphics, simulations, worksheets, statistics, and so on). Any virtual data produced by our environment can be transformed into images, objects or sounds. Data art also presents the underlying links that exist between the ubiquitous algorithms in our lives—figures from databases, raw data, data collected by search engines, calculations and statistics (geographical, political, climatic, financial) and artistic creation."

Some "data art" examples include Flight Patterns: a data art classic visualizing air traffic; a material representation of worldwide communication, made by the pioneer of data art, Aaron Koblin, the Opera Packet Garden; a project depicting people movements on the web portrayed as incredible engineered gardens; and American Varietal, by Jason Salavon, which offers a creative view of American ethnic plurality. Often, these artworks provide a critical look of our society.

In summary, if on the one hand, big data can inspire new paths of development in the arts and humanities fields, on the other hand, the arts and humanities can significantly contribute to the effective exploitation and extraction of meaning from big data in several settings, e.g., business, health care, social life, and so on.

Challenges

Working with any kind of data entails some drawbacks such as privacy and trust, as well as intellectual property and copyright. This is particularly true in the arts and humanities fields.

One of the main social challenges and potential unplanned negative consequences of the rise of big data is related to privacy. Actually, the privacy issue poses a trade-off for consumers and organizations. Sharing more and more information about individuals with organizations and providers allows enhancing customization and driving consumers' choice. On the other hand, consumers want to avoid misuse of the information they pass along to others and the sharing of information revealing an individual's identity. This regards also organizations operating in the arts and cultural fields.

A further important issue regarding a meaningful engaging with data and information on such a large scale is the development of new tools and methods. Nowadays, the capacity to deal with different forms of physical and virtual materials, spanning wide geographical and temporal scales and combining data from different sources, is required. In humanities, analysis of multiple terabytes of heterogeneous data still creates technical and methodological problems. In fact, in the humanities, the problem is that, generally, it is necessary to deal with data from multiple sources, which are all different. The challenge of harmonizing and comparing those data is certainly an area where big data techniques can help (Doorn, 2016). In such a prospect, there is an emerging need for training and skills capacity building in humanities and social sciences.

However, technology development is not enough to meaningfully deal with massive streams of data. Information from data can be more valuable if built on a multidisciplinary approach that involves experts from different fields. As stated by Levi (2013), "humanities and sciences have a lot to learn from each other, and such dialogue will enrich our understanding of the notion of "humanities 'big data'" (p. 35). According to the scholar, humanities have always had "big data." Talking about historians, "what sciences can learn from historians [...] is that sometimes data spread all over the globe are too big to be interpreted or tamed even with 'hard,' computational methods [...] Conversely, humanities scholars have a lot to learn from scientists humanist [...] need to adopt science's exuberant approach to collaborating, sharing data and practices. They also need to learn to look more at the network level, rather than individual stories, and to interweave online data (data that already are 'big data') [...] Finally, humanities scholars need also to embrace and promote technologies that can help bring to light the 'big data' already inherent in humanities" (pp. 35–36).

Additionally, dealing with big data poses some methodological challenges for the nature and purpose of arts and humanities. The rise of big data calls for a new scientific paradigm called "data-driven science" (Kitchin and Dodge, 2014). The focus on discovering hidden or latent pattern in big data seems to imply a renaissance of inductive approach and a sort of return to empiricism. According to Kitchin and Dodge (2014), social sciences and humanities can only benefit from this new approach to attain more breadth, depth, and reliability in current understanding of human behavior. In this regard, Peter Doorn (2016), director at Data Archiving and Networked Services in the Netherlands, has argued that the analysis of big volumes of data opens up new paths of research and makes it possible to answer questions that were previously unanswerable. In fact, what matters in order to drive more value out from the analysis of big data is the issue of starting with the right questions to be answered. As stated by David Thornewill, EVP, IT, Global Business Services at Deutsche Post DHL Group, the hardest thing about big data isn't so much about the manipulation of data itself, rather it is coming up with the right question, and sourcing the right data that can answer that question (Joshi, 2016).

Finally, it is interesting to underline that data are never given, but taken and transformed (Kaplan, 2015). Focusing on the processing pipeline of mass book digitization projects, Kaplan (2015) stresses that "physical books must be transformed into images (digitization step) that are then transformed into texts (transcription step), on which various pattern can be detected (pattern recognition step like text mining or n-gram approaches) or inferred (simulation step) while being preserved and curated for future research (preservation step). This way of presenting the research challenge insists on the fact that data are never given, but taken and transformed" (p. 3). In such a process, a key issue is the data source and data quality, and not just the volume.

Conclusions

Why is big data an important matter for the arts and humanities fields? Can big data work for the traditional goals of arts and humanities or will it create new goals and methods for humanities scholars and arts players in the digital age? Can arts and humanities enrich the informative power of big data? How can technological tools enable the conversation between big data and arts and humanities?

If we consider issues such as predictions regarding better ways to schedule flight times; to design food products or to target goods and services; to analyze matters such as climate change, musical trends, or social changes; and so on, the usefulness of big data and its analytics is almost clear.

Focusing on humanities or arts worlds, their connection to big data is less obvious. Probably this is due to a peculiar trait of these disciplines well underlined by professor Barry C. Smith (2016), director of the Institute of Philosophy and the Leadership Fellow for the AHRC Science in Culture Theme in his post "Big Data in the Humanities: The Need for Big Question." These disciplines concentrate on small-scale objects and their peculiarities, like people, places, and things, often studied not in abstract but in their historical context. Arts and humanities deal with acts and art works that stand in need of interpretation in the absence of well-structured information. However, the progress in data visualization and the diffusion of the digitization of "not born digital" data (e.g., related to historical archives, books and newspapers, and archaeological sites), as well as datafication, offers new interesting opportunities for extracting information and knowledge and discovering unexpected patterns of convergence of key issues events hidden in massive and heterogeneous humanities data sets.

There are several and creative contributions that the arts and humanities can make to the development of approaches to the effective use of "big data" as well as there are opportunities and challenges for transformative research in the arts and humanities disciplines offered by development in the capability to handle, exploit, and use very huge and complex data sets.

There is still much research to be done around the potential of big data in driving a step-change in the way the creative and cultural fields fruitfully engage with data, generating significant benefits and value.

Certainly, taking advantage of big data, which encompasses new approaches to collection and sophisticated analytics, requires tackling significant challenges, some of them novel. A multidisciplinary engagement is the key to deal these challenges and drive value from big data.

References

Arts and Humanities Research Council. 2014. *The Challenges of Big Data*. Polaris House. North Star Avenue, Swindon, Wiltshire.

Boyd, D., and Crawford, K. 2011. Six provocations for big data. A decade in Internet time: Symposium on the dynamics of the internet and society. http://ssrn.com/abstract =1926431; http://dx.doi.org/10.2139/ssrn. 1926431 (accessed July 2017).

Bray, P. 2009. Open licensing and the future for collections. In *Museums and the Web 2009: Proceedings*, ed. J. Trant and D. Bearman, Toronto Archives and Museum Informatics. http://www.museumsandtheweb.com/mw2009/papers/bray/bray.html (accessed July 2017).

Chen, H., Chiang, R. H. L., and Storey V. C. 2102. Business intelligence and analytics: From big data to big impact. *MIS Q* 36, 4: 1165–1188.

Dijcks, J. P. 2012. *Oracle: Big Data for the Enterprise*. Oracle White Paper.

Doorn, P. 2016. Big data in the humanities and social sciences. https://sciencenode.org /feature/big-data-humanities-and-social-sciences.php (accessed July 2017).

Fang, H., Zhang, Z., Wang, C. J., Daneshmand, M., Wang, C., and Wang, H. 2015. A survey of big data research. *IEEE Netw* 29, 5: 6–9.

Gartner, Inc. 2016. Gartner Survey Reveals investment in big data is up but fewer organizations plan to invest. http://www.gartner.com/newsroom/id/3466117 (accessed June 2017).

Grugier, M. 2016. The digital age of data art. https://techcrunch.com/2016/05/08/the-digital-age-of-data-art/ (accessed June 2017).

Jacquesson, A. 2010. *Google Livres et le futur des bibliothèques numériques*. Paris: Editions du Cercle de La Librairie.

Joshi, R. 2016. The CIO's big data challenge: Asking the right questions, connecting the dots. https://www.enterpriseinnovation.net/article/cios-big-data-challenge-asking-right-questions-connecting-dots-459908207 (accessed June 2017).

Judge, A., Stein, R., Walter, M., and Firth, M. 2017. Big data and analytics: What we've learned so far. https://mw17.mwconf.org/proposal/big-data-and-analytics-what-weve-learned-so-far/ (accessed May 2017).

Kaplan, F. 2015. A map for big data research in digital humanities. *Front Digital Hum* 2: 1.

Kitchin, R., and Dodge, M. 2014. *Code/Space: Software and Every Day Life*. Cambridge: MIT Press.

Kwon, O., Namyeo, L., and Bongsik, S. 2014. Data quality management, data usage experience and acquisition intention of big data analytics. *Int J Inf Manage* 34, 3: 387–394.

Levi, A. S. 2013. Humanities 'big data': Myths, challenges, and lessons. 2013 IEEE International Conference on Big Data. Silicon Valley, CA.

Liang, Y., and Kelemen, A. 2016. Big data science and its applications in healthcare and medical research: Challenges and opportunities. *Austin Biom Biostat* 3, 1: 1030.

Lohr, S. 2013. The origins of 'big data': An etymological detective story. Bits blog. https://bits.blogs.nytimes.com/2013/02/01/the-origins-of-big-data-an-etymological-detective-story/ (accessed June 2017).

Marr, B. 2016. *Big Data in Practice: How 45 Successful Companies Used Big Data Analytics to Deliver Extraordinary Results*. Chichester, West Sussex, UK: John Wiley & Sons.

Sashi, C. M., 2012. Customer engagement, buyer-seller relationships, and social media. *Manage Decis* 50, 2: 253–272.

Schreibman, S., Siemens, R., and Unsworth, J. 2008. *A Company onto Digital Humanities*. Malden, MA: Wiley-Blackwell.

Smith, B. C. 2016. Big data in the humanities: The need for big question. https://www.sciculture.ac.uk/2013/11/12/big-data-in-the-humanities-the-need-for-big-questions/ (accessed July 2017).

Tsimonis, G., and Dimitriadis, S., 2014. Brand strategies in social media. *Market Intell Plan* 32, 3: 328–344.

Ularu, E. G., Puican, F. C., Apostu, A., and Velicanu, M. 2012. Perspectives on big data and big data analytics. *Database Syst J* 3, 4: 3–14.

Walter, M. 2016. Data warehousing and building analytics at Cooper Hewitt, Smithsonian Design Museum. https://www.gitbook.com/book/micahwalter/building-analytics-at-cooper-hewitt/details (accessed May 2017).

Ward, J. S., and Barker, A. 2013. Undefined by data: A survey of big data definitions. *arXiv preprint arXiv:1309.5821*.

Wikipedia. 2016. Delpher. https://en.wikipedia.org/wiki/Delpher (accessed July 2017).

Chapter 3

"Never Mind the Quality, Feel the Width": Big Data for Quality and Performance Evaluation in the Arts and Cultural Sector and the Case of "Culture Metrics"

Abigail Gilmore, Kostas Arvanitis,
and Alexandra Albert

Contents

Introduction

Measurement of aspects of the arts and culture to support how decisions are made and performances are assessed has become a source of national, indeed international, obsession (McDowall et al., 2015), although an interest in the importance of arts to society is a much longer preoccupation stretching back before Plato (Belfiore and Bennett, 2008). There has been considerable contemplation by both arts practitioners and arts and humanities academics about how to ascribe value and quantify impact in order to support policy making and account for the allocation of public moneys, improve the effectiveness of arts organizations in satisfying audiences, and develop new business strategies (see, e.g., Belfiore and Bennett, 2010; Crossick and Kaszynska, 2016). As with other sectors, the epistemologies of accountability for publicly funded arts organizations are being changed by shifts in external environments, and the recent attention given to big data and their potential to revolutionize everyday practices of arts management has interested the arts sector greatly (Lilley and Moore, 2013).

The title of this chapter refers to the distinctions between, and competing virtues of, quantity and quality. The phrase actually relates to the practices of tailors in promoting cheaper, wider cloth over finer, more expensive wares (and was the title of a film and television series that featured combative London tailors broadcast in the late 1960s and early 1970s). This chapter concerns the development of methodologies for measuring the quality of artistic experiences and managing the performance of arts and cultural organizations, which now speculatively include the potential use of big data. It presents empirical research conducted for a publicly funded "Digital R&D" project* called "Culture Metrics," which brought together technology partners, arts and cultural organizations, and researchers. Culture Metrics involved the development and testing of a digital platform "Culture Counts," which has been designed to support evaluation. Through a short review of the literature on the developing interest in data science and analysis of the Culture Metrics project as a case study in the changing data culture of arts organizations, we reflect on the emerging rhetoric of big data within the sector and its application to performance measurement, self-evaluation, and data-driven decision-making. We argue that the call for data science represented by initiatives such as Culture Counts presents an attempt to break from the conventions of traditional evaluation for arts organizations that offers a potential solution for quality assurance. However, in its early development stage, Culture Metrics reveals that for this to be successful, the significant tensions surrounding the use of quantitative data for this purpose, the stretched resources for analysis and, most importantly, an overarching absence of big data will need to be overcome.

---

* This program is funded by the National Endowment for Science, Technology and the Arts, Arts and Humanities Research Council, and Arts Council England. Further details can be found at http://www.nesta.org.uk/project/digital-rd-fund-arts

The first section reviews recent literature on big data that has particular pertinence to the growing interest within the arts and humanities concerning the affordances of big data, their use in performance management, and their impact on the "data culture" of the arts sector. We then outline the case study of the Culture Metrics project and the findings of this research, before discussing their implications for arts and cultural organizations in the context of recent debates on measuring quality and value.

Potential of Big Data

There is a gap in the literature between theory and practice in relation to big data and data-driven decision-making in the cultural sector. Crawford (2014) suggests that the current mythology of big data is that with more data come greater accuracy and truth, an epistemological position that is so powerful that many industries, from advertising to automobile manufacturing, are repositioning themselves for massive data gathering. The potential of big data to offer methodological robustness is further strengthened if the data are collected and marshaled in order to overcome methods that compare the incomparable, the "apples and pears," a longstanding preoccupation for the arts sector. This becomes possible as data from initially incompatible sources can be matched and combined in relational databases to examine associations that were previously evasive (Feldman et al., 2015), forming entirely new epistemological approaches and insights born from the data (Kitchin, 2014).

The potential of big data feeds a powerful rhetoric and voracious appetite for data science, machine learning, and algorithms for policy-making. As it becomes easier to manipulate larger numbers of records and collect more observations, the potential for matching ever more diverse sources increases (Feldman et al., 2015). However the automation of data collection and analysis is problematical, particularly for the contentious question concerning the quality of art. This raises the question of how far human judgment and subjectivity can be stripped away from matters of taste and context in the reception of arts experiences. There has been a long-standing recurrent debate about the application of quantitative measures to judge "good art" (Higgins, 2016), but to suggest that these measures are not even applied by humans but rather through machine logic is simply untenable for many. The algorithm may be able to compute across vast landscapes of data, but it does not handle either meaning or context well (Jenkins 2013; Kitchin, 2014). Furthermore, as Beer (2016b: 3–4) warns, the properties of digital technologies and big data have their own agency, which can shape our qualitative understanding: "we play with metrics and we are more often played by them. Metrics…come to act on us as we act according to their rules, boundaries, and limits."

Kitchin (2016: 15–16) claims that we are now entering an era of widespread algorithmic governance, where "algorithm machines" entails new forms of power that are reshaping social and economic systems. These include the diversion of scant resources to never-ending data projects rather than attempts to resolve questions through with currently available data. A deluge of data and powerful rhetoric is sweeping up arts organizations in its tide (Lilley, 2015); however, while all cultural organizations already live in a world of greater volume and variety of data, very few have an integrated strategic approach and the skills and tools to make the most of such potential (Moore, 2016).

The literature reveals discrete but simultaneous areas of work being undertaken in the cultural sector under the guise of big data, adding to the confusion. Some projects highlight the sector's generation and use of big data (e.g., Mateos-Garcia, 2014), whereas others focus simply on the generic use of (any) data and call for an improved data culture (National Endowment for the Arts, 2014) and others explore the use of social media analytics to better understand and engage with audiences (Phillips et al., 2014; Qualia, 2015). Amidst the hype, there is a lack of clarity in the cultural sector around what constitutes big data in practice. Lilley and Moore (2013) advocate the need for the use of big data but do not offer a clear definition. Feldman et al. (2015) choose not to use the phrase "big data" but instead focus on new data frontiers rendered possible by new technologies that have dramatically enhanced the availability, scale, and ability to connect previously disparate data sources.

Big data potentially challenges the dominant epistemologies for social research and societal understanding. While some have defended the importance of the census (Dorling, 2013; Shearmur, 2015), there is also an argument to suggest that it is expensive and outmoded and could be augmented by the voluminous available demographic information from transactional data, such as supermarket loyalty cards to government databases, and triangulated with other sources, such as tax and benefit records, driver's licenses, and household surveys. Furthermore, transactional or "organic" data can identify and respond to trends and changes in almost-real-time and highlight new questions to ask of behavior in ways that traditional survey methods cannot (National Endowment for the Arts, 2014).

But is there actually evidence of big data use in the arts? Big data properties are defined by Kitchin (2013) as high in velocity, created in or near real-time, diverse in variety, exhaustive in scope, fine-grained in resolution, uniquely indexical in identification, and flexible and relational in nature, containing common fields that enable the conjoining of different data sets. The term is mainly used in the computer industry to describe massive, heterogeneous, and often unstructured digital content that is difficult to process using traditional data management tools (Manovich, 2012; Rodríguez-Mazahua et al., 2016). The largest data sets used in the cultural sector are much smaller than those used by scientists; if we use the industry definition, almost none of them qualify as big data. Manovich (2012) suggests that the gap between cultural sector usage and industry definitions will disappear, however, when digital humanists bring together born-digital user-generated content, users' online communication, user created metadata, and transaction data. Web content and data are infinitely larger than all already digitized cultural heritage, which, in contrast to the number of historical artefacts, are growing exponentially.

For cultural organizations to move to using big data, they will need to consider what falls outside of the particular markets or activities being tracked (Shearmur, 2015). For example, in the arts, audience data from box office and other transactional data can miss aspects that are important to audience development, such as data on people who do not normally engage in the arts. The deficiencies of these data have been supplemented by market segmentation approaches, which in turn rely on additional and costly analytical services and commercial big data. Such approaches have their own political economy, requiring recognition of the power dynamics behind the circulation of big data and contributing to and exacerbating what Burrows and Savage (2014) call "the social life of methods." Shearmur (2015) similarly highlights the fact that big data shape, rather than reflect, society, forcing those who use it to opportunistically adapt concepts and needs to the data available.

Boyd and Crawford (2012) suggest that big data reframe key questions about the constitution of knowledge and processes of research, shifting how we should engage with information, and the nature and the categorization of reality. They also underline the importance of the (social) context of data that have to be taken into account in its analysis: for example, big data analyses tend to show what users do, but not why they do it. Similarly, in his discussion of tools for big data analysis, Manovich (2012) proposes that the significance of results should be distinguished by their relevance in relation to the individual or society. The acceleration of big data generation and the meanings of observed data and their analyses therefore pose a number of challenges in relation to the skills required to make sense of such data (Moore, 2016) and the creation of an epistemological approach that enables post-positivist forms of computational social science (Kitchin, 2013, 2014; Ruppert 2013). As Rodríguez-Mazahua et al. (2016) point out, the data growth rate is fast exceeding the ability of researchers to both design appropriate systems to handle the data effectively and analyze it to extract relevant meaning for decision-making.

To summarize, the attractions and appeal of big data are many, but these should be considered alongside the range of challenges described earlier for those who wish to harness their potential for performance measurement and improvement. Sectors like the arts and culture are reliant on public funding and accountability to a range of stakeholders but are also particularly prone to capacity issues for data collection and analysis (Moore, 2016). They are also especially enthusiastic about finding ways to capture and demonstrate value and to measure quality that are credible to themselves and their stakeholders. It is to these issues we turn to next through our case study.

Using Culture Counts: The Case Study of Culture Metrics

The Culture Metrics project involved a consortium of cultural organizations from England who teamed up with independent arts technology consultants based in Australia and the United Kingdom and with the University of Manchester to test and develop an online digital platform (called Culture Counts) for evaluating the quality of arts experiences.* The project was commissioned as part of the "Big Data" strand, accompanying other projects that considered the new possibilities for arts management offered by the generation of data afforded by digital technologies used by the arts. The project's main aim was to develop a data set through which to test metrics, understood as "quality dimensions" (see Table 3.1), as tools for arts and cultural organizations to benchmark and improve their work and to report to public funders. These metrics had been agreed through an earlier Arts Council England (ACE) project involving cultural organizations from the Greater Manchester area, including museums, art galleries, theater, orchestral music, jazz, cinema, and cross-art form organizations (Bunting and Knell, 2014) and had been inspired by a similar project initiated by the Department of Culture and Arts in Western Australia in 2010 (Chappell and Knell, 2012).

The digital platform offered an automated way of aggregating, reporting, and visualizing data collected through postevent surveys. These were conducted with different stakeholder groups involved in the production and reception of specific artistic experiences and included the organizations themselves, their "peers" and funders, and audiences. The survey included statements (corresponding to the metric "dimensions"), which participants could respond to by moving a simple digital slider to record their level of agreement. These scores were then quantified, aggregated across sampled groups, and visualized in a series of bar charts to compare data from the different stakeholder groups and according to the different types of events being surveyed (see Figure 3.1). Longitudinal data could also be compared by collecting from the same groups across different time points: this was particularly important for projects that emphasize the process of participation as the focus for impact and for self-completion by the organizations themselves who wanted to measure the outcome of the event against their expectations during the production process. Respondents could also enter a limited number of words through which to describe their impressions of their experience, which produced a qualitative "word cloud" when aggregated for reporting back to the organizations.

The project combined three main objectives. First was the accumulation of survey data from three types of audiences (self-assessment, artistic peers, and the public) that allows for different perspectives to be evaluated. Second was the use of standardized metrics across organizations that potentially allows for comparisons between them and between different kinds of events and over time. Third was the active involvement of cultural organizations in shaping the metrics and providing insight into how they were used within their everyday data culture for self-assessment, business development, and reporting to funders.

---

* This involved a longstanding collaboration of two consultancies, Pracsys and the Intelligence Agency, which now trades under the name of "Culture Counts." In this article, we refer to Culture Counts to refer to both the consultants, engaged on the Culture Metrics project, and the online platform, to distinguish this from the metrics which were coproduced with members of the arts and cultural sector.

Table 3.1 Quality Metrics Dimensions and Statements

Dimension	Metric Statement
Self, Peer, and Public Assessment	
Presentation	"It was well produced and presented"
Distinctiveness	"It was different from things I've experienced before"
Rigor	"It was well thought through and put together"
Relevance	"It has something to say about the world in which we live"
Challenge	"It was thought provoking"
Captivation	"It was absorbing and held my attention"
Meaning	"It meant something to me personally"
Enthusiasm	"I would come to something like this again"
Local impact	"It is important that it's happening here"
Self and Peer Assessment Only	
Risk	"The artists/curators really challenged themselves with this work"
Originality	"It was ground-breaking"
Excellence (national)	"It is amongst the best of its type in the UK"
Excellence (global)	"It is amongst the best of its type in the world"

Source: Bunting, C., Knell, J., *Measuring Quality in the Public Sector: The Manchester Metrics Pilot: Findings and Lessons Learned*, Arts Council England, Manchester, 2014.

A key feature of the project was that this collaboration between arts sector organizations could establish a credible and representative measurement framework for the UK cultural sector as a whole. Of similar importance was the emphasis on the collation of large data sets and their integration into existing data culture and collection practices. Consequently, our research was organized principally around two research questions, concerning the coproduction of evaluation and the promise of big data for "data-driven decision-making" in the arts. The research methodology involved a literature review on these two thematic areas, stakeholder workshops and an online discussion forum. We also observed test events, conducted

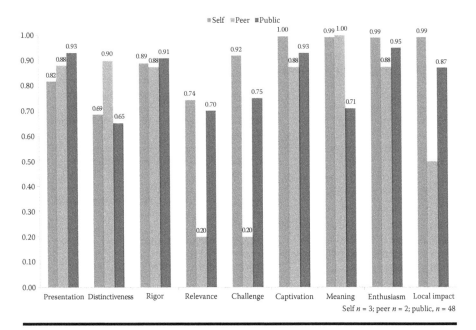

Figure 3.1   Average self, peer, and public scores for Verdi bicentenary concert (awarded after the event). (From Bunting, C., Knell, J., *Measuring Quality in the Public Sector: The Manchester Metrics Pilot: Findings and Lessons Learned*, Arts Council England, Manchester, 2014. With permission.)

qualitative interviews with participants who had a range of different roles within the project, and hosted a policy debate to discuss the potential of big data for the arts (Culturemetricsresearch.com, 2015; Arvanitis et al., 2015).

Our research found that the project was broadly successful in delivering some of its key objectives. Participating organizations were mainly positive about their use of the online platform during test events, although not nearly so many events were managed as had originally been intended, and some had problems with access to Wi-Fi connections, which meant that data were collected through paper surveys (and were not truly standardized). They liked working with the consultants who gave them expert insight and support and who produced reports on the test events to help them understand and analyze results. They were also keen to be recognized for their role in coproducing the metrics and supporting the development of the platform. They were in agreement with the longer-term ambition of Culture Counts to provide automated reporting and a dashboard that can be flexible in encompassing a wide range of monitoring requirements, which might reduce the cost of evaluation compared with other commissioned research mechanisms.

Participating organizations observed that they readily combined the Culture Counts data with other existing data for self-evaluation: for example, they triangulated the analysis with existing audience development and market research or informally through cross-referencing with their own tacit knowledge or feedback through other means, for example, through talking with front-of-house staff on audience reactions to theater productions. Mainly, the use of Culture Counts did not tell them much they did not already know. Rather, by comparing data from the surveys with their informal expectations of how constituent audiences and stakeholders would respond to artistic programming, it helped them to consider changing the interpretation, marketing, and technical aspects of delivery. It provided a way to consider artistic and business processes in combination:

> The ways the Culture Metrics work is [to judge] what you seek to do and how you seek to do it measured against the public and peer expectation of what you're seeking to do and why you're seeking to do it. If they tally then one could argue your plan basis is good. (research participant)

This is a fairly routine way for arts managers to evaluate the outcomes of decision-making and inform future decisions, but the innovation of Culture Counts was to provide standardized questions that lend the assumption of data objectivity. The project failed, however, to provide the means for organizations to benchmark their work with others, however, since too few Culture Counts test events were run to collect enough data for cross-organization or sector comparison, let alone to produce big data. This would only be possible once more organizations and agencies subscribed to the methodology and provided data for the platform.

The project participants felt that their collaboration had resulted in a framework that would provide "a credible account of the quality of cultural productions that has the confidence of the organisations who have participated so far" (Balshaw et al., 2016: 68). The credibility came from their involvement and ownership of the process, through collaboration and coproduction with expert consultants. With their help, organizations hoped to tell their own "value stories," mirroring the Culture Counts marketing slogan: "tell a better story of your impact and value" (Culture Counts, n.d.). This sentiment corresponds to concerns about the voraciousness with which funders require monitoring data on the performance of their funded organizations, which might allow them to tell stories that the organizations do not agree with and cannot control. Overall, there was less interest in "big data" than "just enough data" (Culturemetricsresearch.com, 2015). Perhaps more interestingly, there appeared to be no issue with the overt scoring of "quality" through the online system: that the overwhelming majority of data that Culture Counts produces and presents are quantitative did not seem an issue for the participating arts and cultural organizations.

In the final section, we discuss the implications of this case study for the performance management of quality by arts and cultural organizations, in the context of their approach to using big data.

Evaluating the Promises of Culture Counts

The seductive affordances of Culture Counts seem to lie in its capacity to standardize and frame different stakeholder perspectives and to render sometimes unruly data on arts experiences into a more regimented and legible format, according to agreed and shared measures, with the assurance of expert support.

> This is where the magic starts to happen. Suddenly we in the cultural sector are working together to create big datasets rather than working in small individual silos. Moreover, we're working together to define appropriate metrics for evaluating quality. (Glass, 2015)

The digital platform presents the potential for large amounts of data collection, which, once accumulated, may support some machine learning and algorithmic power. However, since Culture Counts is not based on transactional or organic data, reaching mass data requires considerable further investment into data collection, as well as the involvement of the consultants, who retain sole access to the data collected through trialing of Culture Counts worldwide, as well as expertise and capacity to provide analysis.

Following the end of the Culture Metrics project, a further ACE-funded project was initiated. This "rolled out" the metrics (now called "Quality Metrics") and the Culture Counts platform for further testing with 150 national portfolio organizations, with the aim of developing a larger data set that has since been published online, without analysis, as part of the Arts Council's open data policy (ACE, 2016). The evaluation of the roll-out focused on the participating organizations' perception and experience of using the metrics and the online platform and found that there was general enthusiasm and desire for better "evidence-driven decision making" (Nordicity, 2016: 2) and that the Quality Metrics framework provided an important and innovative step forward through its triangulation of standardized data. However, it identified some significant capacity issues "that undermined the use of data and a positive perception of the framework" (Nordicity, 2016: 3), highlighting the negative impact that the administration of the evaluation framework had on other activities and the inherent skills gap for handling and analyzing data, which led to a lack of understanding and effective use.

Despite the evaluation findings, ACE also announced that they intend to eventually incorporate the metrics within their assessment framework for the national portfolio by rolling them out by the middle of 2017, with competitive procurement for the consultant supplier (Hill, 2017a). This announcement raised significant concerns voiced within the arts press and on social media about the use of a quantitative system for measuring the quality of art (Hill, 2017a). These reiterated issues identified previously in relation to big data and machine learning, such as lack of understanding of meaning and context. They articulated the personal politics of assessing quality:

> You can't take out a ruler and discover how good a play is, though you can measure things that hover around it, such as how many people came to see it and how much it cost. Instead, deciding what is good is a human and subjective thing—and who gets to decide is a tender and touchy subject. (Higgins, 2016)

Paradoxically, the same properties of Culture Counts that are praised for their capacity to standardize data are those that are found wanting: the depersonalization of data through aggregated quantitative metric scores disconnects the appraisal of cultural product from the social context of its reception and undermines the validity of the research. Moreover, there are questions about the robustness of sampling and postevent survey methodologies conducted by hard-pressed arts organizations eager to demonstrate their value to funders (Hill 2017b).

The literature review suggests that there needs to be significant improvements and investment in in-house skills and analytical expertise in order to meet the demands of a truly big data culture in the arts. However, the case of Culture Counts also hints at a broader crisis of expertise and an ambiguity over whose or what forms of knowledge support policy-making. On the one hand, as Higgins (2016) proposes, the debate over quality assessment in the arts reveals the "perceived inadequacy" of previous mechanisms for establishing what counts as quality, which involved the "great and the few" of the Arts Council through selected peer review. The sector leadership and involvement in coproducing the metrics in this sense are statements of intent concerning the right of the arts organizations to perform their own self-evaluation and assessment and to define "good art."

At the same time, data-driven approaches remove the human element: they "no longer rely on specialist knowledge and expertise; algorithms based on mass data sets take the 'knowledge' out of knowledge production" (Chandler, 2015: 847). Beer (2016a: 10) suggests that mass data analytics can potentially democratize analysis: real-time data analytics can make "everyone a quick and nimble data analyst, turning the user into the expert with access to all types of data-informed insights." But while the idea of big data offers potential freedom from human subjectivity and bias, Culture Counts self-consciously provides a particular institutional framing of quality that is accredited through sector involvement, plus the endorsement of the establishment, while maintaining the need to buy-in expertise (Arvanitis et al., 2015).

The findings from the Culture Metrics research suggest that while a digital platform associated with potential big data capture and automated analysis has allure, there is still a preference for an informed, "human" approach to evaluating the quality of art. The platform provides an evaluation tool that has been willingly endorsed and publicly funded by the arts establishment, even as its validity and capacity to produce big data are questioned. As such, one could argue, its commissioning continues a form of value-driven performance management of arts organizations, which remains quite far from the utopian promises of data-driven decision-making. The application of machine logic for evaluating the arts seems not just out of reach but undesirable: arts organizations would rather, it seems, feel the quality in this instance.

References

Arts Council England. 2016. Quality Metrics web page. Retrieved November 20, 2016, from http://www.artscouncil.org.uk/quality-metrics/quality-metrics

Arvanitis, K., A. Gilmore, F. Florack, and C. Zuanni. 2015. *Data Culture and Organisational Practice*. MW2016: Museums and the Web 2016. Published March 20, 2016. Retrieved October 2, 2016, from http://mw2016.museumsandtheweb.com/paper/data-culture-and-organisational-practice/

Balshaw, M., C. Bolton, J. Edgar, M. Fenton, F. Gasper, R. Gauld, A. Gilmore, D. Martin, S. Mead, N. Merriman, D. Moutrey, and J. Summers. 2016. Correspondence: Measuring quality in the cultural sector: The Manchester Metrics pilot: Findings and lessons learned, by Catherine Bunting and John Knell. *Cultural Trends* 25(1): 66–68.

Beer, D. 2016a. The data analytics industry and the promises of real-time knowing: Perpetuating and deploying a rationality of speed, *Journal of Cultural Economy,* 10(1): 21–33.

Beer, D. 2016b. *Metric Power*. London: Palgrave Macmillan.

Belfiore, E. and O. Bennett. 2008. *The Social Impact of the Arts: An Intellectual History*. Basingstoke: Palgrave/Macmillan.

Belfiore, E. and O. Bennett. 2010. Beyond the 'toolkit approach': Arts impact evaluation research and the realities of cultural policy-making. *Journal for Cultural Research*, 14(2): 121–142.

Boyd, D. and K. Crawford. 2012. Critical questions for big data information. *Communication & Society*, 15(5): 662–679.

Bunting, C. and J. Knell. 2014. *Measuring Quality in the Public Sector: The Manchester Metrics Pilot: Findings and Lessons Learned*. Manchester: Arts Council England.

Burrows, R. and M. Savage. 2014. After the crisis? Big data and the methodological challenges of empirical sociology. *Big Data and Society*, 1(1): 1–6.

Chandler, D. 2015. A world without causation: Big data and the coming of age of posthumanism. *Millennium: Journal of International Studies*, 43(3): 833–851.

Chappell, M. and J. Knell. 2012. *Public Value Measurement Framework. Valuing and Investing in the Arts—Towards a New Approach*. Western Australia: Department of Culture and the Arts, p. 3.

Crawford, K. 2014. The anxieties of big data. *The New Inquiry*. Retrieved November 2. 2016, from http://thenewinquiry.com/essays/the-anxieties-of-big-data/

Crossick, G. and P. Kaszynska. 2016. *Understanding the Value of Arts and Culture: The AHRC Cultural Value Project*. Swindon: Arts and Humanities Research Council.

Culture Counts. n.d. Culture Counts website, Retrieved November 14, 2016, from https://culturecounts.cc/uk/

Culturemetricsresearch.com. 2015. Policy week event: Using digital technology to assess quality in the arts, blog post, November 26 2015. Retrieved November 20, 2016, from http://www.culturemetricsresearch.com/new-blog/2015/11/26/policy-week-event-using-digital-technology-to-assess-quality-in-the-arts

Dorling, D. 2013. The 2011 Census: What surprises are emerging and how they show that cancellation is stupid, *Radical Statistics*, 109: 4–13.

Feldman, M., M. Kenney, and F. Lissoni. 2015. The new data frontier: Special issue of *Research Policy*. *Research Policy*, 44: 1629–1632.

Glass, S. 2015. Data at the Deep End: What should we do with our data? *Digital R&D Fund for the Arts*. Retrieved December 8, from: http://webarchive.nationalarchives.gov .uk/20161104001432uo_/http://artsdigitalrnd.org.uk/features/data-at-the-deep-end/

Higgins, C. 2016. Orwellian nightmare or fairer system for all? What Quality Metrics will mean for arts funding. *The Guardian*. 4 October 2016, Retrieved November 20, 2016, from https://www.theguardian.com/culture/2016/oct/04/quality-metrics-arts-council -england-funding

Hill, L. 2017a. Arts Council earmarks £2.7 m for Quality Metrics roll-out, Arts Professional. Retrieved February 24, 2017, from https://www.artsprofessional.co.uk /news/arts-council-earmarks-ps27m-quality-metrics-roll-out

Hill, L. 2017b. Why Quality Metrics is a really bad idea, Arts Professional. Retrieved February 24, 2017, from http://www.artsprofessional.co.uk/magazine/blog/why-quality -metrics-really-bad-idea

Jenkins T. 2013. Don't count on big data for answers. *The Scotsman*. 12 February 2013. Retrieved on 5th April 2018 from https://www.scotsman.com/news/opinion/tiffany -jenkins-don-t-count-on-big-data-for-answers-1-2785890

Kitchin, R. 2013. Big data and human geography: Opportunities, challenges and risks. *Dialogues in Human Geography*, 3(3): 262–267.

Kitchin, R. 2014. Big data, new epistemologies and paradigm shifts. *Big Data & Society*, April–June 2014: 1–12.

Kitchin, R. 2016. Thinking critically about and researching algorithms. *Information, Communication & Society*, 20(1): 14–29.

Lilley, A. 2015. What can big data do for the cultural sector? Retrieved February 24, 2017, from https://www.theaudienceagency.org/insight/using-the-evidence-to-reveal-opportunities -for-engagement

Lilley, A., and P. Moore. 2013. *Counting What Counts: What Big Data Can Do for the Cultural Sector*. London: NESTA.

Manovich, L. 2012. Trending: The promises and the challenges of big social data In: Gold, M.K. (ed), *Debates in the Digital Humanities*. Minneapolis: University of Minnesota Press, pp 460–475.

Mateos-Garcia, J. 2014. The art of analytics: Using bigger data to create value in the arts and cultural sector. Retrieved February 24, 2017, from http://www.nesta.org.uk /blog/art-analytics-using-bigger-data-create-value-arts-and-cultural-sector

McDowall, L., M. Badham, E. Blomkamp, and K. Dunphy. 2015. *Making Culture Count: The Politics of Cultural Measurement*. London: Palgrave MacMillan.

Moore, P. 2016. Big data and structural organisation in major arts bodies: An evolving ethnographic method. *Cultural Trends* 25(2): 104–115.

National Endowment for the Arts (NEA). 2014. *Measuring Cultural Engagement: A Quest for New Terms, Tools, and Techniques*. Washington, DC: National Endowment for the Arts, Retrieved November 14, 2016. https://www.arts.gov/sites/default/files/measuring -cultural-engagement.pdf

Nordicity. 2016. Evaluation of participants' experience of the Quality Metrics National Test Phase. Retrieved February 24, 2017, from http://www.artscouncil.org.uk/sites/default/files /download-file/Nordicity%20Evaluation%20of%20Quality%20Metrics%20trial.pdf

Phillips, M., J. Bennett, E. Jensen, and M. Verbeke. 2014. Measuring cultural value and cultural impact using technology-enhanced methods. Retrieved May 8, 2015, from http://www2.warwick.ac.uk/fac/soc/sociology/staff/jensen/culturalvalue/

Qualia. 2015. QUALIA—A revolution in measuring audience feedback. Retrieved May 8, 2015, from http://i-dat.org/qualia/

Rodríguez-Mazahua, L., C. Rodríguez-Enríquez, J. Sánchez-Cervantes, J. Cervantes, J. García-Alcaraz, and G. Alor-Hernández. 2016. A general perspective of big data: Applications, tools, challenges and trends. *The Journal of Supercomputing*, 72: 3073–3113.

Ruppert, E. 2013. Rethinking empirical social sciences. *Dialogues in Human Geography*, 3(3): 268–273.

Shearmur, R. 2015. Editorial: Dazzled by data: Big data, the census and urban geography. *Urban Geography*, 36(7): 965–968.

Chapter 4

Toward "Big Data" in Museum Provenance

Jeffrey Smith

Contents

The Big Question

Are big data practices useful for searching and mining museum provenance data? The answer is "not yet—but eventually…" when museums have generated enough actual data on the provenance of objects in their collections to create the quantity and quality of information that enables large-scale data-gathering practices.

Challenges

Few museums are able to financially support the time-consuming, ongoing practice of provenance research. Data for ownership and transaction information are burdensome to produce—it requires dedicated, ongoing research and adequate database systems and personnel dedicated to data entry and ongoing maintenance of the information. But this practice will help those that do to understand how their information can be transformed into actual data and how that transformation can become a sustainable method for sharing information more broadly.

Despite the obstacles, the generation and dissemination of provenance information are undergoing a shift from the practice of the written statement of ownership history toward the parsing of that information into both relational and linked data. Doing this without omitting the sometimes nuanced information expressed in the text requires an understanding of *which* data are most useful and *how much* of it is necessary to facilitate productive search. This shift will require a community of museums engaged in the work through a commitment to new tools and practices, and adoption of a common descriptive language for the data.

Linked Data

These new tools and practices largely concern linked data. Linked data is a semantic method of storing information and relating it to other data—it is *designed* to be linked to other data. Linked *open* data (LOD) is linked data that are published under an open license and made available for general use. Linked data is built on the Resource Description Framework (RDF), which translates any data element into three parts: a subject, a predicate, and an object. Known as a "triple," the deceptively simple grammatical structure of RDF makes possible the articulation of individual data elements as they relate to other things. Semantic data can thus be used to identify and disambiguate a piece of information by determining if it is the same or different as another thing, often by linking it to an established authority record for that "entity." Semantic data elements are referred to as entities because each is considered a "thing" existing in the world. Each entity, be it an object, person, place, date, event, or concept, is established as unique by the assignment of a URI, or Unique Resource Identifier—the format for which follows the hypertext (HTTP) protocol for the Internet. Although a URI is unique, the bit of data it identifies may be linked or pointed to an authority record elsewhere as a means of saying "this thing is the same as this other thing." In this way, museums can point to similar or related things in other collections and to sources of information that support that linkage as a fact in their own data.

For large-scale harvesting and analysis of data to become possible, more museums must not only produce many new individual sets of data—those data must be also translated to linked data using a common descriptive language. For the cultural humanities, this descriptive language is the CIDOC-CRM (http://www.cidoc-crm.org/). CIDOC is the International Committee for Documentation, a committee of the International Council of Museums dedicated to the documentation of museum collections and adherence to common standards for institutions to exchange information. The CRM is CIDOC's Conceptual Reference Model, which was developed in 1999 as an extensible model for concepts and information in cultural heritage and museum documentation for libraries, archives, and museums. Built on the protocols for the Semantic Web, an early-1990s outgrowth of the algorithmic search technologies of the 1980s, the CIDOC-CRM provides a set of formal semantics that enables machine-to-machine interoperability and so facilitates information sharing on the Internet, sidestepping the problem of data silos in this realm. The achievements of international cultural heritage projects like Europeana (http://www.europeana.eu/portal/en) and ResearchSpace (http://www .researchspace.org/) have demonstrated the potential of linked data and the efficacy of the CRM to support search across multiple and differing sets of museum data. In the United States, the American Art Collaborative (http://americanartcollaborative .org/) is the most recent effort to provide a body of LOD to search across a consortium of collections.

Linked Open Data

The classes and properties of the CRM have proven comprehensive and flexible enough to allow mapping to many forms of library, archive, and museum data. For the archival works, a mapping of the Encoded Archival Description (EAD) document-type definition set to the CIDOC-CRM was completed in 2001. As archives increasingly adopt the CRM, EAD finding aids and item-level data will be more easily linked. Examples of large-scale mapping of archives are the Getty Provenance Index Databases (http://www.getty.edu/research/tools/provenance /search.html), which are important sources of archival inventories, sales catalogues, stock books, and German sales catalogues pertinent to World War II-era provenance. These data are currently being mapped to the CRM, to be made available as LOD. Completion of this effort will provide an enormous corpus of authoritative source material to the research community.

Unknowns and Ambiguities

An unavoidable fact of provenance is that it often presents unknown and ambiguous information that resists completion yet must be addressed when determining the true picture of what is certain or not known about ownership or custody history. Accounting for this type of data requires a special ontology that can be commonly used to describe such instances. In the world of semantic data, ontologies provide structured formal names and definitions for the types, properties, and relationships of the entities expected within a particular knowledge domain. For example, large sets of meteorological, economic, or biomedical data each depend on ontologies developed within those fields to help map the information. To accommodate unknown or uncertain information, the creation of the CRMinf (http://www.ics.forth.gr/isl/CRMext/CRMinf/docs/CRMinf-07.pdf) offers an ontology for argumentation and inference, critical for accurately qualifying facts in the often-uncertain realm of provenance data.

The use of "?," "probably," and "possibly" as qualifiers for assertions in provenance text is essential, but at the same time, they complicate querying and stating of facts. The CRMinf establishes classes for argumentation, belief, inference logic, and other essential qualifiers of uncertainty with properties aligned with referred classes and properties from the CRM itself. Used alongside a mapping to the CRM, this additional ontology makes it possible to account for stated unknowns and ambiguities that relational data cannot articulate. It may be possible to design search so that queries return data with the use of these argument and inference entities—such functionality would allow users to search *specifically* for instances where data are unknown or uncertain.

For museums to produce quality LOD for provenance, search name authorities such as the Getty's Union List of Artist Names (ULAN), the Virtual International Authority File, and GeoNames must be linked to core entities to support assertions and provide a means for disambiguating variations of spelling or completeness. For provenance research, knowing family relations is of value because custody or legal transfer of works often falls to family members. Being able to link people as determined by birth, marriage, divorce, or inheritance is very helpful. For this information, ULAN's standards for types of person-to-person relations are useful. Where community standards do not exist, museums should generally be the authorities for data in their own collections, and some museums may decide to publish their own authority files and invoke them from within the linked data. But whenever possible, it is advisable to identify and select trusted authorities because it is more efficient and helps cement the community of standards that has arisen to support semantic data.

Although there are name authorities and ontologies from other knowledge domains that can be used, the CRM is able to bridge inherent differences in standards and has proven quite flexible for the cultural humanities. For provenance, it can be effectively used to describe the core object, people, and especially event data, providing a framework for a common ontology that all museums may use. Pioneers in the effort to use the CRM for provenance include the Carnegie Museum of Art and Yale Center for British Art, both of which have provided mappings of the core elements of provenance transactions.

Overall, the transition from provenance narrative text alone to text accompanied by relational or linked data can be described succinctly as

Research > Text > Data > Linked Date > Provenance Search

For museums, this is an iterative, recursive process of determining and then implementing the most efficient and sustainable practices that will lead to provenance data being made available for search and harvesting—iterative, in that practices of phrasing and formatting information are repeated throughout the process so that consistency supports the overall effort, and recursive, in that decisions made for one phase of the workflow inform decisions forward and backward, through the whole of the effort. Each museum must be able to chart its own path through this process, from conducting original research to the sharing of its results.

Research > Text

The recording of ownership history for artworks in museum collections has remained essentially unchanged for many years and often accompanies the core data for an art object in catalogues and books. It has been little affected by the advent of computerized records, networks, and the Internet. The American Alliance of Museums (AAM) has produced a well-documented standard for this format, and most museums follow it, with some variation for their own purposes.

Text > Linked Data

The Carnegie Museum of Art's *Art Tracks* initiative (http://www.museumprovenance .org/) has been at the forefront of this process, by applying the technologies of structured text and linked data to the problem of generating actual provenance data from text.

> *Art Tracks* is an initiative of the Carnegie Museum of Art (CMOA) that aims to turn provenance into structured data by building a suite of open source software tools. These tools transform traditional written provenance records into searchable data, with an emphasis on existing data standards and a strong focus on building tools that are useful (and usable) across multiple institutions.*

The CMOA Provenance Standard (http://www.museumprovenance.org/reference /standard/), a superset of the AAM provenance standard "designed to resolve ambiguities and provide guidance and machine-readability,"† is central to this development. Its standard for acquisition includes related models and provides definitions for the creation of the object as the first instance of ownership and subsequent periods of custody, ownership, and transfer. Commonly encountered situations of

---

* For more information about Art Tracks at the Carnegie Museum of Art, see http://www .museumprovenance.org/ (accessed April 25, 2017).
† For more information about the CMOA Digital Provenance Standard, see http://www .museumprovenance.org/reference/standard/ (accessed April 25, 2017).

transformation of parties, division of custody and ownership, rejoining of custody and ownership, and disappearance of objects are all covered in the CMOA standard, along with models of these processes.

CMOA's Elysa Tool

The Carnegie's approach acknowledges that most museums' provenance focus is the text statement itself. For this reason the CMOA created the open-source "Elysa" application (pronounced "Eliza," one of Andrew Carnegie's housekeepers) to build the text one line at a time, each as a distinct period of ownership or custody, and to select the people, places, and dates associated with each line to that they become data as entities in the eventual set of each object's provenance. The result of this effective approach is the creation of both human-readable *and* machine-readable versions of provenance. It assists with writing provenance because it requires users to carefully account for and standardize the entities that will make up the data, while structuring the text on the back end in a form that can be turned into linked data. While creating each ownership statement, Elysa leaves the typical notes section of the text alone, so that it functions as a "note" for each statement of possession, retaining its rich description for human understanding. Having structured the text, Elysa then transforms it into RDF, using a mapping to the CRM. The Elysa application can potentially reduce or eliminate the need for the large volume of integrated relational data that would be necessary for a more traditional distributed search. For museums considering provenance research programs, this is a significant development.

A great benefit of the Elysa tool is that it can create event data by inferring transfer events between the lines of text that represent instances of ownership. In a relational database, deriving actual event data must be done by deliberately linking people and object data to manually created event records. Some collections management systems do not offer this functionality at all. Those that do lack an integrated workflow to make the work a natural follow-up to record provenance, and this is quite time-consuming. The Elysa tool generates the equivalent of event records on the fly as it evaluates each line. It cannot create unique URIs for these events because if the data are significantly updated and the event parameters change, the data may become erroneous. Elysa's initial solution to this problem was to use blank nodes (or b-nodes), which are an accepted feature of RDF but not recommended for use with the CRM. With a federated search of linked data, use of blank nodes for events would create an impossible situation because each blank node would be indistinguishable from others in the overall graph. The current solution proposed by the Carnegie is to use the elements of string data that make up the actual line of provenance to generate a URI from those characters. This solution would provide a "unique" URI for that specific data, to be replaced by another URI if and when that information changes. Clearly, practical approaches to this problem will be critical for broader-scale adoption of federated search of provenance linked data.

The consensus approach of the Carnegie, Yale, and Freer|Sackler CRM mapping effort is for museums to create actual database event records for the most significant transactions and reference these "authority" event records in the provenance text itself, as a function of a new format standard which recognizes a new fusion of text with data.

Text > Relational Data

But the transition from a solely text-based form of provenance to data can also be enhanced by the use of relational data. Simply by creating relational database records for the people and institutions linked to objects with provenance, museums can provide searchable data to aid research. In a relational database, linked objects, people, and event records can form the backbone for search capabilities to guide researchers to the actual provenance text, with its more nuanced description. On their own, linked database records for previous owners—with their alternate names, geography, dates, associated, family and business relations—serve as authority records for the museum and so help identify individuals referenced within the text or other documentation. Relational data can then eventually be expressed as linked data when the museum has that capacity, creating three forms of provenance data with which to serve several needs.

The potential combination of text with relational and/or linked data is accounted for in an important element of the Carnegie's approach *levels* of provenance. These levels are determined by how much data can be generated from a record's available information. Basic object data, without provenance, is considered "tombstone" information—part of provenance but traditionally recorded outside the provenance data itself. For records with object data and provenance text, but no supporting data, the level is "basic provenance"—the provenance text is considered a document associated with the object and can be searched to determine which records have provenance text. With more complete provenance, a "provenance with entities" level is achieved, and mappings for parties, locations, and associated URL links can be created. The level of "event-based provenance" is warranted when more complete provenance documents the individual lines of provenance text.

These levels establish the degree to which Elysa can parse available information, enabling a museum to create data from its provenance text while indicating the degree of utility it will have in searches of a larger graph of multi-institutional linked data. In moving forward with this approach, it will be important to identify both the minimum amount of useful data necessary for a museum to contribute and the maximum level of data to avoid an overwhelming volume of search results. These distinctions, and the creation of tools that can help avoid an all-or-nothing solution, may enable museums to share their provenance information before they might otherwise be ready.

The combination of provenance text, with relational data *and* linked data, might become a more versatile solution to the administrative load-balancing required for a museum to sustain research-to-search provenance activities. The text would be kept free of repeated references to alternate names and places associated with previous owners, since the database would hold these one-to-many relationships instead. Linked data generated from the text statement would then reference these in-house "authority" records via the provenance text itself. Therefore, in order for text, relational data, and linked data to work in tandem, the format of the provenance text may have to change to accommodate reference to both internal and external authority records cited. The statement itself would need to provide links to other records supporting the text, if tools such as Elysa are to parse the statement and links to such records.

Linked Data > Provenance Search

If, over time, museums are able to retool their approaches to provenance and adopt practices that allow them to generate linked data, the design of search interfaces for this information must evolve in tandem. Stores of linked data (called "triplestores") can be searched by using SPARQL, the query language for RDF. But it is not reasonable to expect researchers to learn and adopt its use, since some experience is required to understand its syntax and returned results. Instead, provenance search interfaces must be designed for the kinds of questions that researchers ask, *in the way they ask them.* Beyond querying objects and people and events, provenance search must also be able to facilitate questions of context, such as "Who bought works of art in Paris between the years 1936 and 1942?" And if the information has gaps and uncertainties, the incomplete data can take its place in the graph alongside more fully described entities. Again, understanding both the minimum and maximum amount of information needed for search—and what to prioritize—will be essential in planning search portals. Discoverability must be a central design principle, so that an iterative process of search, browsing, and reading can expose the connectedness of what would otherwise be separate facts in a large body of information.

Visualization

A powerful feature of linked data is its potential to provide visualization of search results in the form of graphical representations of linked entities, which is how most people intuitively understand its ability to present large sets of information. But researchers may be unfamiliar with such graphic displays and overwhelmed by the amount of information returned. If the key entities are not self-evident, and the properties that connect them to each other not apparent, the information is of limited value. Users may be unable to see which properties are in play in a given results set and then have to click their way through the graph to determine which data are pertinent.

Provenance research is often advanced by serendipitous discovery, so search interfaces must give users selective control over display of the primary entities returned in the graph, with related nodes and linking properties. Useful provenance search will need to combine the power of graph visualization with judicious indexing and faceting, while providing access to related reading material in a drill-down approach. This will be especially useful for links to archival materials, because whether looking at finding aids or item-level records, researchers must be able to see at a glance the existence of supporting documents. Basic text search for data embedded in the set of returned nodes will be important for discovery. And the notes section—the human-readable source of information—can be a rich source for follow-up research. New methods of data representation will need to be combined with more familiar displays of search results to provide a space where researchers can see relationships at a glance yet have access to deeper material within the same space. A search site must also provide users with the ability to cite the data and to save sets of data in a useful form that can support research conclusions. Translation of the information into a humanly readable form that is comprehensible will be essential for success of the round-trip research–to text–to data–to search process.

Conclusion

Finding a sustainable path from provenance research to searchable data will be the work of a collaborative community within museums, universities, and information technology professions. Opportunity lies in what museums and scholars will be able to share and do together—in collaboration with semantic and computer science communities and those rethinking search interface design. Continued partnership between these fields will produce more tools to help create provenance data and to address its complicated issues, such as the need to wrest unique URIs or their equivalents for event data from provenance text. Collaboration will also enable parties to better understand each other's language and priorities. Museums must invest in becoming more conversant and comfortable with linked data, and those who code will need to program and design for a wider, less tech-savvy audience, such as information managers, registrars, and curators.

There are significant opportunities for advancement—large repositories of provenance data such as the NARA Holocaust-era assets and the Getty Provenance Index are being prepared as sources of data for provenance search. The Carnegie Museum of Art's *Art Tracks* program has created semantic models of the core transactional entities of provenance, and more museums are mapping their collections via the CIDOC-CRM to RDF and creating LOD. Over time, as the tools used to generate semantic data and research in museums and universities evolve together, their application to provenance will improve to the point where moving from the standard text statement to accessible LOD will not be the large leap it is today.

The path from text to data to linked data and improved search will become established and will assist with general inquiry and research. And more ambitious "big data" efforts will become possible.

Acknowledgments

The author wishes to acknowledge work of the Carnegie Museum of Art's *Art Tracks* provenance project and his subsequent collaboration with David Newbury of the Carnegie and Emmanuelle Delmas-Glass of the Yale Center for British Art to understand and map core provenance data to the CIDOC-CRM. Thanks also to Duane Degler and Neal Johnson of Design for Context, who were instrumental in helping the Freer|Sackler understand the scope of moving into the semantic realm.

Chapter 5

From Big Data to Thick Data: Theory and Practice

Paul Moore

Contents

Introduction

When NESTA published *Counting What Counts* in 2013, no one involved in its inception was prepared for the impact it would make (Lilley and Moore, 2013). The authors, Lilley and Moore, had offered the short document as an attempt to encourage debate about the role of big data in the arts. There was also an initial attempt to create a formula through which arts organizations might assess where they were positioned in relation to the application of data systems. For the authors, there was always an awareness, and a hope, that, given the speed of change in the big data space, what Douglas Rushkoff (2013) calls the acceleration of the acceleration, *Counting What Counts* would rapidly be superseded by more sophisticated interventions in the debate. Surprisingly, *Counting What Counts* produced two almost diametrically opposed responses. Many arts organizations were outraged by the suggestion that an artistic venture of any kind should be subject to data-driven scrutiny—the words "robots" and "dictated to" were often heard in postconference paper discussions—a response that could often only be countered by the suggestion that funders would at some point want this type of scrutiny, particularly in relation to proof of impact and value for money. Conversely, some of the leading policy and decision-making bodies across Europe showed great interest in the debate, one example being the overwhelmingly positive response of European politicians, academics, and administrators when the *Counting What Counts* thesis was presented at the 2013 European Union Ready for Tomorrow symposium in Vilnius, Lithuania.

What both these responses indicated was the need for a more rigorous examination of the use of big data in arts organizations, and NESTA, with cofunders Arts Council England and the Arts and Humanities Research Council UK, commissioned this further research, the Arts Data Impact (ADI) project, through their Digital R & D initiative.

The ADI project had three related components:

- Partnership with three leading publicly funded arts organizations based in London and working across the areas of music, opera, art practice, and theater. The partner organizations were all using data to greater or lesser extents in their operations
- The appointment of two data scientists in residence (DSIRs) who would work in the partner institutions to develop specific tools for advancing data understanding and usage in the respective organizations, tools that could have a broader impact when tested
- The undertaking of an ethnographic study of the use of data in the partner institutions.

It was this ethnography that was the key element of the project. The decision to use ethnography as the research methodology underlined the conviction that data, and the ways in which data are used, are a cultural rather than a technological problem. It emphasized the crucial point that all technologies are ultimately subject not only to the needs of the user but also to the context in which they are being used. Hence, the ADI project was in effect undertaking what came to be called data ethnography.

This chapter examines this attempt to merge arts (big) data mining with emerging digital ethnography to examine cultural behavior in major publicly funded arts organizations in the United Kingdom. The research, on which this chapter is grounded, hence argues forcibly that arts data are not primarily a statistical tool but are, more crucially, a cultural imperative, since the data become the material from which organizations construct their cultural and contextual narratives.

Digital Ethnography

It has become increasingly apparent that in many aspects of the online, connected space, traditional ethnographic research methodologies need rethinking in order to address the issues and problems posed by developments such as big data. One of the more interesting aspects of the ethnographic process discussed in this chapter is the fact that much of it was conducted in a real-time virtual environment. It was what might be termed an ethnography twice removed. From a methodological point of view, this poses the question as to whether the accepted conventions of ethnographic practice still apply or whether a new set of issues have been introduced to an already complex research ecology. An analysis of the available literature on ethnography in the virtual/digital space indicates that commentators are remarkably sanguine about the possible impact of a removed online experience, suggesting that if the "traditional" ethical and methodological safeguards are followed, then the research outcomes should not in any way be compromised.

The NESTA-funded ADI project was one attempt to develop such a methodology, aimed at examining how large arts institutions are using data at the moment, with a view to developing models of operation that might be useful to other arts providers. It was also, crucially, an opportunity to assess how far data could be used to change and reframe cultural behavior within these complex organizations.

The cultural/behavioral aspects of the research were undertaken using what could be termed a "classical" ethnographic methodology while recognizing the digital context for much of the primary resource. This methodology comprised semiformal interviews with key figures in each of the partner institutions (face-to-face and online), observation-led information gathering in each of the venues, interaction with multiple data archives, and a filtering process through the most relevant theoretical scholarship. For each of the arts partners, a thorough data audit of the available systems and data sets was undertaken. The data audits provided a baseline of the existing systems to uncover key areas to focus on for the development of the ethnographic method. In total, 38 staff members were also interviewed directly with informal engagements taking place with other staff during organizational visits.

The crucial aspect of the ethnography in this context, however, was that it allowed for an analysis of the cultural and everyday interface those using the data technologies had with their primary data sources. This interface was the key focus of the research. Working on the premise that the last thing needed from data analytics is more data, the research explored how far data ethnography offers an opportunity to develop some insight into the process of introducing new and disruptive technologies to a large arts institution.

Ethnography in a Data Context

The positioning of the researcher in a dual context ("real" and digital) raises vital questions about the relationship between observation and participation, particularly in research circumstances where participation is considered by the group being studied to be a key signifier in relation to trust and acceptance. Many ethnographers have argued that the participant observer should, in some way, be passive, receiving data in a raw and untheorized manner from which hypotheses and concepts emerge and evolve. Willis (1980: 89–90) attacks this notion, suggesting that it is actually a means whereby "a secret compact" with positivism allows researchers to treat the subject as an object.

Willis is adamant that there is no untheoretical way to see an object since the observation is always subject to the conceptual constructs of the researcher, with the final account telling the reader as much about the researcher as the researched. The way in which the possibility that theory may "guide" the participant observation is for the researcher to allow scope for surprise, the ability "of reaching knowledge not prefigured in one's starting paradigm" (Willis, 1980: 90). In this sense, it is important to underline the fact that this chapter emanates from a conviction that there has been a seminal shift in the relationship between the individual and communication technologies which—whether in positive or negative terms—alters irrevocably the way in which we negotiate our everyday lives. Laurence Scott (2015) offers the example of an episode from Seinfeld where a decision is made to reverse the security lens on an apartment door so that more could be seen of the outside corridor, not realizing that the entire behaviors inside the apartment could now be viewed by anyone passing, with the related comic results. Scott argues this reversal is exactly what we have done in our online lives, reversing our privacy and leaving ourselves open to the scrutiny of anyone passing by. If this is true in our private lives, then it can be argued that it is also true, perhaps more so given the scale of the technologies involved, of our working lives, although we tend to view work as a siloed activity, unconnected to the practices of our social selves.

While this ethnography is aligned with the accepted conventions of such research methodology, there were a number of aspects, related to the interface with both human subjects and an online, abstract data space, which made this methodology both interesting and worthy of note. A fundamental additional aspect that complicated this "conventional" ethnographic practice was the constant presence of institutional data. Hence, the ethnographic exchanges were filtered and mediated through continual reference to what the data were supposed to be articulating even though this was often at odds with what the interviewee was articulating. The data essentially became a third presence in the ethnographic negotiation, used to justify both decisions taken and organizational positionings. Hence, for example, on more than one occasion, identical data were used by two different staff members to "prove" diametrically opposed responses to the same issue.

The work of the two DSIRs who were embedded in the organization for two days each week examining the data sets available and exploring alternative uses for these data was also invaluable in this context since, crucially, they were also analyzing the interface between staff in the organizations and the available data and supporting the organizations in the development of key questions they needed addressed to enhance their use of data either through increased understanding or the actual creation of tools specific to that organization. The findings of these explorations became a key resource for the developing thick data narrative.

Negotiating this complex data ethnography highlighted a number of issues:

■ Being in their own environment and using data hardware/software of their own choice appeared to make the interview a less stressful experience for the interviewee. Indeed, in comparison with similar interview situations, the interviewer would suggest that the willingness to challenge on behalf of the interviewee was substantially increased by their environment. This led to more robust answers and outcome material.
■ The lack of accepted convention(s) around physical presence and spacial engagement also made for a more relaxed interview. It appeared that the interviewees were quite literally comfortable in the space and hence could concentrate only on the questions being asked.
■ The issue of who was "in control" of the interview was challenged if not reversed. From an interviewer's perspective, it was much more difficult to "guide" the discussion since both body language and facial cueing were difficult, if not almost impossible. One upshot of this was that the interviews were shorter than may have been the case in a real one-to-one although all the material was covered. Interviewees were asked to forward any material they felt was not addressed and one opted to do so.
■ The observational aspects of the research involved not only the participants but also visitors to the venues, since their presence is key to the success of the body in question.
■ The work of the DSIR created additional ethnographic resource since much of their reporting offered what might be termed "unwitting testimony" to practices and attitudes in the partner organizations.

Creating the Ethnographic Narrative

The production of a text from collected data is the central problem for any reflexive researcher. In many research situations, the writing of the final report is a technical problem but one guided by the usual research conventions and notions of neutrality. In the case of ethnography, it is these very conventions the researcher must guard against.

Any attempt to break away from these conventions will involve the recognition that the creation of an ethnographic text is the telling of "a story" and that, in the course of this process, it is inevitable that more than one story must be told. This concept of the story is becoming more vital to the connected space as key players begin to understand the significance of turning data into effective narrative. Hence, in 2014, Google's online journal *Think* argued for a more narrative approach to the use of data in marketing organizations, quoting Rudyard Kipling's assertion that if history were told in the form of stories, it would never be forgotten (https://www.thinkwithgoogle.com/intl/en-gb/articles/tell-meaningful-stories-with-data.html). More recently, in an article examining the apparent failure of data analysis in the US presidential election and the Brexit vote, Ian Warren comments that "The key learning of the last year or so has been that the communication of effective emotional messages is currently beating data alone. This is particularly true in the age of social media which is effectively a delivery system for emotional weapons" (http://election-data.co.uk/how-do-you-feel-dont-ask). The emotional aspects of big data, for example, the way employees feel about their work, can be addressed fully only if operational narratives are constructed, narratives that emerge from a nuanced analysis of the relevant mined data. It is in the construction of this contextual narrative that the arts and humanities can play a key role. Indeed, it is worth arguing that it is only in the arts and humanities that sufficient skill and experience exist to illuminate fully the complexities of arts/big data. As Steve Jobs pointed out—"it is technology married to the liberal arts—the humanities—that makes our hearts sing."

Thick Data

For those researching big data through ethnography, this move to narrative has come to be known as "thick data." The term recognizes the work of Clifford Geertz in developing the idea of "thick description," an account that interprets, rather than describes, this interpretation being what offers greater understanding. The notion of thick, that is, deeply interpretive, data is advanced most eloquently by Tricia Wang in a blog article, "Big Data Needs Thick Data" (http://ethnographymatters.wordpress.com/2013/05/13/big-data-needs-thick-data/). In this article, Wang argues that a concentration on the quantitative data can leave organizations asking the wrong questions in the wrong way, a process that alienates their partners and employees:

> When organizations want to build stronger ties with stakeholders, they need stories. Stories contain emotions, something that no scrubbed and normalized dataset can ever deliver. Numbers alone do not respond to the emotions of everyday life: trust, vulnerability, fear, greed, lust, security, love, and intimacy...Thick Data approaches reach deep into people's hearts. Ultimately, a relationship between a stakeholder and an organization/brand is emotional, not rational.

It should be noted that when the term "story" is used in relation to data, it is not used in any casual sense. There is a difference between an anecdote, which is casual, and a research story, which is intentionally gathered and systematically sampled, shared, and analyzed in order to inspire new knowledge. As Wang points out, "great insights inspire design, strategy, and innovation."

A note of caution is also necessary, however. While the production of a written methodology illustrates the anxiety of a researcher to tell his/her story, it would be misleading to suggest that the detailing of a method then frees the researcher from the ethnographic story. Willis accepts this in *Learning to Labour* (1977), when he draws a dichotomy between narration and analysis, and while this arrangement frees the ethnographic narrative from the constraints of analysis, it has been criticized on the grounds that it makes the links between the portrayal of the culture in question and the analytical superstructure tenuous (Hammersley and Atkinson, 1983: 222). Nevertheless, this arrangement does facilitate the required move from the micro to the macro in terms of the development of general theory.

The outlining of the ethnographic method does not, therefore, exclude the researcher from the ethnographic story, and this recognition has led ethnographers to seek an explanation for their position in theories of narrative associated with structuralism and poststructuralism. Brown (1977: 7) suggests that the extensive use, for example, of irony and metaphor in ethnography makes it particularly apposite that critical theory should hold relevance for ethnographic research:

> For these reasons the critical concepts associated with the novel, poetry and drama—that is, 'poetics'—provide a privileged vocabulary for the aesthetic consideration of sociological theory.

Essentially, therefore, there has to be a recognition that the ethnographer is involved in a process where the ethnographic encounter itself becomes what Clifford calls a "fable of communication...a kind of fictional, but potent kinship," but a fable that has accepted the polyvocality of the ethnographic representation. Hence, any structure is dialogical, the product of a collaboration between the researcher and the researched. This recognition clearly creates problems for any science, such as data science, which claims to move from the particular to the general since the number of distinct registers at work in the written account and the intersubjectivity of its translation from fieldwork to representational account renders any account extremely contingent.

Clifford argues that ethnographies are in effect allegories at the moment they attempt to turn oral accounts into written accounts since they then imply that the written text is saving the culture in some unidentified way. Quoting Benjamin, he suggests that "appreciation of the transience of things, and the concern to redeem them for eternity, is one of the strongest impulses in allegory" (Geertz, 1977). He recommends that the written ethnography recognizes this complication in two ways: by identifying and recognizing the separate allegorical registers in the text and by making explicit the hierarchical structure of power whereby the author's stories "translate, encounter, and recontextualise other powerful stories" (Geertz, 1977).

These arguments have been taken to their logical conclusion, in the postmodern context, by Stephen Tyler (1986). Interestingly, Tyler also sees the process of postmodern fragmentation as the vital link between postmodernism and ethnography. Since all ethnographic experience is, by definition, fragmentary, this makes the ethnographic text the perfect vehicle for postmodern discourse. The most interesting aspect of Tyler's thesis for this context, however, is his insistence that the recording of an interviewee's thoughts steals from them the last vestige of authenticity they have, their voice. The developing ethnographic methodologies grounded in the technologies of the online space would seem to be addressing this concern, and indeed, the challenge to authority constructs noted previously, and the multiplicity of platforms through which the interviewee can articulate and "own" a narrative, may actually be a reversal in the traditional notion of the final narrative always being completed by the ethnographic author. This is especially true where the final narrative is multitextual.

It is clear, then, that the transfer of data from field notes to ethnographic text is a process that has both technical and ethical difficulties. These difficulties are compounded in a situation where the material is dialogic only in so far as the dialogue has been mediated by the author, a situation created by the ethical difficulties associated with recordings or verbatim subscriptions of their accounts. Indeed, some of the most telling comments by staff came in the context of informal conversations at break or lunch times since they were delivered in a context where off-guard remarks were also framed by the proximity of peers.

One tactic to address the complexity of data ethnography as outlined earlier is to complement the ethnographic narrative with visual narrative. Where data have been most successful in driving change and creating new models of understanding, it has been re-presented in ways that complement the narrative being articulated, usually through the use of institutionally relevant (and often institutionally designed) visual metaphors or infographics. Essentially, the infographic method takes raw data and turns them into visual narratives that not only explain but also frame the culture of the body they represent. Hence, this is not merely an aesthetic issue, but a further opportunity for organizations to control the story being presented and to articulate it in ways that underpin the cultural identity of the given organization. It may be argued that this process will add a further layer of complication to an already complex process, but discussions with arts groupings who have moved to such a system would suggest that there is an initial resource commitment in the design stage, but once the institutional templates are established, the resource cost is no more than those associated with any other form of presentation.

A good example is the work of the Danish Agency for Culture in the museums sector. Using a carefully designed visualization of audience segmentation, the Agency has been able to survey, and hence plan, the visitor population map for Danish museums. This has allowed a sophisticated, yet accessible, understanding of the key audience issues relating to this sector and resulted in Danish museums (and incidentally also museums in the geographic region generally) being seen as paradigmatic examples of good practice. The results are published again as an easily accessible publication (in both English and Danish) (Moore 2015).

Organizational Narrative

In the context of an ethnography examining arts organizations grounded in big data, the concept of the story grounded in human observation hence becomes of central significance. As noted, big data is, particularly in the arts context, first and foremost a cultural issue, one embedded in the ways in which data are used to tell stories about the organization in question. The technicist mystification of data, and the fetishization of numbers and figures, is also related to the tendency to see the online space as somehow new and, as yet, not fully understood. It is again the contention of this chapter that this so-called "new" has been mainstream for some time and that we are now in a period that is beyond the "digital," where the active pursuit of supposedly exclusive digital solutions to cultural problems has become counterproductive. The logical extension of this argument is that the idea that big data is somehow "special" needs to be challenged. To adapt and paraphrase Raymond Williams (1989), we have now reached the point where "data are ordinary" and should hence be seen as an integral part of everyday lived experience in the online ecology of arts organizations.

The ethnographic work undertaken in the ADI project indicates that it is the organizational semiotic chains that are most important in the process to make data central to the body's decision-making and planning. This is not merely a question of who speaks to whom but also a question of the kinds of language and shared vocabulary being used to tell the data story. If this fails to happen, then there is a tendency for those involved with data to retreat into secure spaces and protect the data they feel they have ownership over.

The ADI data ethnography illuminated a number of issues that should be of interest to other arts bodies. There was, for example, in some cases a tendency toward a "reverential gap" whereby primacy was afforded to the views and opinions of the artistic director, leaving those involved in data-related work (marketing, ticketing, etc.) with profound frustration. Similarly, there was a tendency for organizations to sustain what could be termed the "intuition myth," assuming that key individuals were capable of making intuitive decisions irrespective of what the data were suggesting. The most worrying aspect of the ethnographic study, however, was the use of data to justify decisions already made. This rearview mirror planning undermined the process of examining the totality of the data resource to identify patterns of behavior that might support informed planning for the future. This pattern recognition, ironically, may be the most important value big data has.

Emergence of Arts Data

While the data ethnography offered a range of interesting outcomes it more importantly gave rise to a more fundamental set of understandings. First, there is the growing acceptance that data are only as strong as the narrative, organizationally and contextually framed, through which they are articulated. This in turn underlines the importance of the arts/humanities in this process since no area of academic practice is better equipped to construct and support the creation of narrative than the arts.

Most crucially, the ADI research confirmed the suspicion that there is a form of data work that can be termed "arts data." It is grounded in the desire to offer thick narrative, to use data as a source of understanding, both on a structural and human level, to find creative and innovative ways to express data visually, and to cement the idea that organizations, especially in relation to data, must acknowledge the ecological nature of daily practices, what Deleuze and Guattari (1987: 8) call the "connections between semiotic chains, organisations of power, and circumstances relative to the arts, science and social struggle."

In conclusion, this chapter, examining the methods and outcomes of a significant arts data project undertaken with large metropolitan arts organizations, argues that the use of data is always a cultural rather than a statistical problem and shifts the primary importance of data away from the mining and representation of that data and into a humanities-based realm of deep interpretation and narrative. This is especially the case in arts organizations, where the impact of an event, performance, or body is difficult to articulate solely through numbers and statistical diagrams. The informed use of big data mediated through an ethnographic intervention offers arts bodies the tools to advance both the internal effectiveness of organizational structures and the external understanding and impact of the work these bodies do. By using the extensive data sets available (both internally and externally), and the developing ethnographic interrogative methodologies relevant to the online space, organizations can construct profound, explanatory narratives—thick data—applicable to the audience being addressed. These narratives can then, in turn, be used to initiate internal change, whether on a personal, institutional, organizational, or even spacial basis. In so doing, arts data and data ethnography celebrate and underline the fact that data are ultimately about people, not technologies, and in so doing represents a more optimistic future:

> For all the possibilities that communication technologies represent, their use for good or ill depends solely on people. Forget all the talk about machines taking over. What happens in the future is up to us. (Schmidt and Cohen, 2013: 11)

References

Brown, R.H. (1977) *A Poetic for Sociology: Toward a Logic of Discovery for the Social Sciences*, Cambridge: Cambridge University Press.

Deleuze, G. & Guattari, F. (1987) *A Thousand Plateaus: Capitalism and Schizophrenia*, Minnesota: University of Minnesota Press.

Geertz C. (1977) *The Interpretation of Cultures*, London: Basic Books.

Hammersley, M. & Atkinson, P. (1983) *Ethnography—Principles in Practice*, London: Routledge.

Lilley, A. & Moore, P. (2013) *Counting What Counts*, London: NESTA.

Moore G.P. (2015) Big Data, Practice and Policy, in Museums: Citizens and Sustainable Solutions (2015) Danish Agency for Culture, Copenhagen.

Rushkoff, D. (2013) *Present Shock*, London: Current.

Schmidt, E. & Cohen, J. (2013) *The New Digital Age: Reshaping the Future of People, Nations and Business*, London: John Murray.

Scott, L. (2015) *The Four Dimensional Human: Ways of Being in the Digital World*, London: Heinemann.

Tyler, S. (1986) "Post-Modern Ethnography: From Document of the Occult to Occult Document," in Clifford, J. and Marcus, G. (eds) *Writing Culture—The Poetics and Politics of Ethnography*, London: University of California Press.

Williams R. (1989) *Resources of Hope: Culture, Democracy, Socialism*, London: Verso.

Willis, P. (1977) *Learning to Labor*, New York: Columbia University Press.

Willis, P. (1980) "Notes on Method," in Hall, S., Hobson, D., Lowe, A., and Willis, P. (eds) *Culture, Media, Language*, London: Routledge.

DIGITAL
HUMANITIES

Chapter 6

Big Data and the Coming Historical Revolution: From Black Boxes to Models

Ian Milligan and Robert Warren

Contents

Traditionally, historians have gone to archives—up in the morning, off to the air-port, flying across the country, or even an ocean, and physically sitting in a read-ing room. These research trips imposed a substantial bottleneck on the amount of primary source research that historians could do. All of this has begun to change in the past three decades with the widespread advent of digitized primary sources, a force that historians are beginning to realize (or should be, in any event) is funda-mentally transforming their research.[1–3] This is a force that touches all historians, be they those who use volumes of digitized primary sources or even just those who use databases or other repositories to navigate newspaper articles or other print volumes. The new bottleneck increasingly relates to the consumption of this abundant information and performing analysis on it.* We used to be limited in the amount of time we could spend in an archive in Washington, DC, for example; now, we are limited in the amount of time we can spend sifting through all of this information online and making sense of it. New tools, methods, and scholarly frameworks are needed to deal with this material.

The shift toward online sources has been positive in many respects, particularly in the global reach it gives scholars, the lowered barriers to access, and the speed by which many historians can find the information they need. Yet it has also come with downsides: a lack of understanding of the Optical Character Recognition (OCR) algorithms that underpin source digitization, inattention to what has *not* been digitized, and, in some cases, the loss of context surrounding individual documents or collections. History, previously the province of painstaking archival work, is becoming a discipline dominated by website keyword searches. This chapter does not indict that process—indeed, we believe, in general, that the more accessible nature of historical research and new technologies has been a net positive—but rather argues that this shift requires a methodological rethinking. Engagement with this new digital world requires critical reflection and interdisciplinary engagement.

This chapter is organized as follows: we begin by reviewing the ongoing problems of data scale within the digital humanities. We then review different models of computational support for the digital scholar and different models of collaboration and publications for scholars. Given our experiences and situation as academics in North America, this largely draws on the professional experiences of that community of practice. Finally, we conclude with observations about the nature of scholarly work and its historic ability to adapt to new tools as they become available.

The Flood: From Close Reading to Black Boxes

As humanists, historians come from a tradition where each document has traditionally been understood through the lens of close reading.[4] This has led to a high degree of interaction between an individual scholar and his or her documents. Achieving this was costly: physical travel to archives and libraries to consult records. With the advent of online archives and databases, historians now have tremendous access to global resources, as well as the opportunity to discover their existence through search engines. Yet, this tremendous access to material has the consequence that the work of actually performing analysis takes up a larger proportion of time.

In short, physical access is no longer the defining factor for a scholar's research. The intimate research relationship with sources that scholars previously enjoyed is

---

* A shift effectively discussed in Roy Rosenzweig, "Scarcity or Abundance? Preserving the Past in a Digital Era," *The American Historical Review* 108, no. 3 (June 2003): 735–762, doi:10.1086/529596.

not necessarily possible at scale. While enormous amounts of gains have been done in the accessibility sense, much remains in the analysis and consumption sense.

This is intimately connected with the rise of the digital humanities as a field of scholarly analysis. Defining the digital humanities is not straightforward, as witnessed by the amount of discussion on that very topic.[5,6] Part of this field considers the data consumption, processing, and analytical and synthesis processes that are used by scholars in order to perform their research, which is intimately connected to the work we consider here. This thus lies at the heart of the paradox of the digital turn. It is now a victim of its own success: the information relevant to the scholar is now present in such quantity that it overwhelms the scholar's ability to consume it. This means that a critical scholarly infrastructure is needed to deal with scale, something that we need to tackle now.

The capacity to process historical information has not kept pace with the capacity to retain digital records. As an example, historians who have studied a small- to medium-sized event in the 20th century, such as the Canadian New Left, can honestly state that they have reviewed much of the extant formally archived primary documentation and drawn a conclusion from it.[7] Nothing is perfect, of course—sources have always been missed, interviews forgotten, memory changed, documents destroyed—but the scale at work meant that quite a bit of the preserved material was reviewed. Scholars reviewing the book would also be familiar with the largest collections and be able to explore their validity.

Scholars of digital era events, facing abundance, will be able to read a much smaller fraction of this information. A period where a social movement, such as Canada's First Nations Idle No More movement, can leave behind over 55,000 tweets in one single day suggests that the percentage of sources that a scholar can directly read has dwindled to a much smaller percentage. While scholarly access to such large repositories is not yet a settled question, the Library of Congress preserves these tweets; increasingly, individual researchers too are creating and storing their own curated data sets of tweets pertaining to large-scale events such as the Women's March, Presidential elections in the United States, and beyond.* We can see this in other events over the last 30 years: the First Gulf War, the e-mail records of the Clinton Administration, the World Trade Center bombings, or the events of the September 11, 2001, attacks.

Fears around digital abundance are not new. Chad Gaffield, a historian at the University of Ottawa, provided an overview of the field in a recent *Digital Studies* article. Indeed, he quotes the president of the American Historical Association Carl Bridenbaugh—*in 1963*—bemoaning the coming tide of data. "Among other ways," Bridenbaugh declared during his presidential address, "bigness has struck us by proliferating sources and editing, thereby deluging us with an overwhelming

---

* The Library of Congress announced that they were working with Twitter to preserve a digital archive of publicly accessible tweets in 2010. Access remains unclear. For a database of available Twitter datasets, see http://www.docnow.io/catalog/.

mass of data for the study of the last one and a half centuries of history."[8] Just as the problem is familiar, so too is the difficulty of exploring this abundance via computing. This quotation from a letter to the American Library Association (in 1962!) is oddly prophetic in the stresses between scholar, information tools and those that build the tools:

> Here is the basic weakness of information retrieval. It can only work with the values of the past. A computer cannot think. It can only remember what someone has told it to remember. Who is to decide what material is relevant to a subject? If he who programs the computer is as capable as the scholar in relating relevant material, he is wasting valuable time. He should be doing research.[9]

This highlights the inherent contradiction at play. On one hand, scholars want the scalability of computational processing while at the same time have concerns around losing control to a black box mechanism they do not understand. For example, when using Google, it may seem straightforward that the first page of responses for "Canadian history" include Wikipedia, the Government of Canada's citizenship guide, and some other projects; but why is the "First Peoples Historical Overview" or the history of the First World War Battle of the Somme relegated to the 10th page, where few will find it? This is an excellent example of how algorithms and computers begin to shape the work that we do.

What does it mean for a historian to turn analysis over to a computer? There is a precedent for this type of arrangement: previously, scholars would often make use of typists and typesetters to convert their manuscripts into publishable form. With the advent of affordable software applications, the difficulty of using computers for word processors has been greatly reduced and scholars now tend to do their own editing. Spreadsheets, for example, have greatly enhanced our ability to perform repetitive mathematical operations and basic statistical calculations.

Hence, the software application is now the mediating element between the computer and the scholar, but only within a limited context. Part of the promise of digital tools is to expand that context so that more questions can be answered by the scholars themselves, either through the use of prepackaged software or by having the scholars themselves write their own software.

Single-purpose, prepackaged software development is a complex endeavor that usually requires a team of specialists. This cost means that only the most generalizable problems are therefore tackled and that the more obscure computational needs of digital humanities need to be tackled by the scholars themselves. An additional complicating factor in the use of an external programmer to mediate these problems is that the addition of such a mediator adds delays and risks of miscommunication. While it is unrealistic to expect historians to learn to become computer scientists or programmers, they at the very least need to be able to use purpose-built programming languages in order to directly manipulate information of interest.

Working at Scale: Digital Collaborations in the Age of Big Data

To realize this, collaboration is necessary. As we move into working at scale, digital historians often find themselves reaching to form collaborations with the science, technology, engineering, and mathematics (STEM) disciplines, especially computer science. These collaborations have not been as widespread as perhaps hoped, however, due in part to tensions between these fields. STEM scholars and humanists often misunderstand each other's objectives, wants, and needs. In the section that follows, we focus on history and computer science given the authors' backgrounds. However, the situations and conclusions may extend directly to related fields.

Computer science is the study of computations, "the branch of engineering science that studies (with the aid of computers) computable processes and structures."[10] Yet to many in the general public, and by extension some humanists, computer scientists can be misconceived as programmers who write computer code. As Michael Fellows and Ian Parberry wrote in 1993, "Computer science is no more about computers than astronomy is about telescopes, biology is about microscopes or chemistry is about beakers and test tubes. Science is not about tools, it is about how we use them and what we find out when we do."[11] Yet the general misconception leads to a warped view where computer scientists are seen as technicians executing precreated plans rather than a field of study.

This preconception has a dramatic impact when projects that attempt to study problems from an interdisciplinary perspective try to bring digital humanist together with computer scientists. "We have the problems and you have the tools to solve these problems" is how the relationship was foreseen by one professor to one of the coauthors. Echoes of this can be seen in the contemporary relationship between digital humanists and computer science. Relationship-building efforts turn sour when one side feel that their role was envisioned to be a data-entry operator, and the other, when they realize that there were no premade tools available.

At the heart of the tension is the notion of what is the meaning of a tool, an algorithm, a protocol, a methodology, and all of its other various materializations. To the computer scientist, computing is a toolbox that is arranged and rearranged to meet the analytical needs of the moment without a set procedure to be followed. To the historian, computing is a computer program to solve a single problem at a time, resulting in occasionally uncritical use that does not fit well with interdisciplinary colleagues.

The concept of "data literacy" is now being used to represent the skill set required to deal with these problems, although in its current incarnation within the humanities, it is primarily about data visualization and manipulation.[12] Analytical and significance training is required to make sense of abundance, however. We know that building good tools to support research is hard and that, in many cases, training is required before somebody can use data tools effectively. Thus, what additional computing or information management training should we create for digital humanities scholars, without having them take a second degree? The ever-expanding world of digital tools requires the development of a critical infrastructure through which to find, process, and analyze these sources. This necessitates a move beyond simply asking questions to get answers. This is a process that has been occurring over the last 15 years, as historians increasingly turn to search portals to begin the process of exploratory research and to primary source databases to find resources of interest. Our fear, however, is to make sure we do not reproduce black boxes that occlude the underlying mechanisms.

A cornerstone of data literacy and the scientific method is the testing of a hypothesis and the development of either a proof or a beginning of a proof on data. Much of the data literacy movement remains at the data manipulation and representation stage, which is worrisome as quantitative empirical analysis requires statistical significance testing as well as data quality checking in order to avoid embarrassing erroneous conclusion.[13] Visualizations and visualization tools such as Voyant Tools are excellent data exploration and communication tools but can lead authors to erroneous conclusions if the hypothesis is not rigorously checked.[14] We note that this does not conflict with the humanist's current research methods (where anecdotal evidence is sometimes required by necessity) but that it is necessary so that the humanist does not come to rely on unsubstantiated results from a black box software package. The answer to these issues, we believe, lies in models.

The Path Forward? How Models Can Bridge the Divide and Attempt to Resolve the Paradox

All of this means that there is an increasingly evident need for humanists that use digital tools—increasingly most of us—to become fluent and understand the underlying mechanisms at work. In the archival age, a historical methodology that consisted of "I went to an archive and found these results" might be sufficient—the simple fact of an archive preserving material suggested potential historical significance—this method does not scale to archives that consist of billions of documents. We can now find citations or evidence for almost any argument, meaning that the contextualization is what matters. Moving forward will require attention to models, not specific tools, and new methods of training and framing the questions.

We thus need to be increasingly rigorous in questioning, interrogating, and challenging the tools that underlie our research. This is not to say that all humanists need to become programmers. Yet they do need enough knowledge to converse intelligently, or read a simplified explanation, to understand models at work.

Models are key. An emphasis on individual tools, implementations, and programming languages is misleading—something our historian coauthor knows all too well, having seen his computer science colleagues move through multiple programming languages in the span of a two-year project (when dealing with large numbers of sources, efficiency gains matter).* At the heart of big data analytics is our essential belief that there is no one tool that can be used to get an answer but an ecosystem of tools that are manipulated in a unique arrangement to create a unique solution. This means that researchers have to be nimble in their thinking and create their solution instead of finding a tool that is the solution. Tools become outdated and dramatically change and algorithms shift. An understanding of underlying principles becomes more important. "What button on what tool do I press to get the answer" may be the unspoken question, but it comes from the wrong place. But how does one operationalize this? We need interdisciplinary engagement, but that is easier said than done. What shape can it actually take?

At a base level of algorithmic and technological awareness, one of the authors is a coeditor of the Programming Historian (http://programminghistorian.org/). Growing out of a series of Python tutorials, the site now hosts over 50 lessons from using the command line, writing sustainably in plain text, cleaning data, and implementing classifiers, OCR, and data mining. Rather than providing "black box" tools for historians, the emphasis is on providing the underlying knowledge to implement and deploy algorithms on a variety of data sets. As expertise is distributed around many disparate universities—it is rare to find a history department that has more than one self-described digital historian, a landscape that will hopefully change over the next few years.

Hubs like the Programming Historian allow us to build up a knowledge base. Other projects such as DH Bridge (http://dhbridge.org/) and the Software Carpentry model bring in-person workshops to institutions and professional organizations. Key to these programs is that the emphasis is not on the tools but on creating the specific tool chains required for the specific analysis.

The success of organizers like Software Carpentry, DH Bridge, and the Programming Historian, however, may speak to the challenges of incorporating digital training into the humanities curriculum within university structures. Despite the lip service given to cross-disciplinary training, the rise of new university budgetary models—in Canada, largely under the gamut of "activity or responsibility based budgeting"—means that departments and faculties can be increasingly reluctant to see their bodies taking classes in other disciplines.† As North American history enrollments are in crisis, students are also increasingly turning to programs that provide (or at least promise) more applied vocational training.

When classes can be mounted, the emphasis, we believe, needs to be on abstract principles and computational theory rather than directly applied technology.

---

* The project is the Archives Unleashed project, at http://archiveunleashed.org/.
† The impact of this is still too early to say. Administrators do need to play a role in trying to counterbalance this, but there is a financial incentive to eschew too much interdisciplinary collaboration at the undergraduate level. For more, see http://higheredstrategy.com /responsibility-centred-budgeting/.

Learn-to-code events are useful but are driven toward creating a demonstrative piece of software rather than solving a computation problem. This is an extension of computer science being seen as somehow synonymous with programming: a specific programming language is being taught to create software rather than using the programming language to solve a problem. Furthermore, there exists a significant difference between creating a modest piece of software and a commercial-grade, end-user friendly application. That distinction is not easily communicated during a single event; software development is a career in itself, which can only leave participants with flawed expectations about tool creation.

Structures at the heart of academia also need challenging. The failure of information technology (IT) is a refrain that is sometimes spoken in organizations in that IT is no longer (or never was) a technology organization but an administrative one. The standardized desktop computer oriented to administrative use, with restricted controls installed for security reasons, is not helpful to academics attempting large-scale computational analysis requiring software that is not on an officially approved list. Yet, IT departments often have de facto control over software packages installed since they control most of the base infrastructure of personal computers. IT service help desks are similarly oriented toward solving specific day-to-day problems such as printing, changing passwords, and occasionally teaching the basics of desktop office-type application. By design, they are not oriented toward supporting digital projects.

The capacity to provide computational support for digital humanities beyond institutional systems is problematic as there is no capacity or understanding of the problems being faced by digital humanities. Initiatives geared toward high performance computing such as Compute Canada and dedicated research support personnel have been extremely helpful in accelerating research in these areas, and we believe that the model should be ported to the digital humanities department.

Lastly, we believe that there is a lot of value in furthering modeling and ontological design initiatives in the digital humanities. Beyond providing machine-readable structures that describe the problems facing digital humanists, we believe that they also serve to increase communications between scholars, even in situations where the amount of data is simply too large for two scholars to "swap spreadsheets." The benefits, beyond sharing the interchange data between projects to enrich analytical capacity, are the communication of the underlying assumptions, methodologies, and intent of the data beyond that which can be communicated through normal database schemas.

Some projects such as the Canadian Writing Research Collaboratory have taken the lead in pursuing the publication of such information in order to foster future collaborations and interoperability with other humanities projects.* Interestingly, a large obstacle to these processes has been the difficulty in getting scholars to define what their viewpoints and definitions are due to the fear of excluding other viewpoints.[15]

---

* http://www.cwrc.ca/

Indeed, the entire point of creating an ontology for one's data is to document our own viewpoint and biases so that others are aware of them when using the data. This is a difficult process even for professionals in that it requires the documentation of processes and underlying behaviors that are long ingrained within the scholar as not to be immediately obvious. A direct parallel in the corporate world is the implementation of Enterprise Resource Planning systems that require much the same process and that succeed in only 58% of cases.[16] Clearly this is a difficult process of introspection even for professionals, although we believe that the coming scale of data used for scholarly research will eventually require it.

Publishing models also play a significant role in inhibiting cooperation between the two academic divides. Humanities disciplines such as history are still largely wedded to the sole-author model: the scholarly monograph is the primary deliverable expected for tenure, with articles showing intellectual progression toward the final product. Research assistants are typically acknowledged in footnotes or the foreword to a book. While STEM publishing models are not uniform, students who contribute substantially to the framing and execution of a project receive authorship in disciplines such as computer science, and collaborative approaches to projects are recognized. A historian seeking tenure may hesitate to substantially collaborate with a computer scientist if it requires credit sharing. While recent moves such as the American Historical Associations Guidelines for the Evaluation of Digital Scholarship by Historians have addressed the "myriad uses of digital technology for research, teaching, pedagogy," adoption remains uneven.[17]

In our experience, fruitful collaborative publishing requires some give and take. One collaboration between a historian and a computer scientist at the University of Waterloo saw initial results published in a computer science conference—prestigious for computer science, whereas for historians, conferences are traditionally lesser-ranked venues for scholarly work. Results were then refined, developed, and published in a computer science journal with an open-access publishing option, allowing the traditional journal format to appear on a curriculum vitae. The rise of open-access models, even the "green" model that allows for submission to an institutional repository, means that a historian can reach audiences even when publishing outside of traditional disciplinary venues.

We believe that different models of collaboration, publication and communications are needed for the digital humanities owing to the complexity of the data, the volume of data, and the inherent miscommunications resulting from the increased exchange of data between scholars.

Conclusion

As with a previous generation of scholars who learned new tools, be they the typewriter, the word processor, or the spreadsheet, the abundance of primary sources requires digital humanists to learn new tools. We do not believe that humanists should become computer scientists or that computer scientists should become humanists, but that better models of collaborations must be found.

Perhaps a limited analogy is that of a sculptor: there needs to be a mix of both technique and artistic talent in order for one to perform the art, and in the most general cases, this is all that is needed. However, a sculptor creating larger-than-life statues that require multiple heavy parts will need specialized engineering support that is beyond the abilities of the average scholar. As with the advent of the word processor and the ability of most scholars to do their own typing and layout, the next generation of scholars will be required to perform a light amount of programming, not to develop software, but to communicate to the machine what the objective of the analysis is. Flexibility in using different models of computing will help to avoid the "I have a hammer and thus everything looks like a nail" trap.

The shift from scarcity to abundance requires that historians and other humanists come to grips with big data. In this chapter, we have emphasized that this is a shift that affects practicing historians of all stripes, not just self-proclaimed "digital" ones. As historians sit in front of their computer, running Google searches to refine an initial thought, exploring ProQuest or JSTOR for primary sources, plumbing the depths of the Internet Archive, or perhaps even engaging with born-digital sources, they are increasingly at the whims of algorithms they may not understand, nor should they be expected to fully do so, but simply to engage with the idea of thinking algorithmically. Pedagogical models like Software Carpentry or DH Bridge help not only the adoption of specific tools but also ways of thinking. Awareness is a good first step.

Ultimately, these are not problems that historians can be expected to tackle or grapple with alone. Cooperation is necessary. In some cases, that may require targeted, specific cooperation such as the current authors, a computer scientist, and a historian, working together on a shared publication. It requires the valuation of the work that all scholarly professionals bring to the table, an understanding that computer scientists are not "just" IT (and, of course, that IT is not "just" IT either, as they sustain systems that enable much of the world around us) and that collaborative work is not necessarily less work or fewer valuable sole-authored publications.

An exciting world is ahead of us. As the barriers to finding information decline, we can spend less time traveling in the case of digitized repositories, which also puts information into the hands of those without travel budgets or time we are facing the prospect of a more inclusive approach to writing history. Critical thought will ensure, however, that we are not in the thrall of the black box.

References

1. Lara Putnam, "The Transnational and the Text-Searchable: Digitized Sources and the Shadows They Cast," *The American Historical Review* 121, no. 2 (April 2016): 377–402, doi:10.1093/ahr/121.2.377.

2. Ian Milligan, "Illusionary Order: Online Databases, Optical Character Recognition, and Canadian History, 1997–2010," *The Canadian Historical Review* 94, no. 4 (2013): 540–569.

3. Jennifer Rutner and Roger C. Schonfeld, *Supporting the Changing Research Practices of Historians: Final Report from ITHAKA S+R*, technical report (ITHAKA S+R, December 2012), doi:10. 18665/sr. 22532, http://www.sr.ithaka.org/wp-content /uploads/2015/08/supporting-the-changing-research-practices-of-historians.pdf.

4. Franco Moretti, *Graphs, Maps, Trees: Abstract Models for Literary History* (London; New York: Verso, 2007).

5. Melissa Terras, Julianne Nyhan, and Edward Vanhoutte, eds., *Defining Digital Humanities: A Reader* (Farnham, England; Burlington, VT: Routledge, 2013).

6. Anne Burdick, Johanna Drucker, Peter Lunenfeld, Todd Presner, and Jeffrey Schnapp, *Digital Humanities* (Cambridge, MA: The MIT Press, 2012).

7. Ian Milligan, *Rebel Youth: 1960s Labour Unrest, Young Workers, and New Leftists in English Canada* (Vancouver, Canada: UBC Press, 2014).

8. Chad Gaffield, "The Surprising Ascendance of Digital Humanities: And Some Suggestions for an Uncertain Future," *Digital Studies/Le Champ Num'erique* (September 2016), ISSN: 1918-3666, https://www.digitalstudies.org/ojs/index.php /digital_studies/article/view/367.

9. Mary-Peale Schofield, "Libraries Are for Books: A plea from a lifetime customer" [in English], *ALA Bulletin* 56, no. 9 (1962): 803–805, ISSN: 03644006, http://www .jstor.org/stable/25696522.

10. *Word Net*, April 2017, http://wordnetweb.princeton.edu/perl/webwn?s=computer +science&sub=Search+WordNet&o2=&o0=1&o8=1&o1=1&o7=&o5=&o9=&o6 =&o3=&o4=&h=0.

11. Michael R. Fellows and Ian Parberry, "SIGACT Trying to Get Children Excited about CS," *Computing Research News* 5, no. 1 (January 1993): 7.

12. Chantel Ridsdale, James Rothwell, Hossam Ali-Hassan, Michael Bliemel, Dean Irvine, Daniel Kelley, Stan Matwin, Michael Smit, and Bradley Wuetherick, "Data Literacy: A Multidisciplinary Synthesis of the Literature," in *Nineteenth SAP Academic Conference Americas* (San Diego, CA, February 2016).

13. Greg Millter, "A Scientist's Nightmare: Software Problem Leads to Five Retractions," *Science* 314, no. 5807 (December 2006): 1856–1857.

14. Stéfan Sinclair and Geoffrey Rockwell, *Voyant Tools*, April 2017, http://voyant-tools .org/.

15. Johanna Drucker, David Kim, Iman Salehian, and Anthony Bushong, "Intro to Digital Humanities," in *Ontologies and Metadata* (Los Angeles: UCLA, August 2014), 119, http://dh101.humanities.ucla.edu/wp-content/uploads/2014/09/IntroductionToDigital Humanities_Textbook.pdf

16. Panorama Consulting Solution, *2015 ERP Report* (Panorama Consulting Solution, 2015), http://go.panorama-consulting.com/rs/panoramaconsulting/images/2015%20 ERP%20Report.pdf.

17. Edward Ayers, David Bell, Peter Bol, Timothy Burke, Seth Denbo, James Gregory, Claire Potter, Janice Reiff, and Kathryn Tomasek, *Guidelines for the Professional Evaluation of Digital Scholarship by Historians* (American Historical Society, June 2015), https:// www. historians. org/teaching-and-learning/digital-history-resources /evaluation-of-digital-scholarship-in-history/guidelines-for-the-professional-evaluation -of-digital-scholarship-by-historians.

Chapter 7

Use of Big Data in Historical Research

Richard A. Hawkins

Contents

Introduction

The executive director of the American Historical Association, James Grossman (2012), has defined big data as "the zillions of pieces of information that traverse the internet." He suggests that "there is something here for historians. Maybe even something Big [sic]." However, historians have been slow to realize the full potential of big data. There are number of reasons. First, in some countries such as Britain, a lot of the big data is provided by commercial publishers, and thus, access requires an individual or institutional subscription/payment. Second, the big data website search engines rely on optical character recognition (OCR), the accuracy of which may be considerably less than 100% such as in the case of pre-twentieth century newspapers. There is a tradeoff between the number of scanned pages and the accuracy of OCR. Third, many historians are unaware of the full extent of the big data available. As Zhang, Liu, and Matthews (2015) suggest, there is a disconnect between the library and information services professionals who are developing the digital humanities resources and the humanities academics who are the intended user community. Fourth, historians also face the daunting volume of digitized historical data. Rosenzweig (2011, 23) observes, "Surely, the injunction of traditional historians to look at 'everything' cannot survive in a digital era in which 'everything' has survived." Fifth, using big data requires historians to adopt a different research methodology. Rosenzweig and Cohen (2011, 31) observe that historians are accustomed to analyzing discrete historical sources with great care, whereas "[c]omputer scientists specialize in areas such as 'data mining' (finding statistical trends), 'information retrieval' (extracting specific bits of text or data), and 'reputational systems' (determining reliable documents or actors), all of which presuppose large corpuses on which to subject algorithms." Sixth, it would also appear that some historians regard digital sources to be of inferior value. Jonathan Blaney (2016), a librarian at the University of London's Institute of Historical Research (IHR), has observed that historians using British History Online (2016), the IHR's digital library of key printed primary and secondary sources for the history of Britain and Ireland, often contact him for the page numbers of the original paper books, articles, or documents. They are unwilling to cite the web addresses of the digitized version of the sources in their publications. Rosenzweig and Cohen (2011, 31) note that with some exceptions, historians have not adopted the research methodology of computer scientists to engage with big data. Historians generally prefer to apply their own minds to analyze data rather than using digital technology to do it for them. The New Economic Historians from the predigitization era are among the exceptions. This school of economic history produced some noteworthy research findings such as Fogel and Engerman's (1974) *Time on the Cross*, which argued that the Ante-Bellum American South had a growing rather than stagnating economy and that slave agriculture was not inefficient compared with free agriculture. Sixth, Zhang, Liu and Matthews (2015, 366) also note that "The unit of currency in DH [Digital Humanities] is not necessarily an article or a book, but rather a project, which is usually published using an open web platform, allowing users to dynamically interact with underlying data." In countries where research funding privileges traditional articles and books, this may result in historians eschewing full engagement with big data.

Grossman is correct to suggest that big data has great potential for historians. This chapter uses case studies from contemporary historical research to explore how this potential might be realized from the perspective of a historian rather than a library and information services professional.

British Library Labs Case Studies of the Use of Big Data in Historical Research

One way the use of big data in historical research might be increased is by the enhancement of the engagement of library and information services professionals with academic historians. The first three examples of historical research based on big data are part of a British initiative that seeks to do this. In 2013, the British Library established British Library Labs, an initiative funded by the Andrew W. Mellon Foundation, to support and inspire the public use of the British Library's digital collections and data in exciting and innovative ways. Several of the projects funded by British Library Labs have been in the area of historical research. They include Melodee Beals' "Scissors and Paste" project, which won the British Library Labs 2016 Research Award. Beals used the nineteenth century British Library Newspapers digital collection to investigate the opportunities for data mining large-scale newspaper databases for reprinted and repurposed news content. She observes that in the nineteenth century, editors often reused content from other newspapers. Her project has resulted in the creation of software to identify strings of this kind of news content. Beals has used case studies, detailed analyses of additions, omissions, and wholesale changes to offer insights into a feature of nineteenth century newspaper editing that has been mostly overlooked by historians (Beals 2016).

Another British Library Labs project in the area of historical research is Katrina Navickas's "Political Meetings Mapper." It builds on the research for her monograph, *Protest and the Politics of Space and Place, 1789–1848* (Navickas 2016), a survey of the rise of mass movements for democracy and workers' rights in northern England from 1789 to 1848. Her project was one of the two 2015 winners of the British Library Labs Competition. Navickas (2015) observes that protest is about space and place. Newspapers are a major source of data on when and where historical protests and political meetings took place. However, before her project, historians had only been able to plot the locations of small numbers of political meetings manually. Navickas's project has developed a tool, the Political Meetings Mapper, to extract notices of meetings from historical newspapers and plot them on layers of historical maps in the British Library's collections. It visualizes the locations of political events in what Navickas (British Library Digital Scholarship Blog 2015) describes as "the crucial era of the 1830s and 1840s, when Chartism, the first and largest movement for democracy in Britain, held thousands of meetings and demonstrations to campaign for the vote. By plotting the meetings listed in the Chartist newspaper, *The Northern Star*, from 1838 to 1844, [she] hopes to discover new spatial patterns in where popular politics happened, and in so doing, help answer the questions of how and why it happened."

Navickas's Political Meetings Mapper inspired another British Library Labs project by doctoral student Hannah-Rose Murray (2016). Her project, which was a finalist in the 2016 British Library Labs Competition, is entitled "Black Abolitionist Performances and Their Presence in Britain." She wants to create a similar digital mapper for black abolitionist speeches. But Murray's project involved a much larger and wider set of data. The black abolitionists travelled to Britain from 1830 to 1900 and gave lectures in large cities and small towns. This meant that their lectures were reported in many metropolitan and provincial newspapers. Murray observes that the scale of her project was perhaps its greatest challenge. She also found that the nineteenth century British Library Newspaper's OCR was imperfect and this meant that the data were not always read correctly. It produced false results and also potentially missed hundreds of references to the black abolitionists. Murray observes, "In order to 'clean' and sort through the 'muddied' OCR and the 'clean' OCR, we need to teach the computer what is 'positive text' (i.e., language that uses the word 'abolitionist,' 'black,' 'fugitive,' 'negro') and 'negative text' (language that does not relate to abolition)." Murray has spent several years transcribing black abolitionist speeches, and most of this will act as the "positive" text. This will ensure that the abolitionist language can be made easily readable. Murray and British Library Labs can then test the performance of this against some of the data they already have, and once the probability ensures that they are on the right track, they can apply it to a larger data set. All of these data are built into what is called a classifier, created by Ben O'Steen, the British Library Labs technical lead. This classifier will read the OCR and collect newspaper references. It measures words by weight and frequency (British Library Digital Scholarship Blog 2016). It is worth noting that search engines have been making use of weight and frequency since the early days of computers (Salton, Wong, and Yang 1975). The classifier also relies on probability, so for example, if there is an article that mentions "fugitive" and "slave" in the same section, it ranks a higher probability that the article will be discussing someone like Frederick Douglass or William Craft. On the other hand, a search engine might read the word "fugitive slave" in different articles on the same page of a newspaper. Murray and British Library Labs are currently processing the results of the classifier and adjusting the data to try and achieve a higher level of accuracy (British Library Digital Scholarship Blog 2016).

Other Case Studies of the Use of Big Data in Historical Research

Australian historians have also used digitized newspapers in innovative ways. The National Library of Australia (2016) has a diverse and growing digital collection, Trove, which included over 510 million individual items as of late 2016. Phillips and Osmond (2015) have used the extensive collection of newspapers digitized for Trove to analyze the history of women's surfing in Australia in the early twentieth century. They note that previous academic writing on surfboard riding has focused on men. In Australian popular culture, Isabel Letham is celebrated as the pioneer woman surfer albeit in a role supporting Duke Paoa Kahanamoku's surfboard demonstration during the summer of 1914–1915. Kahanamoku was a visiting Hawaiian Olympic swimming champion. In the pre-big data era, historical research on women's surfing was constrained by the lack of primary sources. While newspapers had the greatest potential as a source of information in the absence of other primary sources, there were too many pages to search and pre-digital technologies, in particular microfilm readers, were too time-consuming. Philips and Osmond were able to search Trove's digitized newspapers. They discovered a spike in coverage of women's surfing in the 1910s and furthermore that the surfing activity of Isma Amor predated Letham's association with Kahanamoku in 1915.

There has been significant engagement with big data by historians of crime in Britain and Australia. Starting in 2000, the Old Bailey Proceedings Online project (The Proceedings of the Old Bailey, 1674–1913, 2003–2015) digitized the records of London's Central Criminal Court and they are now available for historians to make use of for their research. The project's website provides a fully searchable, digitized collection of all surviving editions of the *Old Bailey Proceedings* from 1674 to 1913 and of the *Ordinary of Newgate's Accounts* between 1676 and 1772. It allows historians to access, free of charge for noncommercial use, over 197,000 trials and biographical details of approximately 2500 men and women executed at Tyburn. These data can be combined with other sources such as the digitized British Library newspapers and English and Welsh census data to create a more detailed picture of the history of crime, criminals, and criminal justice. However, Williams and Godfrey (2016, 401) also observe that apart from the 1881 English and Welsh Census, the digitized data are not in the public domain and freely accessible to historical researchers. The data have been digitized by the British National Archives in partnership with private companies who make these commercially owned data available on pay-per-view websites whose principal users are family historians.

Williams and Godfrey (2016, 399) are part of an Anglo-Australian research project called the Digital Panopticon, which follows from cradle to grave the 90,000 people sentenced at London's Central Criminal Court to either imprisonment in England or transportation to Australia. The lack of full access to the digitized census data sets makes it less easy to analyze the population of inmates awaiting transportation in British prisons and hulks in 1841, 1851, and 1861. Big data can also be used to reinforce studies of English regional crime, as Cox, Godfrey, Johnson, and Turner (2015, 187) have done in their recent study of punishment, recidivism, and desistance in penal policy as experienced in the northwest England in the second half of the nineteenth century and the early twentieth century.

Military historians have also made use of big data. Digitized First World War personnel records are now available for Britain and the white settler Dominions, with the exception of South Africa. As Inwood and Ross (2016) observe, the data contained in these records can be used for research unrelated to the history of warfare, such as the standard of living. This can be done by comparing the height of adult soldiers born in different decades. It would appear that the stature of Australians was declining slightly over time. An even stronger decline can be observed for Canadians. This suggests that urbanization and growing economic inequality in the British colonies were beginning to replicate the adverse health conditions in Britain, albeit in a less extreme form. Another insight from these records is the finding that Scots who emigrated to Canada were taller than those who remained in Britain. Inwood and Ross (2016, 437) observe, "The fact that the emigrants were taller than those who remained in Britain is the first hint from any source that the stream of migrants from Europe to North America involved men and women who were more robust than average within their home societies... If other sources confirm the pattern, we would have reason to think that the emigration of especially robust citizens undermined economic growth in Britain and hastened developments overseas."

Big data can also be used to help fill in gaps in historical knowledge. The author's (Hawkins 2017a) entry on Heinrich Hackfeld for the German Historical Institute Washington, DC's, five-volume project *Immigrant Entrepreneurship: German-American Business Biographies, 1720 to the Present* can be used to illustrate some of the potential of big data too. Hackfeld founded a mercantile business in the Hawaiian Islands in the mid-nineteenth century. By the First World War, it was one of the principal businesses in Hawaii and the largest German-owned company in the US territory. During the First World War, H. Hackfeld & Co. was seized by the US Alien Property Custodian and its assets were sold to a new American-owned company, American Factors. Unfortunately, the company's archive has not survived apart from a typewritten summary prepared in July 1919. Previous histories of the firm provide an incomplete picture of the firm, with basic information such as Hackfeld's family background missing.

Big data provided an opportunity to fill many of the gaps in the history of H. Hackfeld & Co. A German family history website, Oldenburgische Gesellschaft für Familienkunde e.V. (2017), provided genealogical information about Hackfeld and his family missing from previous histories. Hackfeld became a sailor in his mid-teens and the 1919 typescript provided some clues as to his career as a mariner before establishing his business in Honolulu. It was possible to supplement the information in the typescript with reports from two digitized Hamburg newspapers available as part of the Europeana Newspapers project, an aggregated gateway to digitized historic European newspapers available from the European Library (2005–2013) website. The Hamburg newspapers provided additional information about some of Hackfeld's voyages and the ships he sailed on. However, there were some obstacles. The accuracy of OCR for texts using German Gothic script is much lower than that for English Latin script, and it is probable that there were relevant news reports that were not identified by the search engine. Further information was found in digitized historic books such as directories available as part of the Bremen State and University Library's Digital Collection (2010).

After Hackfeld's arrival in Honolulu, other digitized data proved to be very useful. The Library of Congress's (2016) *Chronicling America: Historic American Newspapers* provides access to digitized copies of full runs of one of the first newspapers published in Hawaii, *The Polynesian*, which proved very useful for the early history of Hackfeld's company. This resource also provided many articles from other Hawaiian newspapers published later in the nineteenth century and in the early twentieth century. Some of the men Hackfeld worked with in his early career proved to have left very little trace in the historical record. The Hawaiian Mission Houses Digital Archive (2016) has made available a missionary journal, *The Friend*, which provided additional information, as did some of the books available from the American HathiTrust Digital Library (2016). The HathiTrust collection also includes many historic trade journals, including ones from the sugar industry. These proved useful for additional information about the final years of H. Hackfeld & Co. It also provided access to copies of relevant nineteenth century Hawaiian government publications. The University of Hawaii at Manoa Library's eVols (2016), open-access, digital institutional repository, provided access to relevant historic directories and Hawaiian sugar industry publications.

Almost all of the primary sources used to fill in the gaps in the history of H. Hackfeld & Co. were digital and open access. It would not have been possible to undertake such a project in the predigital age without lengthy research trips to both Hawaii and Hackfeld's native northern Germany. Without OCR, it is probable that many of the news reports and advertisements would have remained undiscovered. Searching unindexed newspaper and journal microfilms or bound volumes would have been prohibitively time-consuming.

The Hackfeld case study illustrates how big data can help researchers fill gaps in their knowledge. Big data can also be used to explore areas where no previous research has been undertaken. The author's article (Hawkins, 2017b) on a Belle Époque Austrian luxury shoe and paprika retailer provides a good example of both the benefits and limitations of big data. This article was inspired by the 2015 University of Wolverhampton Holocaust Memorial Day Lecture. The speaker, Prof. Robert A. Shaw, included in his PowerPoint presentation an intriguing advertisement for a retailing business, Paprika Schlesinger, founded by his grandfather, Robert Schlesinger. Shaw came to Britain in 1939 on a Kinder transport as a refugee child from Vienna. Some of the Kinder transport children's families were associated with significant Central European businesses. The long forgotten Paprika Schlesinger proved to be such a business. However, Prof. Shaw's grandfather had died many years before he was born, so his knowledge of his grandfather's business was rather limited. Paprika Schlesinger had ceased trading before the Second World War and no business records had survived.

Reconstructing the history of Paprika Schlesinger presented an interesting challenge. The Austrian National Library has digitized an extensive collection of Austrian historic newspapers available at Austrian Newspapers Online (ANNO) (2011) and OCR means they can be subjected to key word searches. They generated a significant number of results because Robert Schlesinger recognized the value of publicity from a very early stage in the development of his business. He was particularly keen on newspaper advertising and placed many of his advertisements in the *Neue Freie Presse*, of which a full run is available from ANNO. However, unfortunately, OCR is unable to identify advertisements that use nonstandard fonts or artwork. This is one of the shortcomings of OCR. So many of the advertisements had to be detected by physically scanning multiple issues of this newspaper on a computer, which was very time-consuming. The initial research missed some of the advertisements because they consisted entirely of text, including a very significant one that resulted in Schlesinger's prosecution, conviction, and imprisonment for blasphemy. The advertisements contain information about the development of the business and were supplemented by newspaper articles about the business in the *Neue Freie Presse* and other newspapers available from ANNO. These include a profile of Robert Schlesinger from 1885 in a Viennese satirical magazine, *Die Bombe*. Schlesinger subsequently had a regular column in this magazine for several years in which he reflected on current affairs such as anti-Semitism.

The information derived from ANNO was far from sufficient to write a definitive history of Paprika Schlesinger. Fortunately, other digitized primary sources are available. These include a full run of historic Vienna city directories available from the Vienna Digital Library (Wienbibliothek Digital, 2016). The city directories proved to be a very useful supplement to the information gleaned from the advertisements. The American HathiTrust Digital Library also proved useful in providing access to contemporary publications with additional detail about Robert Schlesinger's charitable donations of shoes to the Viennese poor. However, copyright restrictions meant the HathiTrust website provided access to these particular sources only to users based in the United States. Paprika Schlesinger was one of the most advertised brands in Belle Époque Austria and it attracted the attention of Viennese satirist Karl Kraus. Karl Kraus made caustic observations about Paprika Schlesinger on numerous occasions in his satirical magazine, *Die Fackel*. Digitized copies of this publication are available from several different websites, including the Internet Archive (2016).

Big data has allowed the reconstruction of the life of Robert Schlesinger and his business, Paprika Schlesinger. It would have been prohibitively time-consuming to search microfilm or bound volumes of the Austrian press for relevant material. But gaps remain in the research. For example, digital copies of the historic newspapers published in Bad Ischl, Carlsbad, and Marienbad did not provide any information about the branch stores Schlesinger established in these spa resorts. So far, no obituaries of Robert Schlesinger have been located, notwithstanding the fact he was one of the most well-known Belle Époque Austrian business personalities. It would appear that far fewer obituaries were published in Austria than in Britain or the United States during the same period.

Notwithstanding the great potential of big data, in common with traditional primary sources, it needs to be engaged with critically by historical researchers. The film historian Richard Abel (2013) has observed that digitized newspaper databases may not necessarily provide a geographically or temporally representative selection of newspapers. Technical shortcomings may discourage historians from placing articles in the wider context of an entire newspaper or an extensive set of newspaper issues. Furthermore, one is often alone using digitized newspapers, whereas research using the original newspapers or microfilms in a public library or historical society library brings the researcher into contact with librarians, archivists, and other researchers, who may be willing to exchange information. There may well be a variety of additional primary and secondary sources related to the historian's research available locally.

Big data can also be misused by historians. As Hibbs (2013) has observed, many historians have used the digitized historic newspaper *The Times* as if it was representative of Victorian British journalism. In fact, it is not. However, not all historians make this mistake. Belich avoids the trap of misusing *The Times* (The Times Digital Archive, 1785–2012, 2017) in his history of English-speaking white settlers from 1789 to 1939. He explores the emergence and frequency of usage of the English words "settlers" and "emigrants." He supplements his analysis of articles in *The Times* with full runs of 48 newspapers digitized (as of 2008) by the British Library to represent nineteenth century Britain (Belich 2009, 150–151).

Conclusion

On balance, the emergence of big data has been a very positive development for historical research, as has been shown previously. However, it is important not to exaggerate its impact. As Gooding, Terras, and Warwick (2013, 631) observe, there is a need to make realistic assessments of the benefits of large-scale digitization on scholarly activity. Furthermore, as Sharpe (2015, 339–340) observes in her obituary of the economic historian Joan Thirsk, "As a glance at recent economic history journals makes clear, the meticulous investigation of detail is extinguished by statistical comparisons of what is often meaningless 'big data'... Datasets, often founded on highly spurious hypotheses heaped upon other hypotheses, provide a quick fix in the rush to publish." Sharpe's observation echoes the cautionary articles of Abel (2013) and Hibbs (2013). It is clear that historians need to analyze big data with the same rigor they applied to primary sources in the pre-mass digitization era.

References

Abel, R. 2013. The pleasures and perils of big data in digitised newspapers. *Film History* 25, nos. 1–2: 1–10.

Austrian Newspapers Online (ANNO). 2011. http://anno.onb.ac.at/ (accessed November 29, 2016).

Beals, M.H. 2016. Scissors and Paste. Presentation at the 4th British Library Labs Symposium, November 7. http://www.slideshare.net/labsbl/13-scissors-and-paste-69176125 (accessed November 28, 2016).

Belich, J. 2009. *Replenishing the Earth: The Settler Revolution and the Rise of the Anglo World, 1783–1939.* Oxford: Oxford University Press.

Blaney, J. 2016. Digital citation: Unpublished presentation at Institute of Historical Research History Day, November 15.

Bremen State and University Library's Digital Collection. 2010. http://brema.suub.uni-bremen.de/ (accessed November 28, 2016).

British History Online (BHO). 2016. http://www.british-history.ac.uk/ (accessed December 1, 2016).

British Library Digital Scholarship Blog. 2015, June 16. British Library Labs competition 2015—Winners announced! http://blogs.bl.uk/digital-scholarship/2015/06/bl-labs-competition-winners-for-2015.html (accessed November 30, 2016).

British Library Digital Scholarship Blog. 2016, November 3. Black abolitionist performances and their presence in Britain—An update! http://blogs.bl.uk/digital-scholarship/2016/11/black-abolitionist-performances-and-their-presence-in-britain-an-update.html (accessed November 30, 2016).

Cox, D.J., B. Godfrey, H. Johnson, and J. Turner. 2015. On licence: Understanding punishment, recidivism and desistance in penal policy. In *Transnational Penal Cultures: New Perspectives on Discipline, Punishment and Desistance (SOLON Explorations in Crime and Criminal Justice Histories series)*. ed. V. Miller and J. Campbell, 184–201. Abingdon: Routledge.

European Library. 2005–2013. Europeana Newspapers. http://www.theeuropeanlibrary.org/tel4/newspapers (accessed November 28, 2016).

eVols, University of Hawaii at Manoa Library. 2016. http://evols.library.manoa.hawaii.edu/ (accessed November 28, 2016).

Fogel, R.W. and S.L. Engerman. 1974. *Time on the Cross: The Economics of American Negro Slavery*. Boston: Little, Brown and Company.

Gooding, P., M. Terras, and C. Warwick. 2013. The myth of the new: Mass digitization, distant reading, and the future of the book. *Literary and Linguistic Computing* 28, no. 4, 629–639.

Grossman, J. 2012. "Big data:" An opportunity for historians? *AHA Perspectives on History* 50, no. 3 (March). https://www.historians.org/publications-and-directories/perspectives-on-history/march-2012/big-data-an-opportunity-for-historians (accessed October 6, 2016).

HathiTrust Digital Library. 2016. https://www.hathitrust.org/ (accessed November 28, 2016).

Hawkins, R. 2017a. Heinrich Hackfeld. In *Immigrant Entrepreneurship: German-American Business Biographies, 1720 to the Present: Volume 2: The Emergence of an Industrial Nation, 1840–1893*, ed. W. J. Hausman. http://immigrantentrepreneurship.org/entry.php?rec=285 (accessed April 10, 2017).

Hawkins, R. 2017b. Paprika Schlesinger: The Development of a Luxury Retail Shoe Brand in Belle Époque Vienna. *Journal of Historical Research in Marketing* 9, no. 1: 66–91.

Hibbs, A. 2013. The deleterious dominance of *The Times* in nineteenth-century scholarship. *Journal of Victorian Culture* 18, no. 4: 472–497.

Internet Archive. 2016. https://archive.org (accessed November 29, 2016).

Inwood, K. and A. Ross. 2016. Big data and the military: First World War personnel records in Australia, Britain, Canada, New Zealand and British Africa. *Australian Historical Studies* 47, no. 3: 430–442.

Library of Congress. 2016. Chronicling America: Historic American newspapers. http://chroniclingamerica.loc.gov/ (accessed December 1, 2016).

Murray, H.-R. 2016. Black abolitionist performances in Britain Presentation at the 4th British Library Labs Symposium, November 7. http://www.slideshare.net/labsbl/4-hannah-rosemurraryblackabol-69176116http://www.slideshare.net/labsbl/4-hannah-rosemurraryblackabol-69176116 (accessed November 30, 2016).

National Library of Australia. 2016. Trove. http://trove.nla.gov.au/ (accessed October 6, 2016).

Navickas, K. 2015. Political Meetings Mapper: A presentation at the 3rd British Library Labs Symposium, November 2. http://www.slideshare.net/KatrinaNavickas/political-meetings-mapper-british-library-labs-symposium-2-november-2015 (accessed November 30, 2016).

Navickas, K. 2016. *Protest and the Politics of Space and Place, 1789–1848*. Manchester: Manchester University Press.

OldenburgischeGesellschaftfürFamilienkundee.V. 2017. http://www.familienkunde-oldenburg .de/aktuell/ (accessed December 7, 2017).

Phillips, M.G. and G. Osmond. 2015. Australia's women surfers: History, methodology and the digital humanities. *Australian Historical Studies* 46, no. 2: 285–303.

Rosenzweig, R. 2011. Scarcity or abundance? Preserving the past. In *Clio Wired: The Future of the Past in the Digital Age*. ed. R. Rosenzweig, 3–27. New York: Columbia University Press.

Rosenzweig, R. and D.J. Cohen. 2011. Web of lies? Historical knowledge on the Internet. In *Clio Wired: The Future of the Past in the Digital Age*. ed. R. Rosenzweig, 28–50. New York: Columbia University Press.

Salton, G, A. Wong, and C.S. Yang. 1975. A vector space model for automatic indexing. *Communications of the ACM* 18, no. 11: 613–620.

Sharpe, P. 2015. The history woman: Joan Thirsk (1922–2013). *History Workshop Journal* no. 80: 335–341.

The Hawaiian Mission Houses Digital Archive. 2016. http://hmha.missionhouses.org/ (accessed November 28, 2016).

The Proceedings of the Old Bailey, 1674–1913. 2003–2015. https://www.oldbaileyonline .org// (accessed October 6, 2016).

The Times Digital Archive, 1785–2012. 2017. http://gale.cengage.co.uk/times.aspx/ (accessed December 7, 2017).

Wienbibliothek Digital. 2016. http://www.digital.wienbibliothek.at/ (accessed November 29, 2016).

Williams, L. and B. Godfrey. 2016. Bringing the prisoner into view: English and Welsh census data and the Victorian prison population. *Australian Historical Studies* 47, no. 3, 398–413.

Zhang, Y., S. Liu, and E. Matthews. 2015. Convergence of digital humanities and digital libraries. *Library Management* 36, no. 45, 362–377.

Chapter 8

The Study of Networked Content: Five Considerations for Digital Research in the Humanities

Sabine Niederer

Contents

Introduction

Digital research is taking the humanities by storm. This can be read not only from the many digital humanities programs in education and research in universities around the world but also from the attention for new media practices in humanities and art departments. Famously, and thought-provokingly, media theorist Lev Manovich—strongly rooted in film and media studies—set out to develop a means by which the visual analysis of big data sets of digitized cultural materials could help the study of art and culture transition into the era of big data or, as he calls it, the era of "more media" (Manovich, 2009). Often met with scrutiny by art historians, not in favor of a quantitative approach to the arts, Manovich insisted with this "cultural analytics" program on expanding the study of culture by including the vast amounts of user-generated content. As he wrote as early as 2009: "Think about this: the number of images uploaded to Flickr every week is probably larger than all objects contained in all art museums in the world." Manovich developed the Software Studies Initiative, where he and his team developed software such as Image Plot, for the analysis of large visual data sets. Manovich applies his methods both to digitized materials (such as *Time* magazine covers) as well as—more recently—to born-digital content (such as selfies on Instagram).*

In 2011, Danah Boyd and Kate Crawford presented "Six Provocations of Big Data" (Boyd & Crawford, 2011), in which they critically discuss the ethical and epistemological consequences of big data research. To encourage further thought and discussion about the need for adaptive tools and collaborative methods for digital research, in this chapter, I outline five considerations for the study of online mediated content, attuned to practices in the humanities. Before presenting these considerations, I would like to introduce a novel approach to research on the web. This approach builds on a significant research technique for both qualitative and quantitative analyses of mediated content, which has been developed in the field of communication science and is called "content analysis."

Furthering Content Analysis

Content analysis was incepted to study given or demarcated bodies of content, to analyze both formal features (e.g., the shot lengths of a television show, the column widths and word counts of a printed text, etc.) and meanings (broadly defined to include themes, tropes, terminology, etc.), all in order to make inferences about societal perceptions, cultural change, and trends in public opinion. A famous pre-web longitudinal content analysis study referenced in the scholarly literature is the "Cultural Indicators" program (of the 1960s through 1990s) by George Gerbner et al. that used weeklong aggregations of primetime television footage to record all representations of violence and construct "violence profiles," for this material. These representations were then interpreted and turned into "cultural indicators," which referred both to trends in network television's dramatic content and to viewer conceptions of social reality (Gerbner, 1970). Content analysis has since been described as "indigenous to communication research and [as] potentially one of the most important research techniques in the social sciences" (Krippendorff, 1980).

It is important to emphasize that I understand content analysis to have always been inclusive of *potentially* all content types. By taking mass media as its

---

* For a further discussion of responses to big data from the arts and humanities, see also Niederer and Taudin Chabot (2015).

most prominent raw data source, however, this kind of scholarship tended to be "dominated by content analyses of newspapers, magazines, books, [radio] broadcasts, films, comics, and television programming" as one of its key scholars, as Klaus Krippendorff (1980: 404) pointed out. Krippendorff has made explicit that since content analysis' earliest methodological formation (more or less publicly communicated), data of any kind could potentially be studied through content analysis. He mentions varieties of media "content" as diverse as "personal letters, children's talk, disarmament negotiations, witness accounts in courts, audiovisual records of therapeutic sessions, answers to open-ended interview questions, and computer conferences" and even "postage stamps, motifs on ancient pottery, speech disturbances, the wear and tear of books, and dreams." More theoretically, as a major proponent and methodological innovator of this field of media research, Krippendorff's assertion that "anything that occurs in sufficient numbers and has reasonably stable meanings for a specific group of people may be subjected to content analysis" (Krippendorff, 1980) is a key driver of my own development of "networked content analysis."

If, in practice, content analysis has mostly focused on neatly demarcated sets of texts or other media materials such as television shows, the specificity, dynamism, and networked nature of digital media content poses a myriad of new methodological challenges and opportunities to contemporary content analysts. Digital media content can be published or created on the World Wide Web and enriched with opportunities for navigation and interaction. It can be networked by in-text hyperlinks (creating a so-called "hypertext"), by suggestions of related articles or other recommendation systems or pulled into social media by prevalent "Like" and "Share" buttons on websites, urging users to link content to their own user profiles (Gerlitz & Helmond, 2013). Online content is *networked*. It is dynamic rather than stable; it can change over time or move from the front page to the archive. Social media further scatter content, offering a "live feed" that is referred to as the qualitative and quantitative *real-timeness* of social media data (Back, Lury, & Zimmer, 2012; Marres & Weltevrede, 2013), the content of which can be linked to, copied onto other networks, and archived across the (social) web. These social media platforms each format, rank, and serve content in unique ways, which makes it important to start developing adaptive, digital methods that are attuned to the diverse specificities of these platforms.

Content analysis of such networked content may ask where the content that is under analysis *ends* if all content is (more and less) meaningfully hyperlinked to other related content on other web pages. Indeed, how is it possible to demarcate a website? Is it methodologically appropriate to apply the techniques of content analysis that worked for printed newspapers like the *New York Times* or *The Guardian*, and for television formats such as CNN or Al Jazeera, to online news sites like www.nytimes.com and www.guardian.co.uk, let alone to a content search engine and aggregator like Google News? The answers to these questions as they have been offered by content analysis scholars throughout different phases in the history of the web can be summed up as broadly presenting two distinct approaches. The first, as described by McMillan (2000), argues for a standardization of methods toward the analysis of web content, which McMillan characterizes as a "moving target." A second approach is formulated by Herring in response to McMillan, who proposes to combine traditional content analysis techniques with methodologies from disciplines such as linguistics and sociology to offer a more workable response to the challenges offered by "new online media" (Herring, 2010).

While these two approaches each offer ways forward for the analysis of web content, they are not concerned with the vast differences between different web platforms—the specific technicalities of which contribute significantly to the meaning of networked content. It is important to note that web content currently exists in and through the platforms and engines that produce it, which means that a clean separation of content from its carrier is no longer feasible. Different web platforms and search engines each carry their own (often visually undisclosed) formats and formatting; they have their own scenarios of use and their own terms of service; further, they also output their own results and rankings. Consider the example of Wikipedia, the collaboratively written encyclopedia project on a wiki, where each article has a page, sometimes other language versions, a discussion page, user statistics, and a "history" or archive of all previous versions of the article being accessed, all of which can be used in comparison with the current version of the article, as bots at work continue to edit text and undo vandalism. Differently for Twitter, the social network slash microblogging tool, user-broadcasted messages are bound by a limit of 140 characters per Tweet. They can include images, links to URLs, tags of other users (whether directly connected as "followers" or not), and hashtags to network and aggregate individual content around specific events, issues, opinions, and themes. Content can include retweets of someone else's message (in several distinct ways, as described by Bruns & Burgess, 2011; Helmond, 2015), which generates yet another layer to the networking of content. These specificities of how platforms and engines serve, format, redistribute, and essentially coproduce content are what I refer to as the *technicity* of content.

As online content is networked, I propose the development of "networked content analysis," as digital media-specific research technique, specifically beneficial for social and cultural research, such as the study of societal debates on the web and in social media (Niederer, 2016). Additional to content analysis, the two schools of thought and practice I further build upon at this point, "controversy analysis" (as developed in education at Sciences Po, Paris) and "issue mapping" (as developed by the Digital Methods Initiative at the University of Amsterdam), offer digital means of controversy analysis from similar scholarly traditions but with a distinct angle. While the Parisian school operationalizes Actor-Network Theory to zoom in on a *controversy*, the Amsterdam approach builds on science and technology studies to develop digital method and tools to track *issues* more broadly, be they controversial or not, on the web (Marres, 2015; Rogers, 2009; Rogers & Marres, 2000; Venturini, 2009). Controversy mapping, digital methods for issue mapping, and content analysis, in combination, offer means to study a controversy on the web that include this factor of technicity in the analysis of networked content. The novel challenges posed by the dynamics of web content does not mean we have to dispose of content analysis altogether. On the contrary, as content analysis from the outset has been potentially inclusive of all varieties of content in and across contexts, its methods need to be amended only slightly—building on digital methods and controversy analysis—to suit the technicity of web content.

Critical views on digital methods highlight the methods' and tools' dependency on already problematic proprietary walled gardens and otherwise volatile ever-innovating commercial web platforms, such as Facebook and Twitter (Van Dijck, 2013). Scholars particularly warn of the sheer impossibility of distinguishing between the working logic of web platforms and the exemplarity of "platform artifacts" (Marres, 2015; Marres & Weltevrede, 2013; Rogers, 2013). For example, the most "retweeted" content on Twitter may just be the most Twitter-friendly content; therefore, we may only be finding out more about the logic of the platform itself, rather than the issue under study or the eventfulness of a certain tweet (Marres, 2015). When dealing with online content, therefore, one needs to take into account the sociotechnical logic of the platform itself as part of any analysis (Niederer & Van Dijck, 2010). In fact, with the explosive rise of (big) data, attention to the sociotechnical logics of platforms must be further prioritized as social research increasingly makes use of what has been referred to as "live research" (Back et al., 2012; Marres & Weltevrede, 2013), where masses of content (with specific forms and technicities) are aggregated in real-time, copied onto other networks, and archived across the (social) web. Furthermore, data analysis and the tools that enable this are built on highly dynamic web services. In a critique of the famous "Google Flu Trends" project, David Lazer et al. (2014, p. 1205) write how Twitter, Facebook, Google, and the Internet more generally are constantly changing because of the actions of millions of engineers and consumers. Understanding and studying these platforms as sociotechnical systems for what they are are of utmost importance, as they are "increasingly embedded in our societies" (p. 1205). I would therefore like to propose a novel approach to online content that includes this sociotechnical perspective: "networked content analysis." In the following considerations, I will outline the need for such an approach, which I claim could benefit (digital) humanities research.

1. Online content has a "technicity."

    I have argued in the previous section that technicity of content should be included in the analysis, and therefore, the tools and methods for web research should become adaptive. Here, it is important to point out that the attention to the technicity of content necessitates recognition of the spatial organization and geo-location of content, as well as dislocation and censorship, which all problematize the very idea of a "World Wide Web" of content assumed to be globally available. Internet censorship research has demonstrated how a user's geo-location is crucial to the availability of content, as served for instance by the search engine Google. Research that critically comes to terms with these local differences in search engine results—which can be shown by using a different language version of Google or with VPN connections that access the web from other geo-locations—has been called "search as research" (Rogers, 2013) and presented at international search engine research conferences such as the "Society of the Query" (see also König & Rasch, 2014). What this research underlines is that the web may be "worldwide" in its infrastructure, but it is not in its access to content (Deibert, Palfrey, Rohozinski, Zittrain, & Haraszti, 2010; Deibert, Palfrey, Rohozinski, Zittrain, & Stein, 2008; Rogers, Weltevrede, Niederer, & Borra, 2013).

To attune to these lessons learned from digital research, I propose to try to stay true to the strengths of traditional content analysis for the humanities and social research—the nonintrusiveness of the method, the inclusion of content in all its shapes and forms, and the attention to the context of content—while further developing techniques that better adapt to the specificities of networked content.

2. Online content is coproduced by platforms and engines.

Content currently exists in and through the platforms and engines that produce it, which means a clean separation of content from its carrier is no longer feasible. It is now impossible or, at least, unadvisable to regard a Wikipedia article as entirely separate from its publicly available production process. Who were the authors? Were there bots (software robots) involved? What are being presented as related articles? Which subtopics (of an entry on Wikipedia) have become their own dedicated articles? Which were forked as a means of controversy management? Answers to these questions are likely to be of great interest and utility to those invested in content analysis in a networked era and to anyone embarking on the mapping of a contemporary debate. Krippendorff has laid the groundwork for such analysis, well prior to content analysis having to deal with online content.

3. Online content does not mean the end of traditional media content.

A third consideration is that networked content also *folds in* traditional media content. Television news is published online and discussed in websites; news reports and images populate search engine results, lead to the creation of Wikipedia articles, or are linked to by tweets and amplified by retweets. This leads to the entanglement of news (and other mass) media content, more traditional objects of study of content analysis, and networked content, the object of study in networked content analysis. The entangled nature of any media or content relation is where the focus and benefits of networked content analysis lie.

In the case of Twitter, for instance, the microblogging platform could be approached not only through more conventional news cycle analyses but also through "meme-tracking" (Leskovec, Backstrom, & Kleinberg, 2009). In the latter mode, Twitter as a microblog could then be seen as highly responsive to or even parasitical or imploding of conventional news "sites," echoing and amplifying news snippets by tweeting and retweeting. Further, as Twitter is often moving information faster than the news, Twitter content in some cases *is* news. Of course, for these reasons, Twitter is a popular medium for professional journalists. They bind tweets to their story, and when their work has been published, they may tweet a link to that article, using it as a channel for the distribution of their own work. As news and mass media sources strive to make their content "platform-ready," a term by Helmond (2015), the entanglement of news, other mass media content, and new platforms has entered the next level. Networked content analysis proposes to take this entanglement as a given and demarcate content through the logic of the platform (as developed in digital methods) and thus follow the actors across sources (as key to controversy analysis). The rise of digital media does not mean the end of traditional mass media, but its reconfiguration as part of online networked content.

4. Platforms may offer windows to the world of a cultural or social issue.

Fourth, and more conceptually, I would like to propose that when studying a debate through online content, we may regard the different platforms as different *windows* on the issue. Rather than asking "What does Twitter say about the controversy" or critically asking "Who is on Twitter these days, anyway?" or "Who still uses hashtags?" we may productively ask, "What *kind of* [insert cultural or social issue here] does Twitter present?" and "How does this compare and relate to the [cultural or social topic of interest] presented by Wikipedia (for example)?" In these ways, considering social media platforms as *windows on an issue* is also productive for creating a better understanding of the cultures of use of such platforms.

As an example, in a study of the city of Amsterdam through social media data, a project with the Digital Methods Initiative found that Instagram offers a collected "boutique view" on the city, while meetup.com (a platform for organizing social gatherings) highlights the "tech" and "sports" venues of the city of Amsterdam.* On a methodological level, one could take up the assessment of the possibilities and limitations of studying a place through networked content analysis, assessing how different platforms deal differently with the demarcation of place (Niederer, Colombo, Mauri, & Azzi, 2015).

5. Not all online data are public.

A fifth point worth mentioning is that while Wikipedia offers public views on its technicity, many other platforms do not. Google Web Search, through its terms of service, does not allow for the use of its search engine for anything other than search. So repurposing the engine as a research device

---

* The layered interactive map is available at http://bit.ly/amsterdamcartodb, and the project page is on the Digital Methods Initiative wiki. Its project page can be found at https://wiki.digitalmethods.net/Dmi/TheCityAsInterface.

(as discussed in detail by Weltevrede, 2016) goes against its rules and regulations. Twitter has various application programming interfaces (APIs); however, on an interface level, Twitter does not disclose its mechanisms of ranking and prioritizing content (and neither does Google or any social media platform). This point was central to a critical project titled "The People's Dashboard," which I developed together with Esther Weltevrede, Erik Borra, and others in 2015 and find relevant to mention briefly here.*

The People's Dashboard is a social media platform plugin that visualizes the entanglement of content and users with the platform and its technicity. The dashboard is intended to be a critical layer on top of six different social media platforms: YouTube, Facebook, Twitter, LastFM, LinkedIn, and Instagram, in order to discover and highlight "people's content" as a layer on top of the interface. The plugin, which currently works for the interface of Facebook, color-codes interfaces of social media platforms according to whether it presents the content *of the people* or *of the platform* (Figure 8.1). The project tries to increase understanding around what is actually *social* on social media nowadays. For researchers, such an understanding stresses the necessity to regard technicity as omnipresent and make explicit how it is dealt with. This idea is recognized by scholars working with networked content, such as Marres and Moats (2015), who, in an STS (science and technology studies)-tradition, call for a symmetrical approach to the study of controversies with social media content, in which there is as much attention to "media-technological dynamics" as there is to "issue dynamics." Networked content analysis has a slightly different approach, as it proposes to include technicity by straightforwardly taking the *networkedness of content* into account. In the various case studies, I describe how platforms network content differently, and—as stressed in the first point—how this calls for an adaptive approach to the analysis of networked content, which is amendable to suit the technicity of a platform. Making technicity explicit in this way is comparative to the functionality of The People's Dashboard, as it offers a view on the entanglement of user content with the platform.

The biggest challenge for researchers who want to work with networked content may be the multifariousness of content types, data sources, and technicities, which, in order to be compared, need to somehow be *comparable*. Here, it is useful to consider how both controversy mapping (as developed by Bruno Latour at Sciences Po in Paris) and digital methods approach this issue. Controversy analysis does not strive for a clean objective picture to arise from the analysis of complex issues and debates. Rather than striving for objectivity, controversy analysis tries to reach what Latour calls "second-degree objectivity," which is "the effort to consider as

---

* "The People's Dashboard" is described extensively on the wiki project page (Digital Methods Initiative, 2015b).

Figure 8.1   The People's Dashboard. This mockup of The People's Dashboard was developed during the Digital Methods Winter School of 2015, as a critical layer on top of the interfaces of dominant social media platform interfaces, revealing (through colour-coding) content of the people and of the platform. The tool also highlights mixed content, indicating that people's content has been reordered or repurposed (e.g., Facebook News feed or birthday notifications). The plugin works with Facebook and is available on Github: http://bit.ly/peoplesdash board. (From Digital Methods Initiative, *The People's Dashboard*, https://wiki .digitalmethods.net/Dmi/PeoplesDashboard Digital Methods Initiative, 2015).

much subjectivity as possible. Unlike first-degree objectivity, which defines a situation of collective agreement, second-degree objectivity is attained by revealing the full extent of actors' disagreement and is thereby typical of controversial settings" (Venturini, 2010, p. 270). In second-degree objectivity, it is not necessary to normalize or objectify content in order to make it comparable. Instead, it is the wide array of viewpoints, actors, and sources that build a cartography that Latour himself describes to his students as "observing and describing" (Venturini, 2010, p. 270). As controversy mapping does not offer an operationalization of this approach, let alone how to apply it to networked content, it is useful here to look at digital methods for "cross-platform analysis" (Digital Methods Initiative, 2015a).

Digital methods have proposed three approaches to cross-platform analysis, which are strongly related to the methodological difficulties discussed of disentangling content from online platforms. The first approach can be summed up as *medium research* and takes as a point of departure the question of what the platform *does to the content*. How does the platform rank, obfuscate or amplify specific content, and what do we know of its cultures of use? A second approach is that of *social research.* Here, platform technicities are not included in the study, as the researcher focuses on the story told by the content. A third approach is the combination of the two, asking both what the platform does to the content and what stories does the content tell (Digital Methods Initiative, 2015a). This approach would be most suitable to networked content analysis, where we could explicitly add how the platforms network content and how content is "inter-linked, inter-liked and inter-hashtagged" (Digital Methods Initiative, 2015a). However, noting the size of data sets and the necessity of close reading, the scaling up of such methods remains a challenge, which is dealt with by various scholarly fields (ranging from humanities to data science).

The comparability of content from different platforms and the web also becomes an issue in its visualization or more specifically in its side-by-side representation in dashboards. As analysts, activists, and decision-makers increasingly make use of dashboards, there is increased urgency to developing critical dashboards, as I alluded to in my mentioning of The People's Dashboard. A critical dashboard would show the technicity of content and explain what is left out, what is foregrounded, and what is being amplified by the logic of the platform.

Conclusions

In the era of big data and digital culture, in which websites and social media platforms produce massive amounts of content and network this through hyperlinks and social media buttons, digital research in the arts and humanities needs to become aware of and even adaptive to the many ways in which digital platforms and engines output content. Online content is networked and folds in traditional media content until the two become entangled and even inseparable. Jaron Lanier powerfully describes this development in the preface to his 2010 manifesto *You Are Not a Gadget*:

> It is early in the twenty-first century, and that means that these words will mostly be read by nonpersons—automatons or numb mobs composed of people who are no longer acting as individuals. The words will be minced into atomized search-engine keywords within industrial cloud computing facilities located in remote, often secret locations around the world. They will be copied millions of times by algorithms designed to send an advertisement to some person somewhere who happens to resonate with some fragment of what I say. (Lanier, 2010, p. xiii)

The future of content presented by Lanier, as material increasingly intertwined with its carriers and platforms, is a future of content networked to the extreme. We will find content made for the network, rehashed, redistributed, and copied by network infrastructure and then clicked on, liked, or retweeted by its recipients. The future of content then is content that is written for exponentially *networked technicity*. As content will evolve along with the technicity of its medium, we— as researchers from the humanities, arts and beyond—will have to expand our techniques and tools for networked content analysis, continue to develop a critical vocabulary, and produce further concepts and visual languages for the mapping, analysis, and description of networked content.

References

Back, L., Lury, C., & Zimmer, R. (2012). Doing real time research: Opportunities and challenges. *National Centre for Research Methods (NRCM), Methodological review paper*. Retrieved from http://eprints.ncrm.ac.uk/3157/1/real_time_research.pdf

Bruns, A., & Burgess, J. E. (2011). The use of Twitter hashtags in the formation of ad hoc publics. In *Proceedings of the 6th European Consortium for Political Research (ECPR) General Conference*, 25–27 August 2011. Retrieved from http://eprints.qut.edu.au/46515

Boyd, D., & Crawford, K. (2011). Six provocations for big data. *A Decade in Internet Time: Symposium on the Dynamics of the Internet and Society*, 21 September 2011. Retrieved from http://dx.doi.org/10.2139/ssrn.1926431

Deibert, R., Palfrey, J., Rohozinski, R., Zittrain, J., & Haraszti, M. (2010). *Access Controlled: The Shaping of Power, Rights, and Rule in Cyberspace*. Cambridge, MA: MIT Press.

Deibert, R., Palfrey, J., Rohozinski, R., Zittrain, J., & Stein, J. G. (2008). *Access Denied: The Practice and Policy of Global Internet Filtering*. Cambridge, MA: MIT Press.

Digital Methods Initiative. (2015a). *DMIR Unit #5: Cross-Platform Analysis*. Amsterdam: University of Amsterdam.

Digital Methods Initiative. (2015b). *The People's Dashboard*. Retrieved from https://wiki.digitalmethods.net/Dmi/PeoplesDashboard

Gerbner, G. (1970). Cultural indicators: The case of violence in television drama. *The Annals of the American Academy of Political and Social Science*, *388*(1), 69–81.

Gerlitz, C., & Helmond, A. (2013). The Like Economy: Social buttons and the data-intensive web. *New Media & Society*. Retrieved from http://nms.sagepub.com/content/early/2013/02/03/1461444812472322

Helmond, A. (2015). *The Web as Platform: Data Flows in Social Media*. (PhD). Amsterdam: University of Amsterdam.

Herring, S. (2010). Web content Analysis: Expanding the Paradigm. In J. Hunsinger & et al. (Eds.), *International Handbook of Internet Research* (pp. 233–249). Dordrecht: Springer.

König, R., & Rasch, M. (eds.). (2014). *Society of the Query Reader: Reflections on Web Search*. Amsterdam: Institute of Network Cultures. Retrieved from http://networkcultures.org/blog/publication/society-of-the-query-reader-reflections-on-web-search/

Krippendorff, K. (1980). *Content Analysis: An Introduction to its Methodology* (First Edition). Beverly Hills, CA: Sage Publications.

Lanier, J. (2010). *You Are Not a Gadget. A Manifesto*. New York: Alfred A. Knopf.

Lazer, D., Kennedy, R., King, G., & Vespignani, A. (2014). The parable of Google flu: Traps in big data analysis. *Science*, *343*, 1203–1205.

Leskovec, J., Backstrom, L., & Kleinberg, J. (2009). Meme-tracking and the dynamics of the news cycle. In *Proceedings of the 15th ACM SIGKDD International Conference on*

Knowledge Discovery and Data Mining (pp. 497–506). Paris, France: ACM. Retrieved from http://dl.acm.org/citation.cfm?id=1557077

Manovich, L. (2009). Cultural analytics: Visualizing cultural patterns in the Era of "More Media." *Domus* (Spring). Retrieved from http://manovich.net/content/04 -projects/063-cultural-analytics-visualizing-cultural-patterns/60_article_2009.pdf

Marres, N. (2015). Why map issues? On controversy analysis as a digital method. *Science, Technology & Human Values, 40*. 0162243915574602. http://doi .org/10.1177/0162243915574602

Marres, N., & Moats, D. (2015). Mapping controversies with social media: The case for symmetry. *Social Media + Society, 1*(2), 2056305115604176. http://doi .org/10.1177/2056305115604176

Marres, N., & Weltevrede, E. (2013). Scraping the Social? Issues in live social research. *Journal of Cultural Economy, 6*(3), 313–335. http://doi.org/10.1080/17530350.2013 .772070

McMillan, S. (2000). The microscope and the moving target: The challenge of applying content analysis to the World Wide Web. *Journalism and Mass Communication Quarterly, 77*, 80–88.

Niederer, S. (2016). *Networked Content Analysis: The Case of Climate Change* (PhD). Amsterdam: University of Amsterdam.

Niederer, S., Colombo, G., Mauri, M., & Azzi, M. (2015). Street-Level City Analytics: Mapping the Amsterdam Knowledge Mile. In I. Theona, & D. Charitos (Eds.), *Hybrid City 2015: Data to the People.* Athens: University of Athens. Retrieved from www.media.uoa.gr/hybridcity

Niederer, S., & Taudin Chabot, R. (2015). Deconstructing the cloud: Responses to Big Data phenomena from social sciences, humanities and the arts. *Big Data & Society, 2*(2). http://doi.org/10.1177/2053951715594635

Niederer, S., & Van Dijck, J. (2010). Wisdom of the crowd or technicity of content? Wikipedia as a sociotechnical system. *New Media & Society, 12*(8), 1368–1387.

Rogers, R. (2009). *The End of the Virtual: Digital Methods.* Amsterdam: VossiuspersUvA.

Rogers, R. (2013). *Digital Methods.* Cambridge, MA: MIT Press.

Rogers, R., & Marres, N. (2000). Landscaping climate change: A mapping technique for understanding science and technology debates on the World Wide Web. *Public Understanding of Science, 9*(2), 141–163.

Rogers, R., Weltevrede, E., Niederer, S., & Borra, E. (2013). National Web Studies: The case of Iran. In J. Hartley, J. Burgess, & A. Bruns (Eds.), *Blackwell Companion to New Media Dynamics* (pp. 142–166). Oxford: Blackwell.

Van Dijck, J. (2013). *The Culture of Connectivity: A Critical History of Social Media.* New York: Oxford University Press.

Venturini, T. (2009). Diving in Magma: How to explore controversies with actor-network theory. *Public Understanding of Science, 19*(3), 258–273.

Venturini, T. (2010). Building on Faults: How to represent controversies with digital methods. *Public Understanding of Science, 21*(7), 196–812.

Weltevrede, E. (2016). Repurposing digital methods: The research affordances of platforms and engines. PhD Dissertation, Amsterdam: University of Amsterdam. Retrieved from: http://hdl.handle.net/11245/1.505660

Chapter 9

The English Gothic Novel: Theories and Praxis of Computer-Based Macroanalysis in Literary Studies

Federica Perazzini

Contents

Introduction

As a cultural, technological, and scholarly phenomenon based on the interplay of algorithmic modelling and pattern analysis, the big data revolution has been a major catalyst in changing the way the relationships within and among pieces of information are now seen and understood. In general terms, theorists and critics refer to big data with the umbrella definition of "things one can do at a large scale that cannot be done at a smaller one" (Schonberger and Cukier 2014) in order to extract and uncover hidden patterns capable of revealing new forms of knowledge and value. Needless to say, the versatile potential of big data analytics soon extended its impact beyond the borders of predictive modelling of market trends and customer preferences for which it was developed to conquer the field of literary scholarship. Nowadays, the very existence of billions of bytes of digital information in the form of electronic text archives, along with the web access to this set of data, is forcing scholars to rethink their approach to literary objects, thus allowing the emerging figure of the digital humanist to address questions that were previously inconceivable—inconceivable to a point, however. In fact, as early as 2000. The very idea of a large-scale investigation of the literary system first appeared thanks to Franco Moretti's (2000) "conjectures" on the notion of distant reading that will be fully developed in his *Maps, Graphs, Trees: Abstract Models for a Literary History*. Moretti's distant reading constitutes an alternative approach to the common practice of close text analysis of a few canonical masterpieces in favor of an unusual perspective that takes into account the often ignored 99% of non-canonical works ever published. In his opinion, scholars must widen their horizons to this whole bulk of neglected literature—"the great unread"—so as to surpass the limitations of the traditional methods of reading more or reading closer and embrace the vision of a new quantitative formalism. More than ten years later, in 2013, Matthew Jockers finally gave procedural concreteness to Moretti's standpoint thanks to the experimental methodology of computer-based macroanalysis. In fact, in his pioneering book *Macroanalysis: Digital Methods and Literary History*, Jockers explains how computer-based macroanalysis expands the object of study of literary criticism as never before through the application of the statistical tools and algorithmic protocols derived from computational linguistics that enable the quantitative investigation of thousands of books at once.

In the pursuit of the formalist dream of a "vision d'ensemble" of the literary forms as well as the whole system of novelistic genres, the synergy between Moretti's distant reading and Jockers's practice of computer-based macroanalysis constituted, respectively, the theoretical and the methodological frameworks of reference for my own research—a project that resulted in my PhD dissertation and in two subsequent published works (Perazzini 2013) whose aim was to disclose the laws of "genericity" of one of the most popular and controversial genres of English fiction: the gothic novel. As an unprecedented experiment of fusion between literary criticism and "hard" science methods, my analysis of such a large corpus of digitized novels represented a first attempt to give an account of the stylistic and thematic evolution of the "genome" of the gothic discourse across the decades. In what follows, I will illustrate some of the most rewarding results included in this case study regarding high-frequency lexis, vocabulary richness, and motifs mining. I will conclude with a series of epistemological considerations about the paradigmatic value implied in the computer-based macroanalysis.

Starting the Experiment: Corpus Preparation

Prior to any operation of data extraction and analysis, one must define the sampling frame, that is to say, the entire population of texts from which the sample corpus will be taken. Douglas Biber (Biber et al. 1998) emphasizes the need to clearly define the limits of the population one wishes to study, suggesting the use of comprehensive bibliographical indexes. As far as literary genres are concerned, to determine what the gothic novel population really is, one must first discern how centuries of literary scholarship have used the overencompassing label "English gothic novel." In fact, with its castles, abbeys, and supernatural apparitions, this is a form of fiction that at first glance appears to be a relatively homogenous body of writing in stylistic, thematic, and ideological terms. However, on closer inspection, it reveals its manifold contradictions—a shifting and polymorphic genre of transition built on a series of stereotyped characters and settings—as many have agreed—whose periodization and narrative status are, instead, still in dispute. When does the gothic novel start and when does it actually finish, and how true is the notion that the historical novel subgenre generated its extinction, replacing it as the main novelistic form of the second decade of the XIX century? With these questions yet unsolved, contemporary gothic criticism produced a series of bibliographical studies, like Montague Summers' *The Gothic Quest*, Maurice Levy's *Le roman gothique anglais*, and Frederic Frank's *The First Gothics*, that aimed to reconstruct a clean and comprehensive genre taxonomy to estimate the actual combination of the gothic phenomenon and its temporal frame of reference. Notwithstanding the several merits of such works, in his essay *The English Novel in the Romantic Era* (2000), Peter Garside states that "as source[s] of bibliographical information [the above studies] should be taken with great caution," because none of them is entirely reliable on its own. So after a long procedure of assessment and combination of Summers', Levy's, and Frank's taxonomies, along with a cross-check of each entry with the latest bibliographical surveys of English works of fiction, I ended up with an integrated list of 519 English gothic novels published from 1764 to 1832. This was my population: an ultimate gothic bibliography assembled according to the criteria of documented popularity featuring critical reviews and presence in the "gothic" sections of the circulating libraries' catalogues.

Once the population is defined, one must determine both the sample, that is to say, the corpus of digital texts selected to perform the experiments, and the external model of reference. This latter is a crucial and too often forgotten factor in quantitative cultural analysis for it constitutes one of the few guarantees of representativeness of results since, as Geoffrey Leech (Leech and Short 1981), points out, "without representativeness, whatever is found to be true of a corpus, is simply true of that corpus." In fact, it is the very possibility of comparing the results obtained from the investigation of the sample corpus with those of the randomly assembled external model of reference that allows scholars to generalize their interpretation so as to turn it into an empirically sustained theoretical postulation.

Unfortunately, in the specific case of my research, as well as within the study of literary corpora in general, the sampling methods are inevitably affected by the actual availability of texts in either a digital or a paper format. However, although it is still impossible to select materials entirely randomly, I ended up with an extensive selection of 174 novels: a number that represents exactly a third of the previously reconstructed genre bibliography and stands as one of the biggest textual corpora ever used in a study about literary genres.

These 174 eighteenth and nineteenth century gothic novels were massively gathered from online archives and databases, both open access and private. By definition, a database is a system that allows the efficient storage and retrieval of information, and, in the case of computer-based literary macroanalysis, the kind of information stored is unstructured textual data or, more specifically, corpora of digitized literary texts. I deliberately use the adjective "digitized" for it is essential to introduce a key concept for the understanding of the computational approach: the difference between real objects and objects of knowledge. These concepts don't originally belong to the field of literary criticism but are rather ascribable to an age-old epistemological knot firstly introduced by Ludwig Feuerbach. Concrete in thought and real concrete was the original version of such dichotomy later reprised by both Gaston Bachelard and Louis Althusser. In his *Reading Capital*, Althusser claims that the knowledge of a real object cannot be reached through an immediate contact with the "concrete," but only through the production of the concept of the object itself—in the sense of object of knowledge—as the absolute condition of its theoretical possibility. In my case, a book is a real physical object that for centuries has presented itself in a paper format until recently, when it has become available as an immaterial electronic version that can be read on any device or screen. However counterintuitive, books under such format must still be considered as real objects because what actually constitutes an object of knowledge is an encoded digital text implemented with an apparatus, no matter how essential or sophisticated, of tags and metadata. This is what is called a model, and computer-based analysis can only operate on models.

In this way, digital corpora of encoded literary texts mark the epistemological transfer from a world of concreteness to one of model representations and thus configure themselves as the condition of possibility for all subsequent processes of data retrieval and extraction. So, once the encoding preprocessing protocol was applied to both the corpora (the gothic one as well as the external model of reference), I carried out the three macroanalytic experiments designed to identify the most frequent words (MFWs), the type token ratio (TTR), and the most consistent narrative motifs of the gothic genre, all of which will be presented in the following.

Two Experiments in Genre Stylometry: MFW and TTR

The first experiment, MFW, presents a synchronic portrait of the stylistic character of the gothic genre through the analysis of its high-frequency lexis.

When John Burrows (1987) defines MFW as "the real nitty gritty" of a text, he refers to the fact that the words we tend to use the most not only reveal the authors' idiolectic imprinting but also something about the semantic structure of their writing. In the field of computational analysis of literary forms, for instance, the study of the MFWs of a corpus has been used as a clustering force capable of isolating the specific traits that differentiate one genre from another (Allison et al. 2011). As previously mentioned, for this and all the other experiments, my sample corpus of 174 English gothic novels was compared to an external model of reference (from now on called countercorpus) of 174 nongothic English novels that were randomly collected from the Stanford Literary Lab database dating from 1764 to 1834. Each year presented exactly the same number of books for both the corpora; e.g., if the year 1797 has seven entries for the gothic novel, the same amount of texts was provided for the nongothic countercorpus.

As a computer can read text only in terms of continuous streams of input, two main propaedeutical parsing procedures are required to determine the word count and its grammatical structure: tokenization and stemming. In this sense, tokenization is configured as an act of segmentation of the single texts into individual units of meaning, which in most cases coincide with proper words but may also include contiguous strings of alphanumeric characters or punctuation marks. Thanks to a specific script, I subsequently determined the exact number of word occurrences for each text in each corpus (gothic and nongothic), obtained a list of common words appearing in both corpora, and then calculated their frequency mean and normalized the data according to the expected rate of occurrences (average corpus mean). Such a procedure, called statistical standardization, associates to each word a z-score: a positive or negative value reflecting a word's distribution above or below an expected average corpus mean according to their frequency. In this way, as shown in Figure 9.1, I identified the MFWs of the gothic novel by simply isolating those tokens that presented a higher differential z-score between the gothic and nongothic corpus. Figure 9.2, instead, shows a possible semantic clusterization of the different lemmas.

In conclusion of this section devoted to the analysis of the high-frequency lexicon of the gothic novel, data have shown that the gothic discourse discerns itself from other literary forms in five main features:

1. A dynamic narrative structure particularly focused on verbs related to the semantic fields of generic actions, adventurous quests, temporal and location marks, verbs of motion and displacement.
2. The statistical relevance of spatial characterization and exploitation of the time factor as suspense catalysts (expressed in the differential z-score of adverbs such as "every" and "immediately" or nouns such as "hour," "anxiety," etc.).
3. The use of a system of adjectives and nouns ascribable to the macrosemantic area of abstract values, typical of early romances and adventurous novels.

word	#tokens_	#tokens_	Ztokens_	Ztokens_	Ztokens_gothic-nongothic
the	23953090	1179234	74.04437	67.93435	6.110021
of	13750971	706075	44.2887	38.95088	5.337819
to	13629721	685642	43.00373	38.60642	4.397307
my	2641147	174278	10.84546	7.388699	3.456758
his	5188123	274344	17.13833	14.62447	2.513863
her	5347159	271664	16.96979	15.07628	1.893516
which	2273549	126715	7.85435	6.34438	1.509971
from	1852027	107517	6.647041	5.146867	1.500174
by	2269928	118963	7.366849	6.334093	1.032756
your	1212764	68851	4.215443	3.330768	0.884675
lord	333921	28598	1.684043	0.834041	0.850002
every	450460	32558	1.933076	1.165119	0.767957
this	1885928	97340	6.007038	5.243177	0.76386
their	1088108	59283	3.613738	2.97663	0.637108
heart	393509	27256	1.599648	1.003326	0.596322
he	6030932	281414	17.58294	17.01883	0.564118
who	1295470	67305	4.118219	3.56573	0.552489
with	4032147	190741	11.88077	11.34043	0.540343
me	2033321	100195	6.186581	5.66191	0.524671
him	2334568	112434	6.956258	6.51773	0.438527
lady	580012	32988	1.960118	1.533167	0.426951
father	333572	21069	1.210565	0.833049	0.377516
de	325391	20452	1.171763	0.809807	0.361956
power	134207	11332	0.598232	0.266668	0.331564
whom	285231	18140	1.026368	0.695716	0.330652
length	93606	9388	0.475979	0.151323	0.324655
friend	268800	17184	0.966248	0.649037	0.317211
thy	87563	8974	0.449943	0.134156	0.315788
yet	431392	24312	1.414508	1.110948	0.30356
an	1381136	67003	4.099227	3.809101	0.290127
return	145511	10848	0.567794	0.298782	0.269012
appeared	112094	9309	0.471011	0.203846	0.267164
heaven	87539	8181	0.400074	0.134088	0.265986

wordstats-gothic-nongothic.1000 | dati MFW e scarto | graphs | +

Figure 9.1   Gothic MFW, Excel screenshot.

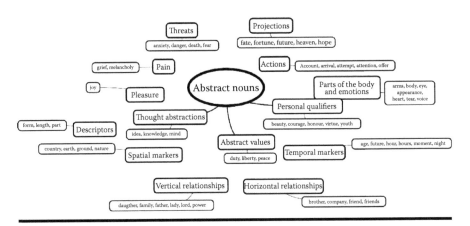

Figure 9.2   MFW, semantic clusters.

4. The high distribution of descriptors related to specific parts of the body expressing the manifestation of emotions and sentimentalism ("countenance," "eye," "arms," "tears," "heart").
5. The relevance of the themes of power and possession indicated by the marked representativeness of possessive adjectives, among the grammatical words, and nouns belonging to the semantic domain of vertical relations.

Moving on to the second experiment, TTR is a traditional method of measuring the lexical diversity of a given text. The distinction between a *type* and its *tokens* is an ontological one between a general sort of thing and its particular concrete instances. In this way, types are generally referred to as the abstract class of words that concretely occur in the particular form of tokens. From the study of the ratio between the quantity of unique word types and their actual occurrences in a single text or a corpus derives a series of speculations about how rich, diverse, and complicated to read a text, or a specific genre, can be. In this perspective, following the same standardization procedure as in the MFW experiment, I calculated the indexes of vocabulary richness for each of the 348 novels belonging to both the sample gothic corpus and the nongothic countercorpus. I then proceeded with the extraction of the results and the graphic output of the vocabulary richness z-score values arranged chronologically. In the Figure 9.3 histogram, the bars in

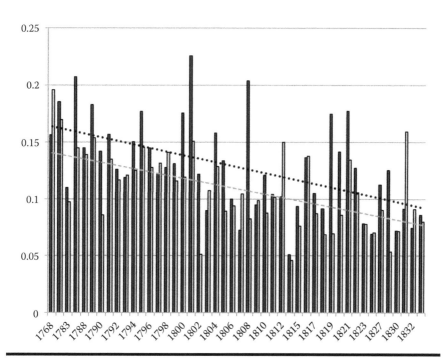

Figure 9.3   TTR sample gothic corpus vs. nongothic countercorpus.

black indicate the scores of the gothic corpus, while the light-gray bars represent those of the nongothic novels.

As this chart shows, the gothic corpus turns out to be lexically richer and more varied than the nongothic countercorpus, with an average of 1.78%. This means that as one gets closer to the years of massification of the novel in the mid-nineteenth century, the gothic genre maintained a higher degree of lexical variety even in the face of the general trend of simplification and repetitiveness of the literary market. This richness index undergoes significant changes in the period of maximum diffusion of the genre and is inversely proportional to the popularity of the single bestselling novels.

So to summarize the practical contribution of this section, the TTR experiment shows a clear evolutionary pattern of the gothic genre (which is seen as "physiological" to most literary forms) articulated around an initial tendency toward originality and diversification of the language, followed by a phase of lexical impoverishment that coincides with the moment of maximum genre dispersal. In fact, it is right in the years when the gothic reaches and exceeds its point of critical mass, establishing itself as the unquestioned hegemonic form of the literary market, that its prose becomes more modest, repetitive, and simple. Not only does this experiment empirically prove the connection between readability and saleability indexes, but it also shows how such connection lies at the basis of the very mechanisms of canon formation.

An Experiment in Narrative Patterns: Mining the Motifs

In addition to high-frequency lexis (MFW) and vocabulary richness (TTR), another experiment in the study of literary genres from a distant point of view is the analysis of narrative motifs. In fact, according to the theoretical commonplace that genres originate from, the reiterated and conventional correlation between formal and thematic choices, narrative motifs can be seen as the minimal constitutive units of themes. This begs the question of how computers can detect such units. Following Ted Underwood's (2012) definition of topic as a "collection of words that have different probabilities of appearance in passages discussing certain discourses within a collection of documents," recent experiments in computer-based macroanalysis have succeeded in developing an algorithmic procedure, called topic modelling, that extrapolates such discourses through the correlated frequency of words that could have generated them. So assuming that each novel in the English gothic corpus is made of a mixture of recurring themes and motifs, topic modelling represents a computer-based syntactic way to infer the semantic structures that are latent and constitutive of the whole genre itself.

Figure 9.4 Gothic consistent motifs: *usurpation, seduction, lunacy,* and *confinement.*

But how does it work in detail? First, an algorithm categorizes the words in each document of the corpus into mathematically correlated clusters. This procedure is unsupervised, meaning that with no human input to instruct the machine about what actually constitutes a theme or a narrative motif, the resulting model collects the distribution of co-occurring words within segments of the whole corpus. Topics are returned in the form of a word-cloud that scholars can examine in order to verify if a common theme can be spotted in each of the word clusters. The ease with which these resulting word clusters can be associated to specific themes is referred to as topic coherence or topic interpretability.

Once the computational logic at the basis of topic modelling has been illustrated, it is possible to interpret the results regarding the motifs of the gothic discourse and proceed with their diachronic visualization throughout the temporal frame of reference of 1764–1832 previously defined. The graphs in Figure 9.4 reveal what motifs survived the challenge of time by attesting themselves as the most consistent of the genre.

Interestingly enough, *usurpation*, *seduction*, *lunacy*, and *confinement* establish themselves as the thematic cores of the gothic discourse. What these four elements have in common is that they all constitute a drift from an institutionalized orthodoxy, an illegitimate desire or behavior that exceeds the norm. In the case of *usurpation*, for example, we witness an illicit acquisition of a right or a property, whereas *confinement* and *seduction* are respectively related to a double process of objectification and appropriation of an individual through imprisonment or sexual abuse. Despite gothic novels featuring the previous transgression as a prerogative of characters like pervert aristocrats or dissolute clerics (both of which belonged to a feudal imagery still at hand), such motifs may work as a symbolic correlative of three "ghosts" haunting the solidity of the bourgeois status: the legitimation of class identity, the concept of luxury, and the obligations of the modern social contract, all of which will be discussed in what follows.

Making Sense of Numbers: Interpreting the Gothic

I opened with an ambitious introduction in which I connected Moretti's distant reading with Jockers's computer-based macroanalysis in order to frame the theoretical and methodological premises for a new large-scale perspective in the study of novelistic genres. I then presented the different phases of my case study experiment about the English gothic novel defining the object of study, the sample corpus of reference, and the units of analysis. The primary purpose of my investigation was to clarify some of the contradictions implied in the gothic label by identifying the components and the rules of its genericity through empirical and measurable units.

So, if we were to define the gothic genre from a synchronic point of view, it would result as a complex novelistic form constituted by the juxtaposition of narrative motifs and stylistic elements attributable to the semantic domain of danger and threat, ontological hesitation (projection into the unknown), hierarchies of interpersonal relationships, and, of course, the use of supernatural. Among the stylistic and formal elements at the basis of the DNA of the gothic discourse, there are grammatical determiners, especially definite articles and possessive particles, adverbial forms of temporality (frequency, temporal determiners, immediacy, and duration), as well as forms denoting verbal action, motility, and perception. The picture is further enriched by the use of adjectives connected to the semantic domain of abstract values (i.e., personal qualities), as well as a series of noun classes ascribable to the field of physical emotions, spatiality, temporality, vertical, and horizontal relationships.

Specificity, spatial and temporal markers, abstract values, sentimentalism, adventurous digressions, and relational power structures have been identified as the common distinctive units of the gothic stylistic character. However, as the second experiment has demonstrated, the patterns of gothic genericity are perfectly traceable also in the consistency of certain narrative motifs. In fact, among the functions that emerge the most for chronological and percentile stability are the forms of villainy such as *usurpation, seduction, lunacy,* and *confinement.* Each of these motifs is deeply rooted in the sense of transgression of an implicit norm of social behavior moved by self-interest and greed. Furthermore, *usurpation, seduction, lunacy,* and *confinement* can be read as narratological clues of the discomfort of the rising middle class in its attempt to exorcise the "ghosts" and paradoxes that threatened the legitimation of its own identity, namely, the values at the basis of the bourgeois status, the hazardous ideal of luxury, and the relationship between individual and society within the new borders of the social contract.

The first "ghost" has to do with the English bourgeoisie's urge to define itself. If Robinson Crusoe served as the original myth for the rising "middle station of lower life" whose founding values were work, self-discipline, continence, and comfort, such was not the case during the nineteenth century, when that same class shifted toward a more entrepreneurial and financial acception typical of the industrialized and capitalized world. In this new order of things, the old hegemonies of aristocracy and clergy became the symbolic containers to which the bourgeois consciousness could oppose itself to. Sobriety, industriousness, and accumulation of credit through the mobility of capital and trade were now juxtaposed to excess, indulgence, and savage debt based on an idea of wealth typical of the noble class where land ownership was transmitted vertically. Yet, despite the middle-class had made of such restraint and moderation its own birthmark, the looming spirit of modern capitalism unveiled greed and consumerism as an ironic incongruity intrinsic to bourgeois morality.

The second "ghost" evoked by the gothic genre exposes the earlier paradox of reconciliation between the concepts of commodity and luxury with the principles of the protestant ethic. If, on the one hand, the bourgeois cannot but linger hungrily into the consumption of luxury in order to reach the proper level of comfort and welfare that the chosen ones deserve, on the other hand, in doing this, the same is actually betraying the constitutive features of his class identity primordially based on frugality and moderation.

After addressing the issue of class identity legitimation and the paradox of capitalist consumerism, the last bourgeois "ghost" reflected in the shadows of the gothic genre deals with the relationship between the individual and his collectivity. If one of the undeniable achievements of the Enlightenment was that of rationalizing and regulating every aspect of the public sphere, then the gothic discourse gives voice to the cry of the selfish modern "I" who is forced to come to terms with the clauses of a social contract that presents itself as a compromise between public order and individual freedom. But what is the price of such an enlightened management of social stability? What are the collateral damages of bourgeois contractualism? The gothic novel answers with images of centralized power, unavoidable control, and confinement, with all the interpretative and ideological consequences these imply.

Conclusion: Some Epistemological Considerations

In many years of passion for literature and its intriguing stories, I've come to realize that the most successful plots, the most beautiful ones, stem from an act of transgression. On the contrary, it seems to me that as a discipline, the story of digital humanities rises to recompose a transgression: a subversive act that dates back to November 1609, when Galileo Galilei pointed his telescope to the night sky. The empirical evidences of the Galilean observations marked the schism between hard and soft sciences, in which the experimental measurements of the scientific method deprived philosophy, and literature along with it, of the need of objectivity. In this perspective, little or no importance lies in whether the projects and experiments exposed so far have convinced the reader of their unprecedented contribution in bringing new knowledge in the field of literary studies. In fact, even if the answer were to be negative and the reader were to conclude that the tools and methods of computer-based macroanalysis can but confirm something already known and disseminated by traditional criticism, the true question would then regard how to consider such validations. Are they just a disguised form of failure of the quantitative approach with respect to the qualitative one?

An untainted way to address this question is by embracing an epistemological perspective that recognizes Popper's principle of falsifiability as the guarantee of hermeneutical validity. This is because entering the field of quantitative methodology in literary research means sticking to a binding premise where everything in the humanities is and can be intuitive and in computer science must become something formalized and formalizable. This assumption strongly emerges in Moretti's article entitled "Operationalizing," in which the very concept of measurability, borrowed from physics and hard sciences in general, provides the scholar with the means to make a concept actual in a continuously negotiable dialogue between theory and reality. Here, Moretti illustrates how the transformation of a concept in a series of testable and quantifiable operations constitutes both the condition of possibility for the application of computational tools to the study of sheer literary objects, as well as the essence of a new literary criticism that is no longer theory driven but data driven (Moretti 2013). In this way, the nonelusive nature of empirical verification forces the literary scholar to embrace broader perspectives and move from the usual level of close-reading to the new paradigmatic frontier of quantitative criticism, of which my own research is but a first attempt.

Bibliography

Archer, D. (ed.). 2009. *What's in a Word List: Investigating Word Frequency and Key Word Extraction*. Farnham (UK): Ashgate.

Allison S., R. Heuser, M. Jockers, F. Moretti and Michael Witmore. 2011. Quantitative Formalism: An Experiment. In *Stanford Literary Lab, Pamphlet 1*. https://litlab.stanford.edu/LiteraryLabPamphlet1.pdf.

Althusser, L. and É. Balibar. 1970. *Reading Capital* [1968]. London: Verso, New Left Books.

Biber, D., S. Conrad, and R. Repper. 1998. *Corpus Linguistics, Investigating Language Structure and Use*. New York: Cambridge University Press.

Bollier, D. 2010. *The Promise and Peril of Big Data*. The Aspen Institute Publication Office.

Burrows, J. F. 1987. *Computation into Criticism: A Study of Jane Austen's Novels and an Experiment in Method*. Oxford [Oxfordshire]: Claredon Press.

Frank, F. S. 1987. *The First Gothics: A Critical Guide to the English Gothic Novel*. New York: Routledge.

Garside, P. 2000. The English Novel in the Romantic Era: Consolidation and Dispersal. In *The English Novel 1770–1829: A Bibliographical Survey of Prose Fiction Published in the British Isles*. Garside P., J. Raven, R. Schöwerling (ed.), Oxford: Oxford University Press.

Jockers, M. 2010. Digital Humanities: Methodology and Questions. Blog entry. http://www.matthewjockers.net/2010/04/23/digital-humanities-methodology-and-questions.

Jockers, M. 2013. *Macroanalysis: Digital Methods and Literary History*. Urbana-Champaign: University of Illinois Press.

Jockers, M. 2014. *Text Analysis with R for Students of Literature*. New York: Springer.

Leech, G. N. and M.H. Short. 2007. *Style in Fiction: A Linguistic Introduction to English Fictional Prose*. Upper Saddle River (NJ): Pearson Education.

Levy, M. 1995. *Le roman gothique anglais: 1764–1824*. Toulouse: Albin Michel.

Moretti, F. 2000. Conjectures on World Literature. In *New Left Review, 1* https://newleftreview.org/II/1/franco-moretti-conjectures-on-world-literature.

Moretti, F. 2005. *Maps, Graphs, Trees: Abstract Models for a Literary History*. London: Verso.

Moretti, F. 2013. "Operationalizing": or, the function of measurement in modern literary theory. In *Stanford Literary Lab, Pamphlet, 6*. https://litlab.stanford.edu/LiteraryLabPamphlet6.pdf.

Perazzini, F. 2013a. *Il Gotico @ distanza: Nuove prospettive nello studio dell'evoluzione dei generi del romanzo*. Roma: Nuova Cultura.

Perazzini, F. 2013b. *Nascita del romanzo gotico*. Roma: Nova Logos.

Schonberger, V. M. and K. Cukier. 2014. *Big Data: A Revolution That Will Transform How We Live, Work, and Think*. London: John Murray.

Summers, M. 1940. *A Gothic Bibliography*. London: The Fortune Press.

Summers, M. 1964. *The Gothic Quest: A History of the Gothic Novel*. Westerham (UK): Russel & Russel.

Underwood, T. 2012. Topic modelling made just simple enough. Blog entry. http://tedunderwood.com/2012/04/07/topic-modeling-made-just-simple-enough/.

MANAGING BIG DATA WITH AND FOR ARTS AND HUMANITIES

Chapter 10

Toward a Data Culture in the Cultural and Creative Industries

Cimeon Ellerton

Contents

Introduction

The word "data," in my opinion, has some challenges in the context of the cultural and creative industries. It is such a generic term, covering any type of information, and it can be perceived as rather dry and extensive, almost the opposite of creativity. Yet those with the right skills can bring these data to life for people and find stories within it that have an interest or practical meaning for others. I have been engaged in ongoing exploration into the challenges, trends, and opportunities of big data in order to put audiences at the heart of our cultural institutions. This exploration has taken the form of technical experimentation, action research, and ethnography, in particular the following:

- Aggregating and analyzing data for audience development
- Rapid-prototyping through collaboration between tech and culture specialists
- Ethnography into the cultural and structural barriers to data driven decision-making

When given the right tools, big data can help organizations build resilience while supporting creative risk taking. Furthermore, the rapid expansion in available information about who our audiences are (and are not) sets the stage for a radically transparent understanding of whom our public arts organizations are serving, who decides what goes on in them and how we communicate that to the public. Evidencing approaches to cultural democracy versus the democratization of culture should impact how we interpret the mission and policies of those that create and fund artistic activity. If, for example, Arts Council England's vision is centered on achieving "great art, for everyone," a conversation needs to be had about what "great" and "everyone" really means and how we measure it. Until then, we will lack as a sector the strategic framework and vision to use big data, so even the best audience, technological and organizational development will have limited impact. In the following, I discuss some learning from key projects that led me to this viewpoint. It should also be noted that while the findings have relevance across the creative and cultural industries, much of our exploratory work has focused on the subsidized touring companies, theaters, concert halls, museums, and galleries in England.

Barriers Are Cultural Not Technical

Throughout all the research projects, we have found that the most significant barriers to effective use of data within the organizations are not technical, but cultural and attitudinal. The data exist, but it is not always clear who has the means and rights to use them. We have found that this uncertainty is a common challenge across organizations, both large and small, and in every art form. Equally, there are pockets of excellence, but the cultural sector and, in particular, the subsidized part thereof are not necessarily of great scale or easily scalable. This is a fundamental challenge to the adoption of truly big data techniques, where size does sometimes matter when it comes to the data set. Many cultural organizations whose existence involves presenting new work to the public must also constantly seek to find a market for what are effectively new products. We are not like a supermarket or grocery store. Nobody needs what we offer in the same way they need food, and individually, we do not have hundreds of products on offer to suit every mood or situation. So while our analysis shows that the loyal core audience remains relatively stable across art forms and organizations, the churn of new audiences to any one venue is huge, in the region of 60% to 80% per year. The question of whether this is good or not cannot be answered by the data. The cost of maintaining such high churn rates can. We have found that business and technical terminology is itself a barrier. Terms such as "data-driven decision-making" (DDD) can be off-putting to many leaders in the subsidized arts sector, who believe that the use of such language and techniques is the top of a slippery slope leading to a purely commercial, transactional relationship with audiences and the cultural sector becoming just another part of consumer society. When delivering a talk on DDD to chief executives of arts organization, Anthony Lilley* was asked:

> You're telling me a computer should programme my venue?
>
> **Participant in a leadership workshop**

This is not a silly question. The hype of big data has promised extraordinary levels of automated decision-making. However, experts such as Nate Silver make a strong case for the human intervention in understanding the meaning of data analysis. In his book, *The Signal and the Noise*,[1] Silver writes about the limitations of automated analysis techniques to prescribe the action that should be taken on the basis of any analysis.

> We're not that much smarter than we used to be, even though we have that much more information—and that means that the real skill now is learning how to pick out the useful information from all this noise.

We at The Audience Agency have come to call this the "so what" question, and I will talk in more detail about this later in the chapter. What is clear is the importance of context and experience that, combined with values-driven business models, cannot—at least for the foreseeable future—replace people as the final decision-makers. We are some way off the prescriptive analytics of the "Gartner Model of Data Management Maturity."[†] What is within reach is the application of big data techniques to move beyond the merely descriptive and toward the predictive.

Aggregation and Collaboration

Forecasting the likely interest in an exhibition or event and the likely impact of a marketing intervention could drastically improve resilience in arts organizations while simultaneously increasing the capacity for creative risk-taking. However, truly big data in the arts—of the scale available to telecoms and finance—cannot

---

* Anthony Lilley is a media practitioner and theorist with a background in creative, policy, and academic spheres. He is the chief creative officer and chief executive officer of Magic Lantern Productions Ltd.—an award-winning interactive media and multiplatform creative house and consultancy.

† See https://www.gartner.com/doc/3044517/use-gartner-mdm-maturity-model

be generated by a single organization within the cultural sector. There are large theater operators that might come close, but even they would be paddling in the shallow water in comparison to, for example, a supermarket chain. Furthermore, for the analysis to be of use, it must be actionable. In the case of theaters, our research shows that it is usually the local venue with which audience members feel they have a relationship and not some larger parent organization or visiting company, which has implications for who is best placed to use any analysis of captured aggregated data, as well as the previously described difficulty in achieving the volume of data required for these advanced analytics.

To quantify the challenge of generating truly big data in the arts, we can see in our Audience Finder* ticketing data warehouse that an average UK box office contains around 149,000 transactions. Those transactions relate to a smaller number of bookers, of which many will be walk ups providing no further information to that transaction than a date, time, value of purchase, etc. It does not help us get to know who those walk ups are. Compounding this for any individual organization is the fact that of those bookers for whom we do have personal information, on average, only 20% of those will have attended more than once and so these "oncers" are giving little away in terms of overall frequency, interest, or value. There is an answer to this challenge. Aggregating data provides much greater volumes at greater velocity than any individual organization can generate on its own. Aggregating just the transactional information of the subsidized performing arts venues has produced over 49 million records. The nonticketed organizations can also gain from this approach. Again using Audience Finder as an example where at current count, 379 organizations are collecting data using a standardized audience survey methodology, over 2000 audience responses per week are being collected, giving us more than just behavioral information, but also attitudinal and demographic information. The power of the two combined is yet to be fully explored but has the potential to fundamentally shift the level of insight we have about our audiences. Where organizations are able to be supported in making use of the combined data sets, this has practical implications for individual organizations.

> A bespoke audience segmentation project for an organisation predicated on box office patron and transactional data identifies groupings of patrons with similar behaviours and preferences. The portraits for each segment are then enhanced using customer profiling,† and the aggregated cohort dataset to see what each of these grouping's preferences are

---

* Audience Finder is a free national audience data and development tool developed and managed by The Audience Agency, for and with the cultural sector, and is funded by the National Lottery through Arts Council England. It enables cultural organisations to understand, compare, and apply audience insight.

† In this case, the Audience Spectrum system developed with funding from Arts Council England.

elsewhere, and then further enriched with data from primary research. By linking survey responses to box office patron IDs it is possible to analyse the survey responses by segment to better understand demographics, experiences and motivations. In the same way that preferences elsewhere using box office data can be identified, motivations to attend a particular organisation can also be set in a wider context for each segment for instance.

Penny Mills
Consultancy Director

However, it is not all plain sailing. Thanks to the policy intervention and investment from Arts Council England,* the aggregated data set now exists to provide the source material for a data-driven approach to audience development. However, there are still structural challenges that prevent the effective use of the insight from this big data. For best results, we believe that organizations should be working together in a coordinated way to use big data as a way to put audiences at the heart of our cultural institutions. Organizations involved in touring work have the potential to benefit dramatically from this approach, where "relationships with the areas and audiences that the work visits are often shallow and fleeting," according to Catherine Love in the paper *What Can We Do about Touring.*[†]

Traditional touring models have been about people dropping into each place, performing and then moving on to the next place. What we're trying to do is build a relationship with audiences and communities.

Kate McGrath
Codirector of Fuel

Without working together to build and maintain audiences, the offer may not be broad or frequently changing enough to attract the widest scope of potential audiences. Equally, it may also feel uncoordinated and without a clear brand. The real opportunity is not about developing relationships based on an existing offer, but on understanding the scope and variety of the offer required to meet a bigger market. Going back to the industries that have so far made most use of big data, these tend not only to have a high volume of transactions, they also have a broad range of products. By working together, cultural organizations stand a better chance of being able to not only maintain but also grow the active pool of arts attenders by promoting a joint offer to existing and potential audiences.

---

* See http://www.artscouncil.org.uk/document/data-sharing-and-requirements-national-portfolio
-organisations and accompanying guidance on audiencedatasharing.org.
[†] Commissioned by Fuel as part of the New Theatre in your Neighbourhood project.

Skills and Silos

Assuming that the barriers to generating the data are overcome, there are still barriers in analyzing and understanding the data. An organization's information technology (IT) capacity and policy can cause some serious issues around data, especially where IT is purely a service (whether internally provided or externally sourced) and understood to operate as a technical support function rather than a key layer of operations across all departments. This can lead in some instances to the emergence of a single data guru, who is most often physically positioned in the IT department and who owns the means to capturing and analyzing the data and concentrates a great deal of power, knowledge, and responsibility in this one monopoly. This colocation of function and knowledge creates a silo that reinforces the cultural barriers to using data that are often found in parts of the cultural sector. It is worth noting that there are also many examples of organizations working happily and creatively with technology and data across the organization. We would, however, also note that these organizations generally have technology built into the mission and model of the organization. Few organizations not set up in this way bridge the division between the arts and sciences that is too often embedded in the structures of our society and education system. Nesta,* in a publication titled *Fix the Pipeline for STEAM Talent in the Creative Economy*,† states that "50 years after C.P. Snow's Rede Lecture, we still have Two Cultures," but it does also offer two solutions:

> Government should remove the perverse incentives that currently riddle secondary education deterring young people from combining arts and science subjects, and reward universities that succeed in developing rigorous, multi-disciplinary courses valued by industry.

How do cultural institutions attract the data scientists and economists who can break the colocation of function and knowledge described earlier and derive value from these big data sets against the social and cultural divide? The Alan Turing Institute‡ is now actively seeking data science research in the arts and cultural sector, but outside of academia; where are the roles and budgets in our organizational structures to fit these new skills? We have previously been advised by the then Technology Strategy Board, now Innovate UK, that any organization would struggle to recruit to such a role with a less than £60,000 salary and that major supermarket retailers struggled to recruit into £100,000 posts. That's not to say we

---

* Nesta is an innovation foundation with a mission to help people and organizations bring great ideas to life.
† See http://www.nesta.org.uk/blog/fix-pipeline-steam-talent-creative-economy#sthash.zLSQA 8UT.dpuf
‡ Alan Turing Institute is the national institute for data science, with headquarters at the British Library.

should assume it is impossible. There are many reasons why we choose to work in the cultural sector, and salary is rarely among them, but it does raise a question of how competitive our offer is to the potential workforce. The good news is that the Chartered Institute of Personnel and Development published findings in June 2016 stating that "working in a non-profit organisation is so satisfying it is the equivalent of a salary increase of £22,000 per year."

It would be remiss to ignore the skills that we do have in the cultural sector, and there are concentrations of these in and around marketing and commercial departments of the organizations and specialist agencies like ours. However, the supply-led rather than demand-led nature of some cultural organizations means that the skills and knowledge of these staff will often be brought to bear on organizational decisions once they have already been made. It is more than a convention that cultural organizations seek to find an audience for the offer rather than let the audience inform the offer. This is backed up by the findings of the Warwick Commission,* which stated that "low engagement is more the effect of a mismatch between the public's taste and the publicly funded cultural offer." In a world in which public subsidy is increasingly justified by the cultural sector's ability to attract a wide cross-section of society, mission and monetary realities demand a move toward models in which the voices and interests of the many are meaningfully represented. Despite years of striving to democratize the existing cultural offer as curated by the cultural elite, we still find ourselves superserving 10% of the population and providing for just about 50%. The evidence increasingly suggests that if we want the majority of society to engage in the public culture, we will need to enter into an age of cultural democracy. The possibility of using big data in a nuanced and creative way stops this idea being a provocative theory and makes it a question of pressing potential. Already, data are describing the potential of experimental, community-led programming (such as Creative People and Places[†]) to build and sustain relationships with so-called unengaged communities. Data scientists have a potentially important role to play if we can begin to incorporate them into our organizations and, critically, their knowledge into our decision-making processes.

> If art and culture are to matter to more people, they must provide them with value.

Steven Hadley
Postgraduate researcher at Queen's University Belfast[‡]

---

* In November 2013, the University of Warwick launched a one-year commission, chaired by Vikki Heywood, CBE, to undertake a comprehensive and holistic investigation into the future of cultural value.
† Funded by Arts Council England, there are now 21 independent Creative People and Places projects in areas where people have fewer opportunities to get involved with the arts.
‡ See article at http://www.artsprofessional.co.uk/magazine/article/democratising-arts

Data science can help to create mechanisms whereby the behaviors and attitudes of audiences are understood and considered in order to provide the value that audiences are seeking.

The Implementation Gap

The Arts Data Impact* project identified key ways that data science can be embedded within organizations to support not only the analysis and understanding of data but also the practical and everyday application of that data. Alongside breaking down the silos and cultural barriers described earlier, the way in which data is presented is critical in helping make sense of them and therefore being able to act on them. Statistical representation—charts, bar graphs, and so on—is by far the easiest and most universally recognized way of presenting data. However, it is those who understand data who design the ways in which they are presented, and this can hinder decision-makers from being able to identify patterns that might then underpin effective forward planning. Charts, visualizations, and maps—so-called infographics—provide more engaging and intuitive ways of understanding the data for nonspecialists. There are specialist skills involved in formulating, designing, and creating infographics that require the combination of graphic design skills with a deep understanding of statistics and cognition. This combination is in great demand but in limited supply and adds further weight to the movement encouraging a move from STEM to STEAM[†] in education, such as that proposed by the Cultural Learning Alliance in its 2014 paper STEM + Arts = STEAM.[‡] Our own experience suggests that at the current evolutionary stage, a reassuring data-confident interpreter, who is of the sector and recognized as being experienced in the sector, is also needed alongside the data scientist in order to give the confidence and ability to act on any findings from data analysis. Our ethnographic research with Professor Paul Moore[§] (University of Ulster) finds that there is a clear fracture (with different levels of severity) between the work of those involved with data and those we could call the "artistic" gatekeepers, with the artist/aesthetic generally having primacy. This causes a number of problems in applying the insight,

---

* Arts Data Impact was an initiative supported by the Digital R and D Fund for the Arts that introduced the first ever "data scientist for the arts" in residence to three large arts organizations—the National Theatre, English National Opera, and the Barbican. They were responsible for encouraging staff across the organization to recognize and use the data resources available to them. From this, opportunities were identified as potential prototypes for data tools.

[†] The Cultural Learning Alliance is a collective voice working to ensure that all children and young people have meaningful access to culture.

[‡] See http://www.culturallearningalliance.org.uk/images/uploads/STEAM_report.pdf

[§] Professor Paul Moore is Head of School of Creative Arts and Technologies at Ulster University and chairs the NI Media Literacy Hub.

what we at The Audience Agency have termed the implementation gap. Despite the challenges described in generating large and coherent data sets for big data analysis, Moore finds that many larger or more complex organizations are simultaneously reaching data saturation point. There seems to be a scramble to adapt the most recent technological innovations with the result that the full value of these is not realized, data sets cannot communicate with each other, and staff are feeling stressed and pressured about not "doing enough" with their data. One outcome of this is that the data tend to be used mainly to explain or justify present or past decisions and positions, for the purpose of political advocacy on platforms internal and external. The use of data for forward planning is often happening by default. Similarly, fetishization of new software as a solution to decision-making problems encourages a model where organizational needs are shoehorned into software packages that may not be suitable for that organization.

Evidence versus Intuition

Every organization studied in the ADI project had at least one individual who had taken on or been given the mantle of "gifted through intuition." This allowed the individual to have status because they understand supposedly innately what should be done in any given situation, be it planning, programming, or some other area of business. Sometimes, these individuals thereby attained a control beyond the usual remit for such a position. This intuition myth can work against effective data utilization, and in fact, initial research would suggest that the intuition so lauded is often built on a detailed understanding of the data combined with deep experience, which is then articulated as intuition because the decision-making structures and processes within the cultural institutions we studied are sometimes more receptive to these decision stories than a clearly data-led one. This reinforces the earlier assertion that it is knowledge combined with experience that makes for powerful DDD. However, no single person is infallible and no experience always true. Here, confirmation bias takes a role in generating unassailable truths. The natural human tendency toward seeing only the evidence that points to a predetermined world view or hypothesis can lead to previously good observations becoming embedded in organizational thinking but which over time become untrue. Daniel Kahneman, Paul Slovic, and Amos Tversky's research into judgment under uncertainty[2] provided the means for understanding the effect of these heuristics on decision-making in 1982. The sector's ability to adopt strategies to reduce the negative effects of these biases will be greatly enhanced, although by no means eliminated, by the adoption of a data culture.

All of this is not to say that intuition does not have an eternally vital part to play. As one data-convert and director of a successful repertory theater told us recently, being able to predict the outcomes of her programming decisions with much greater, data-informed accuracy has enabled her to take far more artistic risks than ever before. The predictive power of big data makes it starkly clear how often you can afford to take risks, as well as quantifying the level of risk a decision may actually represent. Being able to calculate risk in this way perversely makes it all the easier to throw business caution to the winds when something unprecedentedly inspiring comes along.

Conclusion

Organizational and cultural change is a slow process, and the arts sector is making important steps toward that change. Bringing data scientists and analysts into the center of organizations will be key to promoting and delivering that change. But data delivered in the appropriate way can and should provide a new string to the bows of professionals across the sector, especially those who are committed to a more inclusive culture. As the general public and, therefore, the audiences for culture become used to omnichannel and personalized experiences, cultural organizations will have to adapt to using data-informed techniques at a strategic and operational level. This technologically driven proliferation of communication channels creates ever-increasing workloads for marketing departments trying to build and maintain relationships with audiences. A more sophisticated approach to understanding and responding to a diverse society's thirst for culture is going to be vital in navigating the rapid changes in public expectations. In the words of Todd Yellin* at Netflix, a company that has done much to challenge the business model of both film and TV industries and needs to understand the full diversity and interests of its audiences:

> Here's a shocker for you, there are actually 19-year-old guys who watch *Dance Moms*, and there are 73-year-old women who are watching *Breaking Bad* and *Avengers*.

Not only does Netflix know this, but they act on it, in what they commission, program, recommend, and communicate. Could the sector use this as a template for data-led cultural democracy in action?

What we can see is that there is a need for data to be understood across all levels of staff in an organization—particularly those in senior decision-making roles, to ensure that not just marketing but also program decisions are based on data. This could be one way to increase cultural democracy by developing offers that are both high quality and appeal to a diverse public.

---

* Vice president of Product Innovation at Netflix.

References

1. Nate Silver. *The Signal and the Noise: The Art and Science of Prediction.* Penguin Books, 2012.
2. Daniel Kahneman, Paul Slovic, and Amos Tversky. *Judgment under Uncertainty: Heuristics and Biases.* Cambridge University Press, 1982.

Chapter 11

Arts Council England: Using Big Data to Understand the Quality of Arts and Cultural Work

Carl Stevens

Contents

Introduction

Arts Council England (2013) champions, develops, and invests in artistic and cultural experiences that enrich people's lives, supporting a range of activities across the arts, museums, and libraries. The Arts Councils strategic framework is underpinned by a determination to support the arts and cultural sector to pursue excellence in all it does, acknowledging that excellence is difficult to define and will always be the subject of debate but committed to working with the sector to agree to more rigorous definitions. The Arts Council is clear that excellence cannot be separated from the people who value it and that this relationship is relative, subtle, and complex.

Since 2013, the arts and cultural sector in England has been developing and testing a set of quality metrics and accompanying quality evaluation framework that offer a new approach to understanding quality. A total of 137 National Portfolio Organizations and Major Partner Museums trialed the quality metrics over 374 events between November 2015 and May 2016, using a digital big data platform that enabled them to capture a wide range of self, peer, and public responses to their work and analyze them in real time. Combining responses to the metrics with detailed metadata and basic demographic information, the trial produced the largest ever standardized data set on the quality of cultural experiences in England.

This chapter begins by outlining the difficulty of understanding and measuring the quality of artistic and cultural work and the current approach Arts Council England takes to this. We will then explore the development of the quality metrics framework, discussing the importance of its coproduction by arts and cultural organizations. Following the linear development of the framework through to the recent trial, we will demonstrate how this quantitative approach begins to address the three key difficulties traditionally associated with understanding and measuring the quality of arts and cultural work: first, that creative output is too diverse to be measured in a standardized way; second, that our experiences of arts and culture are subjective; and third, that we don't have a common language for describing them. We will finish by summarizing the benefits the framework can offer, both as a self-reflective tool for individual organizations and as a powerful instrument to help the sector understand and communicate the public value it creates.

Why Artistic and Cultural Quality Is Difficult to Understand

Understanding, measuring, and communicating the value and impact of arts and culture are challenging, yet there is an ever-increasing need for publically funded arts and cultural organizations, and policy bodies such as the Arts Council, to be able to understand, evidence, and communicate this value. This can lead to a tendency for arts and culture to be measured more by its instrumental impact, the impact derived from its wider social or economic benefits, rather than the intrinsic impact of the work on the audiences that experience it.

Arguing against the increasing instrumentalism of cultural measurement in his essay "Capturing Cultural Value," John Holden (2004, p. 21) remarks that "audience numbers and gallery visitor profiles give an impoverished picture of how culture enriches us." They are important indicators but say very little about the creative work itself. However, the effect that a piece of work has on the people experiencing it, the thing that makes it what it is, the reason it was created, is harder to measure. It can be subjective and personal. It can't easily be defined nor counted.

In 2013, Wolf Brown completed a literature review to better understand the different methods in place for measuring the value and impact of arts and culture (Carnwath and Brown 2014). Two common themes in the review relate to the challenge of understanding the intrinsic impact. These are a reliance on in-depth qualitative feedback from those experiencing a piece of work and a suggestion that value cannot be measured consistently across different art forms. Three key factors arguably underpin those challenges. First, arts and cultural output is too diverse to be compared; what constitutes a high-quality experience in a visual art gallery is different from that of a theater. Second, arts and culture affects different people in different ways. Their experience of it is subjective and personal. And third, there is no shared language commonly in use for describing a high-quality experience.

Arts Council England invests in 663 National Portfolio Organizations and 21 Major Partner Museums. These arguments are at the heart of the challenge in fully understanding the quality of the work produced by those organizations. The breadth of activity they deliver is extremely diverse. The Arts Council wants to support organizations to deliver high-quality work that reaches as greater and wider audience as possible. Audiences engage with arts and culture in many different ways, from attendance at events and exhibitions, to immersive participation, to cocreation. Some will be experts in their field and some will be first time attenders.

Arts Council's Current Approach to Understanding Quality

In "Supporting Excellence in the Arts: From Measurement to Judgement" (2008), Brian McMaster argued that excellence, innovation, and risk taking were being constrained by top–down targets and recommended that funding bodies adopt a new assessment framework based around self-assessment and peer review. Following this, Arts Council England implemented a peer review program of Artistic Assessment in 2010 and relaunched it as the Artistic & Quality Assessment program in 2014 to incorporate assessments of museums and programmed and participatory work. Assessments are undertaken by a range of independent sector professionals. The assessors' role is to experience the work of a funded organization and write a report for the Arts Council assessing the quality of that work.

The program commissions in the region of 1000 assessments each year but provides only a subjective snapshot of an organization's work rather than an understanding of the views of the multitude of people experiencing work across their wider program. The qualitative nature of the assessments makes it difficult for organizations to compare and learn from each others' reports. It is also difficult for policy makers such as the Arts Council to get a collective understanding of the quality of work produced, in order to support the sector and effectively make the case for public investment in arts and culture.

Quality Metrics

Since 2013, the arts and cultural sector in England has been developing and testing a set of metrics and accompanying quality evaluation framework that offers a new approach to understanding quality.

Quality metrics is a sector-led metrics framework that uses self, peer, and public assessment to capture the quality of arts and cultural work. The quality metrics themselves (Figure 11.1) are a set of statements developed by arts and culture

Dimension	Statement	Respondent type		
		Self	Peer	Public
Concept	It was an interesting idea	✓	✓	✓
Presentation	It was well produced and presented	✓	✓	✓
Distinctiveness	It was different from things I've experienced before	✓	✓	✓
Captivation	It was absorbing and held my attention	✓	✓	✓
Challenge	It was thought-provoking	✓	✓	✓
Enthusiasm	I would come to something like this again	✓	✓	✓
Local impact	It is important that it's happening here	✓	✓	✓
Relevance	It had something to say about the world in which we live	✓	✓	✓
Rigor	It was well thought-through and put together	✓	✓	✓
Risk	The artists/curators were not afraid to try new things	✓	✓	-
Originality	It was ground-breaking	✓	✓	-
Excellence	It is one of the best examples of its type that I have seen	✓	✓	-

Figure 11.1 Core quality metrics used in the 2015/16 trial. (Reproduced from Knell, J., Whitaker, A., Quality Metrics final report: Quality Metrics national test. http://www .artscouncil.org.uk/sites/default/files/download-file/QualityMetricsNationalTest _Report_Knell_Whitaker_2016_0.pdf, 2016. With permission.)

organizations that describe the different dimensions of quality artistic and cultural work. The metrics are administered through a digital survey platform that allows organizations to collect, analyze, and share self, peer, and public feedback on their events, exhibitions, or performances in real time.

The metrics correspond to the different high-level impacts that arts and cultural work is expected to have on the people experiencing it. Rather than metrics that ask respondents to express whether something is good or bad, they ask respondents to rate each dimension of quality in order to describe, albeit in a quantitative manner, how they feel about the work they have experienced.

The work takes its inspiration from a similar project initiated in 2010 by the Department of Culture and the Arts in Western Australia.

Manchester Metrics Pilot

Having heard about the work in Western Australia, a group of arts and cultural organizations in Manchester approached the Arts Council for support to trial something similar in England. This group of organizations, known as the Manchester Metrics Group, consisted of 13 arts and cultural organizations of varying size and discipline.*

Stage 1 of the Manchester Metrics pilot took place between April and July 2013 and facilitated development of the framework, testing of the concept, and formulation of an initial set of metrics. Stage 2 of the pilot enabled the consortium to refine the metrics and test them in practice across eight arts and cultural events in the North West of England between November 2013 and January 2014.

Rather than using the metrics already developed in Western Australia, the Manchester Metrics Group started with a blank sheet of paper to devise a set of metrics suitable for them. This approach to coproducing metrics was intended to ensure that they would be relevant to the way work is produced and presented in England and would be applicable across multiple art forms and organization types, a first step in addressing the argument that quality cannot be measured in a standardized way due to the diversity of output.

The coproduction process was also intended to provide the sector with a sense of ownership of the metrics, an important step in addressing Lilley and Moore's (2013) argument in their report on big data in the arts, *Counting What Counts*, that for many cultural organizations, "gathering and reporting of data is seen as a burden and a requirement for funding rather than an asset."

---

* For a list of participating organisations, see Bunting and Knell's 2014 report, *Measuring Quality in the Cultural Sector. The Manchester Metrics Pilot: Findings and Lessons Learned.*

In his report on stage 1 of the project, John Knell (2014) highlights that despite the diverse range of organizations making up the Manchester Metrics Group, they quickly agreed on a set of key outcome areas that were not dissimilar to those in use in Australia. This suggested that despite the varied output of arts and cultural organizations, there are commonalities in terms of the impact they hope their work will have on the people experiencing it. The more challenging work for the Manchester Metrics Group was translating the outcome areas into a small set of standardized metric statements that are understood by peers and audiences and are applicable for the range of work produced by arts and cultural organizations. This stage of work began to address the challenge of not having a shared language to describe quality.

At this early stage, the group agreed that it was important to use the metrics to provide a pre-event and postevent self-assessment in order to allow organizations to outline their creative intentions for their work and express whether they felt those intentions had been achieved. The pre-event self-assessment provides a weighting for each individual metric, meaning that if an organization expects their work to score highly for *enthusiasm* but lower for *risk* and *originality*, they can express this in their pre-event survey.

This is an important feature of the framework as it shifts the objective from "obtaining a high score" to gathering a nuanced understanding of how a piece of work delivers on its specific artistic aims. Setting intentions enables organizations to use the framework as an evaluation tool, while weighting metrics provides the context that allows a consistent set of statements to be used across a wide range of work, as opposed to only using the metrics that a piece of work is intended to receive positive responses to.

The Manchester Metrics Group trialed the framework across eight events, aiming to receive in the region of five peer responses and at least 50 public responses per evaluation in order to capture a wide range of opinion.* By providing insight into how different pieces of work resonate with different audiences and how those responses relate to the intentions of the organization, the framework shifts from a tool that's primary purpose is to report on quality to a more sophisticated quality evaluation framework that provides organizations with insight that can be used to improve the way they operate.

National Pilot

Following the two-stage pilot, the Manchester Metrics Group commenced a project to build on findings from the trial and further develop the metrics themselves, the online platform, and the technology that supports them. The consortium involved

---

* Findings are presented in John Knell and Catherine Bunting's 2014 report *Measuring Quality in the Cultural Sector. The Manchester Metrics pilot: Findings and Lessons Learned.*

a wider range of organizations from outside of Manchester in the process and tested the metrics across over 70 events.*

This phase of the work started to consider how organizations might use findings from the quality metrics surveys to make data-driven decisions to inform their creative and commercial practice and the potential policy value of a standardized quality evaluation framework to funding bodies such as the Arts Council.

The report from this pilot argues that one of the key reasons the quality metrics framework and Culture Counts platform was received positively by the organizations adopting it is that unlike more complex big data analysis, which requires specific skills, tools, and expertise not widely available within arts and cultural organizations, collecting standardized responses from a range of respondents through a platform that can provide automated real-time reporting is a relatively simple and familiar mechanism.

The report from this pilot also recognizes that the use of data and technology to support and inform the way organizations operate is relatively underdeveloped within the arts and culture sector. A shift will be needed in order for even a relatively familiar survey-based framework such as quality metrics to be used to its full potential whereby organizations are collecting robust data, asking the right questions of it, and using their insight to inform what they do.

An interesting piece of research that took place through this phase of the work was the comparison of responses to a Royal Opera House production of Swan Lake both in a live theater setting in London and in live cinema events in Manchester and Peterborough. On average, audience responses were slightly more positive at the cinema events than the theater. However, the findings also highlighted that the theater audience were considerably younger and engaged more regularly with dance than those experiencing the work in the cinema.

What the data alone don't tell us is why these responses differed. It does, however, provide a starting point for further investigation and demonstrates the potential for the metrics to provide insight that can be useful both for individual organizations and in a wider policy context, particularly when used in conjunction with data related to audience demographics and motivations. For example, through wider evaluation using the quality metrics and comparison of live and screened events, the sector can begin to understand more about the impact of those experiences on different audiences.

This is also where the framework begins to address the challenge of subjectivity. By asking a large group of people from different places and with different levels of expertise to respond to the same piece of work in a standardized way, it is possible to begin to understand how the notion of a high-quality experience can differ or correlate between different groups, broadening the conversation about artistic quality and what it means to different people in different settings.

---

* Findings are presented in the 2015 report, *Home: Quality Metrics, Research and Development Report*.

Metadata	Field examples	Obtained
Nonquestion survey data	Timestamp, respondent ID	Automated via culture counts software
Organization data	Registered area, region, organization size	Arts Council England open data
Event data	Event art form and art form attributes, event location	Supplied by organizations
Geomapping data	Rural status	Office of National Statistics open data

Figure 11.2 Metadata framework from the 2015/16 quality metrics trial. (Reproduced from Knell, J., Whitaker, A., Quality Metrics final report: Quality Metrics national test. http://www.artscouncil.org.uk/sites/default/files/download -file/QualityMetricsNationalTest_Report_Knell_Whitaker_2016_0.pdf, 2016. With permission.)

National Test Phase

Having seen the potential of the quality metrics framework at a relatively small scale, the Arts Council wanted to test the validity of the metrics and the wider framework across a larger and more diverse group of organizations and to learn more about the insight that could be gained from analysis of the aggregated data collected by organizations using the framework.

During the national trial, 137 National Portfolio Organizations and Major Partner Museums organizations completed 374 quality metrics evaluations between November 2015 and May 2016, receiving 19,800 audience responses, 1,358 self-responses, and 921 peer responses.[*]

Through this phase of the work, organizations used the Culture Counts[†] platform to collect self, peer, and public responses to the core quality metrics. Organizations aimed to receive a minimum of one self-response, five peer responses, and 30 public responses per evaluation. Self-assessors provided pre-event and postevent responses. Peer and public respondents provided postevent responses only.

The Culture Counts platform allows respondents to respond to each metric question using a sliding 0–100-point scale. This means that an audience member responding to the nine metrics can produce a highly diverse combination of answers, enabling an individual to express his/her personal response to a piece of work in minute detail. Organizations also collected basic demographic information (age, gender, and postcode) from public respondents. This was matched with metadata (see Figure 11.2) to

---

[*] Findings are presented in Knell and Whitaker's 2016 report, *Quality Metrics Final Report: Quality Metrics National Test.*
[†] https://culturecounts.cc/uk/

enable insightful aggregate analysis that moves beyond the basic comparison of art form or event scores, to more intelligent comparison of similar events and types of work.

Aggregate Analysis

Aggregate analysis (see Figure 11.3) of the responses captured through all 374 evaluations showed that, on average, the work presented throughout the trial received a broadly positive response from all respondent groups. Organizations demonstrated confidence and satisfaction with their own work, scoring it relatively highly in their pre-event and postevent surveys and largely met their creative intentions as demonstrated by the alignment between organization's pre-event scores and audience postevent scores. Notably, three of the metrics rated by all three respondent groups (challenge, distinctiveness and relevance) scored considerably lower than the other six.

Several readings can be made from these overall findings. One is that a greater percentage of work presented through the trial was enjoyable and well presented rather than innovative and challenging. Another is that the metric descriptors for challenge, distinctiveness, and relevance require respondents to provide more considered responses. For example, being asked to consider whether a piece of work had something to say about the world today requires the respondents to think about events outside of the work they are experiencing. This is different from the more immediate response required to something being well produced or presented. Likewise, it is a harder test for a piece of work to score highly for "it was different from things I've experienced before" than "it was an interesting idea."

Further analysis has also revealed that respondents were much more divided in their responses to these lower-scoring metrics than those that were higher scoring. So although the average scores are around the 0.7 mark, individual responses to these metrics had a larger range than those of the higher-scoring metrics. This could suggest two things. First, that some work evaluated through the trial was considered highly relevant, challenging, and distinctive, while other work was considered to the contrary. And second, some of the work evaluated divided the audience, meaning that some respondents gave particularly high responses to these metrics and others gave low responses to the same piece of work.

This standard deviation issue has been a point of interest throughout the development of the framework and an important one to note. Receiving similar scores from all respondents is not necessarily the sign of a high-quality piece of work, especially if those scores are around the midpoint of the scale, as this could suggest it didn't resonate strongly with the people experiencing it.

Arts and culture can often be divisive, and work that has a strong positive impact on one person may have a decidedly negative one on somebody else. So if those average scores are actually formed from a combination of high and low scores, particularly for those metrics that require a bit more consideration, the work could be seen to have had a stronger impact, even if this meant that some people didn't

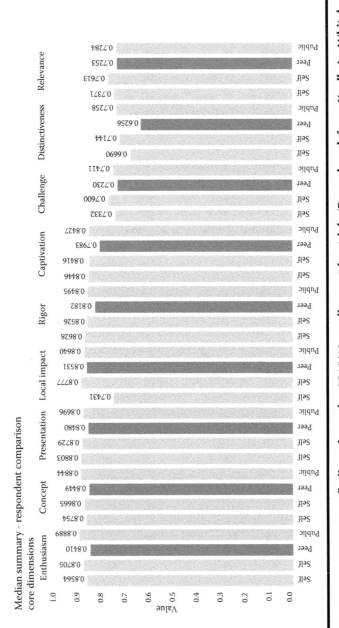

Figure 11.3 Average aggregate findings from the 2015/16 quality metrics trial. (Reproduced from Knell, J., Whitaker, A., Quality Metrics final report: Quality Metrics National Test. http://www.artscouncil.org.uk/sites/default/files/download-file /QualityMetricsNationalTest_Report_Knell_Whitaker_2016_0.pdf, 2016. With permission.)

like it. Enabling organizations to explore audience responses at this level of detail is another step in tackling the issue of subjectivity. Respondents provide their individual views, but these can be explored in the context of others.

What this aggregate analysis highlights is that a considerably more sensitive form of analysis is required in order to extract real meaning from the data and fully address the challenge of comparability. It does however provide a useful benchmark to aid further investigation.

Art Form Analysis

The art form attributes built into the metadata framework enable examination of the findings beyond simple comparisons between main art forms such as visual arts or theater, allowing for more meaningful comparison of similar types of work or work that has a shared characteristic such as being immersive or participatory. The range of work produced even within a single art form doesn't necessarily lend itself to direct comparison. Examining data at a more detailed level provides greater insight and opportunity to debate what constitutes a high-quality experience within a particular type of work.

Looking at the findings for circus (see Figure 11.4) demonstrates how different art forms impact on the overall aggregate scores. It also demonstrates how art forms began to form distinct profiles throughout the trial. Circus proved to be particularly popular with the public, scoring highly across the generally high-scoring dimensions, higher than average on the generally lower scoring dimension of *distinctiveness* but particularly low for *relevance*.

It is important to reiterate that these findings are from a limited trial and are presented in this chapter as an example of how the data can be used, rather than as research findings. However, the evidence in Figure 11.4 suggests that the circus produced through this trial was presented to a very high standard (presentation) and that audiences found the work distinctive (distinctiveness) and enjoyed their experience (enthusiasm). This is an interesting finding in itself and suggests that, perhaps, one of the things the audience enjoy about circus is the distinctiveness of the art form. This paints a very different picture to a set of responses, suggesting high enthusiasm for indistinctive work.

The lower score for *relevance*, however, suggests that the circus work evaluated through the trial didn't appear to have much to say about the world. This is perhaps unsurprising for an art form like circus, which is not associated with strong narrative; however, audience responses fell notably short of the intentions outlined by the organizations, suggesting that the intended meaning and relevance were not picked up upon by the audience.

This could provide useful information to circus companies, helping them realize and act on the need to do more to convey the meaning of their work. This is where it would also be useful for circus organizations to compare their responses.

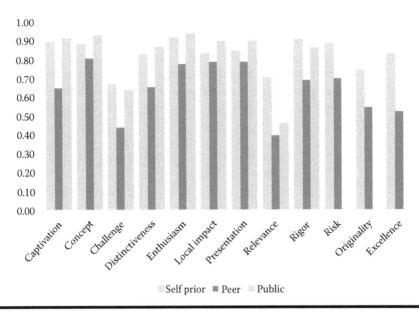

Figure 11.4   Average aggregate circus findings from the 2015/16 quality metrics trial. (Reproduced from Knell, J., Whitaker, A., Quality Metrics final report: Quality Metrics National Test. http://www.artscouncil.org.uk/sites/default/files /download-file/QualityMetricsNationalTest_Report_Knell_Whitaker_2016_0 .pdf, 2016. With permission.)

For example, if one circus company consistently receives stronger responses for relevance than others, questions could be asked to find out why and this learning could be shared to help others convey the meaning of their work in a stronger way.

The data about particular types of work act as a starting point to prompt questions and encourage further discussion and learning. It provides a platform for organizations producing similar types of work to share findings and really think about what quality looks like within the context of their discipline in relation to others.

Enhancing Understanding of Quality and Driving Improvement

The quality metrics framework has the potential to help improve our collective understanding of artistic and cultural quality in several ways, addressing the problems raised at the beginning of this chapter around subjectivity, comparability, and language.

Coproducing a set of easy-to-understand metric statements that are applicable across art forms and embedding them in a quantitative evaluation framework begins to create a shared language that acts as a starting point for organizations to understand the quality characteristics of their work and how they impact on their audiences.

Allowing organizations to set their own intentions for the work they are evaluating, in essence providing a weighting to certain metrics, enables the same framework to be used to evaluate different types of work and shifts the emphasis from scoring highly against each metric (in which case organizations would only want to use the metrics most relevant to the piece of work they are presenting) to a more sophisticated quality evaluation framework that provides organizations with insight they can use to inform their decision making.

Gathering data from a wide range of people, from industry professionals to first-time attendees, on their experience of the work in a consistent and comparable way and analyzing these responses in relation to other audience data such as demographic information and engagement levels help us begin to understand what quality means to different people and across different art forms.

The data provide real-time insight for individual organizations to allow them to understand what different people think about their work. Using standardized metrics allows them to easily share findings and learn from organizations producing similar work, providing useful information that can be used to better tailor their offer, inform creative output, and improve quality. Increasing data and evaluation skills across the arts and cultural sector will also increase resilience, enabling organizations to operate more effectively in the digital economy and evidence their impact to stakeholders in funding applications and evaluation reports.

As more organizations adopt the framework, the bigger and more complex the data will become, and with sensitive and detailed analysis, will present a rich picture of the quality and value of arts and cultural work in England. This will provide academics and policy makers with national quality and impact data to explore alongside existing data sets and more qualitative means of evaluation, to further enhance our understanding of what quality means and how best to support the sector to produce work of the highest quality.

The framework also has the potential to improve decision-making and accountability among policy makers and funders such as the Arts Council, enabling arts and cultural organizations to evidence the quality of their work in a consistent way and funding bodies to create a better account of the effectiveness of their investment and make a strong case for continued investment in arts and culture.

Conclusion

Rather than providing a reductionist good/bad assessment of quality, quality metrics is a nuanced framework with the potential to provide useful insight into what quality means to different people in different contexts. The work has highlighted the difficulty of measuring quality across a large and diverse portfolio of arts and cultural organizations but demonstrated how quality metrics can address this difficulty and provide information that is useful at both organization- and sector-wide levels. A large standardized data set on the quality of cultural experiences in England has already been produced, and wider adoption of the framework will produce larger and more complex data sets that offer a number of potential benefits to the arts and cultural sector, funders and policy makers, and academics.

Bibliography

Arts Council England. 2013. Great Art and Culture for Everyone: 10 year strategic framework.

Bunting, C. & Knell, J. 2014. Measuring quality in the cultural sector. The Manchester Metrics pilot: Findings and lessons learned. http://www.artscouncil.org.uk/sites/default/files/download-file/Manchester_Metrics_Final_Report_May_2014.pdf

Carnwath, J. & Brown, A. 2014. Understanding the value and impacts of cultural experiences. http://rraceweb01.aws.rroom.net/sites/default/files/download-file/Understanding_the_value_and_impacts_of_cultural_experiences.pdf

Holden, J. 2004. Capturing cultural value: How culture has become a tool of government policy. https://www.demos.co.uk/files/CapturingCulturalValue.pdf

Knell, J. 2014. Manchester Metrics pilot: Final report of stage one. http://www.artscouncil.org.uk/sites/default/files/download-file/Manchester_Metrics_Stage_One_Report_Dec_2013.pdf

Knell, J., Bunting, C., Gilmore, A., Florack, F., Arvantis, K., & Merriman, N. 2015. Home: Quality Metrics. Research and development report. http://artsdigitalrnd.org.uk/wp-content/uploads/2014/06/HOME-final-project-report.pdf

Knell, J. & Whitaker, A. 2016. Quality Metrics final report: Quality Metrics national test http://www.artscouncil.org.uk/sites/default/files/download-file/QualityMetricsNationalTest_Report_Knell_Whitaker_2016_0.pdf

Lilley, A. & Moore, P. 2013. Counting What Counts: What big data can do for the cultural sector. http://www.nesta.org.uk/sites/default/files/counting_what_counts.pdf

McMaster, B. 2008. Supporting excellence in the arts: From measurement to judgement. http://webarchive.nationalarchives.gov.uk/+, http://www.culture.gov.uk/images/publications/supportingexcellenceinthearts.pdf

Chapter 12

Visualization of Scientific Image Data as Art Data

Jo Berry

Contents

> Artists have a distinct approach to understanding and communicating ideas that can illuminate and challenge perceptions within society. (Wellcome, n.d.)

> We easily forget that research is actually a creative process. When we want to explain things, we often look for illustrations on the internet, instead of creating our own illustrations of conceptual insights. If we would dare illustrate and visualise our research, we might get both new insights and better contact with the general public. (Ericson, University of Gothenburg, 2016)

This chapter maps how art created from scientific image data from different imaging laboratories can help and influence how such data can be visually communicated, and how working closely with imaging specialists and scientists was an opportunity to present new insights into the application, use, and analysis of advanced imaging technology and data in new visual depictions. The research project described is situated within contemporary visual arts and communication, drawing upon the knowledge of the discipline as practitioner and academic. This chapter maps out important aspects of this research investigation as it unfolds while working in the field and in the studio. It is a "multi-dimensional zone of considerable complexity" (Kemp, 2016: 217) originating from experiencing science in action. It provides a straightforward process of engagement and a fertile arena for interaction where useful insights into scientific research themes are discussed, establishing an accumulative understanding of methods of observation that are impacting positively on both fields of expertise.

Interest in industrial technologies, material exploration, color, and light* had already been developed by the author over 15 years of art practice, which led to working with pharmacists in the Life Sciences Department at Nottingham University from 2010 to 2012 on a project called "Hijacking Natural Systems."† This highly successful project was nominated by the University for The Times Higher Education Award and cited by the Wellcome Trust as an exemplar of a successful Arts and Engagement project.‡ And over the last nine years, work with scientists who use highly sophisticated imaging technologies and processes has resulted in projects such as "Light It Up: Brains, Psychosis, Neuroimaging & Us"§ and "Bridging the Gaps."¶ The rationale for this current study is an exploration of advanced imaging and microscopy from a visual arts practitioner's perspective, where this artist engages in a constructive manner with scientists to interpret data differently. The new visualizations (as shown in Figure 12.1), which are being created, offer new insights into scientific imaging, which have value beyond pure science, as these scientific data are visually rich and have the potential to be exploited from a visual viewpoint. The work being created is generating interest for exhibition and commission, on web platforms to show to the general public.

---

* 2001–2005, "Light drawings: a contemporary artistic medium." Advanced Research Fellow funded by the Arts & Humanities Research Council (AHRC) and Loughborough University (£52K).
† 2009–2011, School of Bio-medical Sciences, Nottingham University, funded by Wellcome Trust Arts Award (£29K) and ACE (£28k).
‡ This project was funded by Wellcome (£29k), ACE (£28k), Derby City Council (£500), and Derby Museum & Arts Gallery (£2K).
§ 2013–2015, Neuro Translational Imaging Department, Nottingham University, funded by ACE (£29K).
¶ 2012 ESPRC Funded Award, the Organic Chemistry and Fine Art Department, Loughborough University.

Figure 12.1   Radiolarian: a digital drawing rotated at a 5° angle six times.

As technologies become more sophisticated, ways of viewing samples (static and live) are continually being developed. The super-high-resolution machines that scientists use today to image samples are not normally accessible to nonscientific specialists, yet imaging technologies present a rich, underexplored area for artistic exploration. All scientific collaborators see this exchange as an opportunity to generate interest and understanding about their research among expert and nonspecialist audiences. They recognize that their working methods can appear extremely opaque to the public and difficult to understand but believe that key concepts normally beyond those who might attend science exhibitions or read scientific literature can be communicated to audiences using a different perspective. They acknowledge that scientific images are increasingly travelling outside laboratories and entering news magazines, courtrooms, and media and understand that these images rely on cultural preferences to create persuasive representations. They have identified this artist/designer with her skills, knowledge, and experience as an ideal candidate to share findings and to generate impact outside the scientific context.

From September 2015, work began with three different laboratories to gain first-hand experience of working with research scientists using advanced imaging as an important visual tool in their scientific investigations. Each academic research institution is a core-teaching facility, allowing scientists the space, time, and resources to collaborate and gain knowledge without direct commercial pressure. The resulting research project involving these specialists is designed to offer new understanding in the topic of data visualization through the lens of an artist working as an equal on three different themed case studies:

I. Experiencing internal structures of cells using microscopy with different imaging technologies.
II. Versatile imaging as a three-dimensional sketch.
III. Dermal drug delivery—how to increase bioavailability in viable skin.

The first three sections of this chapter describe appropriate aspects of this investigation, which already have extended knowledge and appreciation of cutting-edge imaging experiments and scientific procedures. Acting as a participant and observer using the model cited by Robson after Spradley (Sutton, 2011), observations are recorded (space, actors, activities, acts, events, time, goals, and feelings) in a process of analysis that is extending knowledge of these art–science collaborations by establishing an accumulative understanding of the precedents of art and science conceptualizations where methods of observation arise through enquiry and reflection.

The fourth section describes how pure scientific data are being reprocessed within a reflective, constructivist, and systematic visual framework, where digital technologies are being employed to expand visual possibilities and where this practitioner is researching through creative action and "reflecting in on action" (Schon, 1983). Digital drawing is being used as an explorative, generative tool, leading to design decisions (Schaeverbeke, 2016). Industrial process production methods (laser cutting and three-dimensional [3D] printing) and moving image and animation are employed to further explore complex ideas and structures (Doloughan, 2002), giving rise to new visualization and material models and revealing new insights into the study of complex systems invisible to the naked eye. This is an example of research *through* practice where experimental methods are evidenced (Rust, Mottram, and Till, 2007: 21) and where a range of innovative ways are identified in which creative practice can add to research knowledge.

The fifth section describes how this inquiry is centered on critical feedback from the collaborating scientists, who will be invited to inspect new visualizations and material models and reflect and comment on their understanding of this approach. This visualization process is being undertaken and used as a vehicle to create a "space" for new interaction and new responses, building mutually beneficial relationships over a sustained period of time, which impacts positively on both fields of expertise. By comparing viewpoints, it is expected that this information will contribute to the production of more refined visualizations.

Experiencing Internal Structures of Cells Using Microscopy from Different Imaging Technologies

One aim of the research project is to show how capturing and understanding data (Coffey and Atkinson, 1996: 85) through visual processes can make a valuable contribution to understanding scientific image data so that they can be communicated and distributed effectively to new audiences. The project described here is based at the Cell Signalling and Pharmacology Group (CS&PG), University of Nottingham. The School of Life Sciences Imaging department encompasses three units, all under one consistent structure: the Advanced Microscopy Unit, Cell Signalling Imaging, and Super Resolution Microscopy. This department houses some of the most sophisticated imaging technologies available, providing cutting-edge imaging facilities to researchers across the university and external collaborators. They are trying to understand how cell systems work, right down to a molecular level, examining in detail individual cell mechanisms. Advanced imaging is used as an important analytical tool to collect a range of data. It is the scope of advanced imaging methods and data that is proving so fruitful for the other research aim: the creation of art.

Over the last year, observations of individual members at work on practical scientific activities have taken place, with in-depth discussions about the major themes and imaging techniques being investigated. This experience enriches understanding of scientific concepts and how scientists use a range of data. As it is important to have some understanding of technical and analytical methods used in the acquisition of data, the following paragraphs detail specialist scientific procedures from observed experiments.

A highly developed imaging and processing technique used frequently is confocal microscopy (CM). CM illuminates the sample through the objective lens,[*] which is set as a pinhole to focus a laser beam of light.[†] The microscope adjusts to fluorescent molecules[‡] that excite the sample at a certain wavelength of light and uses a special dichroic[§] mirror to direct different wavelengths of light[¶] to allow light longer than that wavelength through. Fluorescence, a member of the luminescence family[**] of processes, is an important visual imaging tool used with this technique. Fluorescence lights up live and fixed cells with luminous color to create extremely complex and visually interesting imaging experiments. From formal scientific experiments that follow a rigid protocol, super natural microscopic fluorescent images of cells can be seen on screen and captured in a number of ways. This technique can be refined to achieve highly detailed ways of seeing samples. As the laser scans over the plane of interest, a whole image is obtained, pixel by pixel and

---

[*] For articles about objective lens see, for example, https://www.microscopyu.com /microscopy-basics/properties-of-microscope-objectives

[†] For articles about galvanometer-based scanning system, see, for example, https://www .olympus-lifescience.com/de/microscope-resource/primer/techniques/confocal/confocalintro/

[‡] For articles about fluorescent molecules, see, for example, https://www.ncbi.nlm.nih.gov/pmc /articles/PMC3805368/

[§] For articles about dichroic mirrors, see, for example, https://www.rp-photonics.com/dichroic _mirrors.html

[¶] For articles about wavelengths of light, see, for example, https://www.microscopyu.com /microscopy-basics/resolution

[**] For articles about luminescence family, see, for example, http://zeiss-campus.magnet.fsu.edu /articles/basics/fluorescence.html

line by line. Longer, slower scan times result in a better-quality, higher-resolution image with a lower "signal-to-noise ratio."*

The CM computer system interface uses a range of different ways of viewing cells as 2D and 3D projections. One technically interesting method of obtaining data from cells can be imaged as a Zed stack.[†] By changing the position mode and scanning, a 3D Zed stack image is produced where an image is taken from the ultimate bottom of the slice of the cell to the optimal top of the cell to build a 3D image. The laser reads and captures features from each slice of the cell to construct an image. By mathematically enhancing the cell's appearance, a flat cell can be made to look thicker by configuring the software and making a 3D projection.

One observed assay (an experimental test) of a confocal imaging experiment using fluorescence microscopy on an eight-multiwell plate[‡] was especially productive in terms of acquiring image data. Five healthy cells in each well were selected and imaged. The computer accurately marked the position of each cell so that an image could be captured before and after the drug had been added. The information obtained was relatively small but was important as it revealed whether the membrane receptor had internalized.[§] The images acquired show visually beautiful and structurally unfamiliar, brightly colored human-stem-cells-derived cardiomyocytes.[¶]

One of the newest fields of imaging experienced, and of great visual interest, was superresolution microscopy** (SRM). SRM is an emerging and rapidly evolving field of microscopy. It is a form of light microscopy that captures images at a higher resolution than the diffraction limit of light. This process is set up to counteract the fact that high-resolution microscopes are not infinitely sharp. Today, through the development of technology, optical imaging processes are progressing into the realms of electron microscopy. Through understanding how data are acquired, unique opportunities to exploit data as a visualization tool are becoming apparent. This exploitation is influencing how data can be used creatively to visually communicate extremely complex ideas.

One superresolution encountered breaks the diffraction limit of light by using mathematics to calculate the distances between individually blinking dyes attached

---

* For articles about signal-to-noise ratio, see, for example, http://www.olympusmicro.com /primer/techniques/confocal/signaltonoise.html

[†] For articles about Zed stacks, see, for example, https://greenfluorescentblog.wordpress .com/2012/04/29/basics-in-confocal-microscopy-and-image analysis/

[‡] For articles about the multiwell plate, see, for example, http://www.museion.ku.dk/2010/11 /the-history-of-microplate-technology/

[§] For articles about membrane receptor internalization, see, for example, New England Bio labs at https://www.neb.com/applications/cellular-analysis/receptor-internalization

[¶] A medical definition of cardiomyocyte, Sigma-Aldrich (no date), can be seen at http://www .sigmaaldrich.com/life-science/biochemicals/biochemical-products.html

** For articles about Zeiss systems, see, for example, Zeiss online campus at http://zeiss-campus .magnet.fsu.edu/articles/superresolution/index.html

to proteins to increase resolution. A major barrier to increasing the resolution of the image is the wavelength of light. This technique uses a pointillist application of light, calculating its mathematical optimum in relation to a sample's ideal excitation value. This enables scientists to increase the resolution of the microscope to see individual receptors on a cell membrane.

Scientists can push the boundaries of imaging by utilizing their knowledge of fluorescent properties, fluorescent molecule behavior, optics, and computer software. Scientists today can hit the live cell with low enough power to image a single molecule and look at localizing individual molecules and see them shine. By altering the laser excitation wavelength, molecules can be turned off and on. The process of superresolution is extremely difficult to grasp as a nonspecialist observer, but it is a very interesting process to view and demonstrates how the manipulation of a number of factors impacts the acquisition of data. The resulting imaging data focuses on minute details of complex and fascinating visual scientific information. This is seen during a number of imaging sessions. One in particular is when the scientist records the surface of regular bacteria where individual frames were taken at 1/10th and 1/30th of a millisecond to produce a movie. The position of each flash of light is recorded as a pixel on a charge-coupled device (CCD)* camera. A map of their locations is created, and from this, an image is derived. Another observed SRM assay tested how deep the microscope could image the tissue with oil- and water-based immersion solution. This was from a fixed sample, stained with antibodies of neurotissue from the spinal cord of a mouse, using structured illumination microscopy. By using this system, the difference between wide-field microscopy, where the image is out of focus, and SRM, where the image is detailed and resolved, can be seen. A large data set of imaging experiments was acquired as brightfield, structural illumination and Zed stacks. Files are saved at the highest possible resolution, which becomes 15 times smaller after processing. These acquisitions are aesthetically interesting. They are categorized and selectively reprocessed into a range of visual outputs that rely primarily on digital applications.

For a visual practitioner, there are particular technical details of considerable interest and conceptually important to understand. First is the fact that once the sample was set up on the stage,† everything is then viewed, imaged, and processed via the computer screen, and second, images are calculated using a 16-bit number of shades that encompass 65,000 gray-scale shades. No screen or printer could print these nuances, but it is there as digital information and can be seen if the color histogram on screen is stretched. A stereomicroscope is used to view the high pixel definition visible on screen, made up of a tight grid of millions of red, green, and black squares. The grid pattern is shifted or rotated in steps between the capture of

---

* For articles about CCD cameras use in SRM, see, for example, http://zeisscampus.magnet.fsu .edu/articles/superresolution/palm/practicalaspects.html

† For articles about Zeiss systems, see, for example, Zeiss online campus at http://zeiss-campus .magnet.fsu.edu/articles/superresolution/index.html

each image set, creating what could be described as a Moiré (interference) pattern. Viewing these beautiful colored images on screen, it is difficult to comprehend that they are made from optical technology and mathematical strategies but they open up possibilities for a visual practitioner to play with all the modalities of this system to build new information in collaboration with imaging specialists.

Versatile Imaging as a 3D Sketch

Thus, whatever the particular scientific technique being explored, the artist is seeking to explore the visual results while, through collaboration, reflecting the processes involved. At the Core Research Laboratories Imaging and Analysis Centre, Natural History Museum, London, over a three-day period, samples were selected to image on scanning electron microscopes (SEMs). SEM is used to investigate the fine structure of biological and inorganic material *by making visible the invisible*. The specimens selected were chosen because they contained much structural information and are highly detailed. Two different SEM systems were used: the Zeiss Ultra Plus and the LEO 1455VP. Each system uses a beam of accelerated electrons to produce strikingly detailed images at up to a 100,000 times magnification of the sample. The intention is to reveal and describe unexpected structural details, such as the strange calcification objects that are attached to the main structural body of these microscopic samples (as shown in Figure 12.2).

One of the new processes being piloted at NHM is photogrammetry, which involves creating a large data set of images of a specimen over a 360-degree rotation. This builds up a wealth of visual information, which is then used to create a 3D digital representation. This is processed using 3D software and outputted as a 3D print. Ideas using these techniques will be tested to generate data from a range of specimens.

Dermal Drug Delivery—How to Increase Bioavailability in Viable Skin

A rich source of imagery came from a study of how to increase bioavailability in skin. Skin is important to us and has many important functions; it is our largest organ and is designed to help keep our bodies working properly. A multidisciplinary project at the Centre for Cellular Imaging (CCI) Sahlgrenska Academy Gothenburg University, Chalmers University, and Malmo University is applying optical microscopy techniques within experimental skin research, such as creating a mechanistic understanding of how a topical drug delivery system can be designed to target, for example, eczema at exactly the right place and not to be systematically taken up by the body.

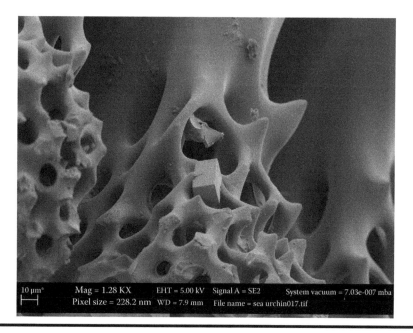

Figure 12.2 Acquired original Zeiss Ultra Plus SEM image of the details of a sea urchin spine.

Through participating in a weeklong imaging and analysis project, it was possible to see how scientists investigate the release of drugs in the skin and how they collect data to demonstrate their hypothesis. Multiphoton microscopy* was used to image "deep" samples of the skin and to test different creams. Pig skin samples were used as it has similar properties to human skin. The main benefit of this method of imaging is that by using two exciting photons,† pulsed at the same time, less energy is used and deeper samples can be imaged. What is fascinating to view is how the ultrafast laser system images data by concentrating more visible light on one point of a sample as an instant pulse measured in femtoseconds‡ and the fact that the two-photon absorption spectra excites two fluorophores equally well with less power.

---

* For articles about multiphoton microscopy, see, for example https://www.nikoninstruments.com/en_GB/Learn-Explore/Techniques/Multiphoton-microscopy
† For articles about photons, see, for example, http://www.olympusmicro.com/primer/techniques/fluorescence/multiphoton/multiphotonintro.html
‡ For articles about femtosecond laser, see, for example, https://www.rp-photonics.com/femtosecond_lasers.html

Skin, when imaged, naturally emits light, called autofluorescence,* which allows the deeper layers of collagen to be imaged without adding extra fluorescent dyes. In this experiment, images were taken after being treated with three different creams: immediately, after 6 hours, and at 24 hours. Each experiment was repeated three times and reaped a rich reward of still images, 3D movies, and Zed Stacks. The data collected, describing how the fluorescent dye and cream interact as they travel through the different layers of the skin (stratum corneum, epidermis, dermis, subcutis, and collagen), are visually captivating as they are richly colored, with each layer detailing the complex framework of the anatomy of the skin.

After an interesting and productive week of study, the scientists commented that having an artist as part of the team brought a new perspective.

Evolving Data Sets through Creative Visual Reconstruction

The research project discussed in this chapter is a pioneering multidisciplinary visual arts enquiry about new modes of utilizing data. It is a distinctive process of visual investigation to analyze and interpret scientific data from the viewpoint of the visual artist to find out if this process and the strategies employed can lead to new translations. Using experimental, avant-garde art and design strategies to extend the scope of this enquiry, the methodology employed is centered on the notion of play and visual probing that is happening in both the scientific computer laboratory and the studio and selecting for reprocessing any material considered to have potential visual qualities. Data used include equations, words, figures, graphs, computer-generated imaging material, and pure scientific image information. Characterization of the new data visualizations is emerging from using a range of different digital technologies and material processes. In the laboratory, software image data are categorized, selected, and reprocessed using a range of scientific software programs, including Zen, Fuji Image J, and Q-capture Quo.† The strategies and techniques employed to reprocess material expands the possibilities and enhances conceptual ideas, and by reworking material using different digital commands, complex visual iterations are developed, which dramatically restructure data both as 2D and 3D outputs (as shown in Figure 12.3). Instructions used include scale, color editing, timing, maximum-intensity projection, flying speed, Z scaling, 2.5 projections, histograms, rotation, surface, map-ortho, plane, rendering, and interpolation. Scientific terminology such as intracellular, binding,

---

* For articles about autofluorescence, see, for example, https://www.microscopyu.com/techni ques/multi-photon/multiphoton-microscopy

† For articles on scientific software, see for example, https://www.zeiss.com/microscopy/us /products/microscope-software/zen.html Fuji and https://imagej.net/Fiji and https://www .qimaging.com/products/datasheets/qcapturepro7.pdf

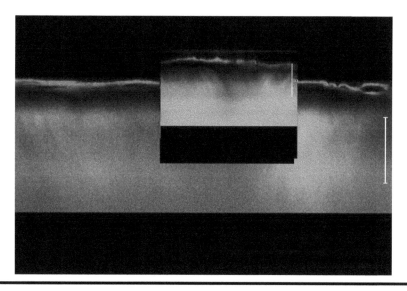

Figure 12.3 Reconstructed image of skin (stratum corneum, epidermi, dermis, subcutis) treated with Ovixan001 for 6 hours.

fixed-concentrations, internalization, transfected, synthesis, localize and track, downstream, chain reaction, and cycle are being used to further stimulate ideas.

In the studio, research is concentrating on three important elements to further extend the scope of this study: drawing, 2D and 3D prototyping, and the moving image. The work produced at this point is speculative and responsive in order to try out visual ideas and to expand the design-thinking process.

Data are reconfigured as complex, multilayered, structurally intricate digital design drawings, making use of a subtle interplay of visual information. An intense period of investigation is required to create highly detailed design drawings, which are produced by hand using digital drawing software from extensive observation (see, for example, Figures 12.4 and 12.5).

This drawn investigation of the photographic image is a process of identification. It picks out and maps important structural shapes and elements—what could be described as the "deep organising building principles behind natural form" (Kemp, 2016: 19). The drawing's intent is to reveal the mathematically precise pixellated image underneath in a simpler manner. The drawings pick out negative and positive shape through tracing elements of the shapes and structure of scientific data. Simple squares are used to construct and define shapes that are then amalgamated with a tool called Pathfinder.

The generative character of drawing and its activity is an inherently iterative process where one drawing inspires the next. In this situation, drawing is used as a tool for thought and for communication, as the act of drawing and its "extended states help to gradually explore and clarify design thinking" (Schaeverbeke, 2016).

Figure 12.4 Fixed human stem cell (with antibody marker for cardiomyocytes). An image compilation from pure scientific image data, 2.5-D projection stills, digital drawing.

It is intended in the next phase of this inquiry to create 2D and 3D prototypes using these drawings as a core element in the construction of both 2D and 3D prototypes, where a series of design features including structure, movement, and rotation can be examined.

The other intended development is the production of a series of animated films that interweave documentary film footage with image stills inspired and sourced from the library of collected reprocessed image data.

Analysis, Reflection, and Feedback

Central to this inquiry is critical feedback from the collaborating scientists, and there will be a range of opportunities to gather these data, creating new insight

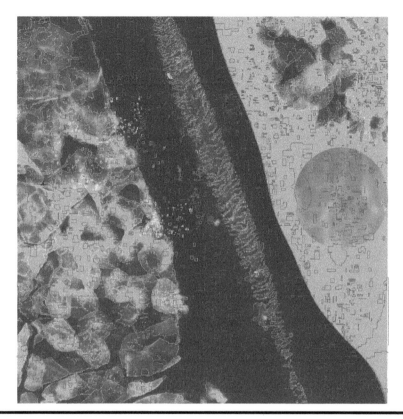

Figure 12.5   Bitesize, a deconstructed digital drawing compilation of skin imaged on a multiphoton microscope.

into image data visualization and contributing to the production of more refined visualization models. This feedback/communication enhances professional working knowledge for all collaborators, who can exchange ideas fluidly through the use of digital platforms.

Direct observations have already been recorded from interaction and dialogues with scientists. One has been pursued with Dr Joelle Golding,* an experienced postdoctoral researcher. These image data, remodeled using Zen Software and Adobe Illustrator, have been presented as examples of successful art–science collaboration at national and international conferences and published in international magazines (*Gothenburg University Magazine*, 2016; Varoom, 2016a, 2016b). The scientific collaborators at the University of Gothenburg, who had never worked with an artist

---

* Dr. Joelle Golding is a senior postdoctoral researcher working at the Cell Signalling and Pharmacology Department at the School of Life Science at Nottingham University.

before, stated that this experience had already had a transformative impact on their practice. As Dr. M. Ericson commented:

> We easily forget that research is actually a creative process. When we want to explain things, we often look for illustrations on the internet, instead of creating our own illustrations of conceptual insights. If we would dare illustrate and visualise our research, we might get both new insights and better contact with the general public. We can actually get inspiration from artists, and maybe this will make it easier to get funding because we can then show our research in a really interesting and new way! (*Gothenburg University Magazine*, September 24, 2016)

There have also been opportunities to publish research at a local, national and international level (*Gothenburg University Magazine*, 2016; Varoom, 2016a, 2016b; Cumulus Conference, Open Design for Everything Hong Kong), and research is being presented at a number of academic presentations for scientific specialist audiences and interdisciplinary, creative audiences. Opportunities for the exchange of information are being showcased and explored through various exhibitions, now and in the future (including "Bridging Nordic Imaging, Enabling Discoveries from Atoms to Anatomy," 2nd Symposium, Gothenburg.)

Conclusion

"Artists have a distinct approach to understanding and communicating ideas that can illuminate and challenge perceptions within society" (Wellcome, n.d.). The Wellcome Trust in this statement credits the arts with having an invaluable role to play in engaging the public with science, inspiring interdisciplinary research that benefits both artists and scientists. In *Art & Science,* Sian Ede (2012) identifies art and science as creative disciplines with common rationales, claiming that there is immense value in art engaging with science in complex and nondirect ways. Explaining how artists knowledgeable about the natural and scientific world approach this formal academic scientific world in an unconventional, personal, and emotive manner, Ede demonstrates her conviction about the immense value in art engaging with science in complex, and nondirect ways. The relationship between research and art practice in this research project is like an "iterative cyclic web," with activity alternating between practice and research (Smith and Dean, 2009: 19). This activity illustrates how the connectivity of ideas can work with many different strands as information is redirected and represented in new ways. And it works particularly well because it uses digital platforms. It exemplifies a process in which documentation, theoretical frameworks, contextualization of artwork, and the creative process of making it can offer knowledge of distinctive systems of investigation, enquiry, and reflection.

A fundamental premise for this visual investigation is to see how art and design strategies can impact in a positive manner on this seemingly formal academic scientific world, where unorthodox visual methods and strategies can add value to how scientific data can be interpreted and visualized. The new conceptual models reveal how expert visualizations can make intelligible ideas visible, offering a credible way of representing science in an original manner, creating significant new representations that can enhance scientific concepts (Faure Walker, 2013). It aims to critically engage different audiences, from scientific specialists, the arts, and the general public, by generating new work for exhibition, publication, and social media production. Importantly, the project is also providing insight into how big data can be managed. Accessibility to a wide range of subject specific software and the transferability of information through digital platforms is immense and can be overwhelming. But from an artist's/designer's perspective, data have much visual potential to be explored and novel data visualization through art can support communication and distribution. This research project has spotlighted a methodology of working and of data visualization that is ripe for development not only in science and in art but also potentially in other fields of expertise.*

References

Coffey, A. and Atkinson, P., 1996. *Making Sense of Qualitative Data*. Thousand Oaks, CA: Sage.

Doloughan, F.J., 2002. The language of reflective practice in art and design. *Design Issues*, 18(2), pp. 57–64.

Ede, S., 2012. *Art & Science*. 3rd edition. New York: I.B. Tauris.

Faure Walker, J., 2013. *Perceptions of Knowledge Visualisation: Explaining Concepts through Meaningful Images*. Idea Group, IGI Global, and USA.

Gothenburg University Magazine. 2016. Available at: http://www.GUJ4-2016English (accessed October 28, 2016).

Kemp, M. 2016. *Structural Intuitions Seeing Shapes in Art and Science*. Charlottesville and London: University of Virginia Press.

Rust, C., Mottram, J., and Till, J. 2007. *Review of Practice-Led Research in Art, Design & Architecture*. UK: Arts and Humanities Research Council. Available at: http://shura.shu.ac.uk/7596/ (accessed April 8, 2017).

Schaeverbeke, R., 2016. *Extended Drawing (Learning from the In-between)*. Available at: https://lirias.kuleuven.be/handle/123456789/545188 (accessed May, 2017).

Schon, D. 1983. *The Reflective Practitioner*. New York: Grune & Stratton.

Smith, H. and Dean, R.T. 2009. *Practice-Led Research, Research-Led Practice in the Creative Arts (Research Methods for the Arts and Humanities)*. Edinburgh: Edinburgh University Press.

Sutton, C. 2011. *Social Surveys: Design to Analysis*. London: Sage.

---

* Contextualising the key areas of knowledge, foundational theories and critically reviewing the discourse for national and international networks can be accessed at http://www.joberry.co.uk

Varoom. 2016a. VaroomLab Visionaries—Scientific Images. http://theaoi.com/varoom
-mag/article/v31-varoomlab-visionaries-scientific-images (accessed October 28, 2016).

Varoom. 2016b. Still and static digital representations made from scientific images. http://
theaoi.com/varoom-mag/article/varoomlab-journal-issue-four/ (accessed October 28,
2016).

Wellcome. n.d. Website of the Wellcome trust. http://www.wellcome.ac.uk (accessed
May 8, 2016).

Educational Resource and Training References

• http://nottingham.ac.uk/life-sciences/facilities/research-and-teaching-facilities.aspx
• http://www.ammrf.org.au/myscope/
• http://micro.magnet.fsu.edu/primer/
• http://microscopyu.com
• http://zeiss-campus.magnet.fsu.edu/articles/basics/fluorescence.html

Chapter 13

Museums, Archives, and Universities—Structuring Future Connections with Big Data

Jane Milosch, Michael J. Kurtz, Gregory J. Jansen, Andrea Hull, and Richard Marciano

Contents

Introduction

Big data's value to the arts, humanities, and other disciplines is contingent upon the integrity, verification, and safeguarding of its information—its "provenance." For art museums, provenance research on its collections and acquisitions attempts to establish an unbroken chain of ownership from an object's creation to its present owner. This information is traditionally either departmentally "siloed" within an institution or between institutions or, in Germany, for example, is the intellectual property of the researcher. With the advent of digital humanities, enabled by big data, the discipline of art history is encouraged to expand beyond its traditional bases in connoisseurship and history of collecting to encompass broader fields of study.*

In Maxwell Anderson's 2015 essay, "The Crisis in Art History: Ten Problems, Ten Solutions," first presented at a 2011 College Art Association of America meeting, he notes that art historians have become "a fragmented pool of experts," and in order to "elevate the importance of their discipline in the hearts and minds of academics and non-academics alike," it is necessary to build stronger connections between the "life of mind," surviving works of art, and the public. He also encourages a new generation to "devote their lives to the study and care of cultural heritage."[1]

Provenance research—fundamental to the histories of art and of collecting—might be the fulcrum on which to balance these new efforts Anderson calls forth. In the United States and in Germany, recent museum exhibitions drawn from their permanent collections have taken provenance as one of their guiding themes, organizing the presentation of the artworks to capitalize on the diverse stories provenance research can tell. These exhibitions have been popular with the public and critics alike, as they reveal new links between artists, collectors, dealers, and the markets in which they meet. The result of curators working with provenance researchers and archivists, they move compelling provenance stories from back of the house to the front of the house. Stories that engage the public and young scholars alike will become increasingly available when digital humanities and big data

---

* In October 2016, The Phillips Collection in Washington, DC, and the University of Maryland in College Park, Maryland, organized a symposium, "Art History in Digital Dimensions," aimed "to unite diverse audiences and practitioners in a critical intervention for the digital humanities and digital art history, providing a cogent and inclusive road map for the future." In the public keynote lecture, "Digital Art History: Old Problems, New Debates, and Critical Potentials," Paul B. Jaskot, professor of art history at DePaul University, gave a brilliant summary of the challenges and goals of digital humanities for art historians, which formed the backdrop of the lived-streamed discussions about "collaborative, trans-disciplinary models of research; the implications of data-driven approaches to art history and the humanities; legal and ethical obligations of scholars and museum professionals engaging art history in the digital world; and the innovative array of objects for study presupposed by digital art history," which followed at the University of Maryland. See http://dah-dimensions.org (accessed April 24, 2017).

progressively inform museum exhibition practices. Because museums are unique in the scholarly world in that they engage extensively with the public, such exhibitions will help ensure the continued vitality of the discipline of art history.

New Strategies

Museum curators who conduct provenance research on art objects in museum collections traditionally record their results in narrative format only and then turn over their texts to registrars and other data-entry specialists, who enter it into one of several different collection databases that museums use.

With the coming of big data, many emerging art historians and museum professionals are working toward recording their research not only in narrative format but also in new formats that enable the sharing and exchange of these data across collections and institutions—they understand that it is no longer enough to work only in isolation and on a single track. Museums have much to gain from making their material attractive to aggregators, virtual museums, educators, and others, who are seeing that the benefits of collaborative scholarship enabled by digital humanities are increasingly valuable to better contextualize their objects and build richer stories around them.

American museums are ahead of most museums in Europe (let alone those of other geographical areas that were prolific creators of art, such as Africa, India, and China) in digitizing their collections. In most instances, their provenance information is automatically updated and shared with the public in real time and includes images of the objects. Concurrently, museums have a strong interest in protecting the integrity of their research resources and results from accident, corruption, and malfeasance and to illuminate gaps in provenance data that indicate need for further research. Many, if not most, objects have gaps in their ownership histories— particularly decorative and graphic art objects, often produced in multiples. And because provenance data and records are often dispersed over many collections, databases, and archival holdings siloed in institutions around the world, sometimes, establishing true ownership is quite complex.

Currently, linked open data (LOD) appears to offer the best path to address these issues. Through LOD, with widespread adoption of a single standard for recording provenance data, provenance information will, at some point, be viewable across institutions and collections, allowing museums to ask more nuanced questions about the lives of their objects—the people and places through which the object has traveled—telling a more complete history of art, and its place in a larger socio-historical narrative.*

---

* For more information about the launch of the "Art Tracks: Standardizing Digital Provenance Documentation for Cultural Objects" project at the Carnegie Museum of Art, visit http:// press.cmoa.org/2015/12/17/cmoa-neh-art-tracks/ (accessed April 24, 2017).

New Efforts to Aggregate Collections Data

Although the road to get there may be a long one, several institutions are taking their first steps on the Research to Provenance Search path outlined in Chapter 4 of this book. The Smithsonian's online search platform, Collections Search Center (collections.si.edu), provides a user-friendly search interface for navigating Smithsonian collections information and associated digital media. Smithsonian museums and research centers contribute data to this site by mapping new information to an Index Metadata Model, and Smith has launched new initiatives to help bring provenance data together in new ways.

Development of World War II-Era Provenance Research

Let us now back up a moment—to 1997, when the Association of Art Museum Directors (AAMD)* convened a task force to draft guidelines on how its members should handle art looted by the Nazis and not previously restituted. These guidelines informed the "Washington Conference Principles on Nazi-Confiscated Art" drafted by the 1998 Washington Conference on Holocaust-Era Assets. Forty-four governments and 13 nongovernmental organizations met to discuss how best to ensure that museums conscientiously research the provenance of artworks potentially looted during the National Socialist era, addressing Jewish losses in particular and concentrating on painting and sculpture, books, and archives.

In May 2001, the American Association of Museums (AAM) issued a series of guidelines for helping identify and publish potentially confiscated works held in American museums and in 2003 launched the Nazi-Era Provenance Internet Portal (NEPIP; http://www.nepip.org/) to provide a searchable central registry of these works and their histories, accessible to the public. After a decade of NEPIP, nearly 30,000 objects from 179 participating museums are listed there. During that time, many museums, archives, and research institutions rapidly digitized records to help identify objects in US collections that had changed hands in continental Europe between 1933 and 1945, to help fulfill the objectives of the Washington Principles.

Since 2000, to honor its commitment to the Washington Principles, the Smithsonian Institution has financially supported the work of provenance researchers at its museums and in 2004 launched the "Smithsonian Institution WWII Provenance Web Site," which includes a publicly searchable object database and other resources.

In 2009, the Smithsonian Provenance Research Initiative (SPRI)† was founded as a pan-institutional program to advance the institution's ongoing,

---

* For more information, visit https://aamd.org/object-registry/resolution-of-claims-for-nazi-era -cultural-assets/more-info (accessed April 24, 2017).
† For more about SPRI, http://provenance.si.edu/jsp/spri.aspx (accessed April 24, 2017).

serious commitment to provenance research of its collections—prioritizing objects in its collection that might have been misappropriated during the Nazi era—and to the preservation of cultural property and heritage, both considered integral parts of the Smithsonian's mission of increase and diffusion of knowledge. In service to the field of museum provenance generally, SPRI is leading the construction of an international network of museum professionals and researchers who deal with various aspects of provenance research (concentrated on World War II [WWII]-era, but expanding to include postcolonial and antiquities), training emerging museum professionals who will take up the challenges of twenty-first century provenance, and assisting the development of new technologies that will enable provenance research, so long isolated in individual institutions, to enter the arena of large-scale social investigations enabled by big data and the digital humanities.

In 2011, in recognition of the need to build comprehensive international exchanges on provenance research, the National Archives and Records Administration (NARA), under the direction of Michael Kurtz, launched the International Research Portal for Records Related to Nazi-Era Cultural Property (Portal)* to fulfill the objectives of the 1998 Washington Conference on Nazi-Confiscated Art, the 2000 Vilnius Declaration, and the 2009 Terezin Declaration to make all relevant records and information publicly available. The Portal is a collaboration of 18 national and other archival institutions with records that pertain to Nazi-era cultural property working with other expert national and international organizations to extend public access to widely dispersed records through this single Internet Portal.

In conjunction with the launch of the Portal, NARA partnered with SPRI and, working with the AAMD and the AAM, hosted a two-day seminar in which museum professionals and others interested in provenance learned about new electronic tools, collaborative projects, and strategies for research. Experts guided discussions about using these resources and shared results of recent and ongoing research projects. A total of 150 people attended, including 35 guest speakers and representatives from 60 museums, 34 US states, and 10 European countries.[†]

---

* For more information about the International Research Portal for Records Related to Nazi-Era Cultural Property (Portal), visit https://www.archives.gov/research/holocaust/international-resources (accessed April 24, 2017).

[†] For more information about the World War II Provenance Research Seminar, May 2011, visit https://ww2provenanceseminar.wordpress.com (accessed April 24, 2017).

Identifying Key Challenges

In the aftermath of the Portal launch and symposium, two observations stood out: one, the realization that when results of their provenance research cannot be broadly shared, nor resources accessed easily throughout the community of professional researchers and interested parties, museums' scarce financial and human resources are squandered. When each museum must constantly "reinvent the wheel," with exhaustive duplication of efforts in a proliferation of digitized provenance information, this is not sustainable in the twenty-first century. The second observation is that, although it was a monumental accomplishment to bring these 18 organizations together on the Portal, it was not searchable in a federated, or other meaningful, way, thus limiting its utility to museums and the field in general.

Around this time, the Freer|Sackler recognized that their provenance research and digitization efforts needed to be synchronized more effectively, to better share and exchange research and collection data with other Asian art museums and collections. The Freer and Sackler galleries, together considered one of the world's finest collections of the arts of the Far and Near East, have a long history of working to ensure complete access to their provenance research, beginning with its founder Charles Lang Freer's insistence on documentation to accompany his acquisitions.

The Freer|Sackler's provenance project, supported by SPRI, brings to the forefront scholarly interest in Euro-American aspects of the Asian art market before, during, and after WWII. In 2014, after the Freer|Sackler completed extensive research on nearly 400 Chinese objects with WWII-era provenance gaps, the museum quickly realized that this information was still of limited use because the information was neither contextualized nor searchable.

To contextualize its research of these objects, Freer|Sackler devised an approach to link 50 WWII-era Asian art collectors and dealers biographies with art objects and associated archival data. Funded by a grant from the David Berg Foundation, this project became known as the Asian Art Provenance Connections Project (Figure 13.1)* and was launched in the spring of 2016. Its web pages (http://www .freersackler.si.edu/collections/provenance-research/) hyperlink objects with the collector/dealer biographies and with other Smithsonian-wide archival documentation. By creating a search interface that exposes relationships articulated through the data, the project promotes international awareness, supports more effective research methodologies, and facilitates international collaboration and information exchange between museums and the public concerning Asian art provenance.

---

* For more information about the Freer Gallery of Art and Arthur M. Sackler Gallery of Art's provenance research efforts and resources, including the Asian Art Provenance Connections Project, visit http://www.freersackler.si.edu/collections/provenance-research/ (accessed April 24, 2017).

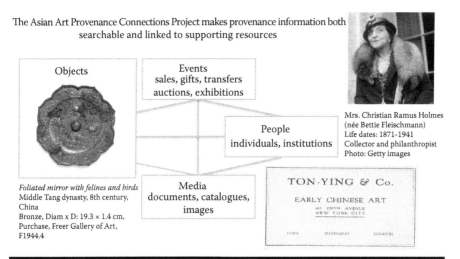

Asian Art Connections Project artwork

The Asian Art Provenance Connections Project makes provenance information both searchable and linked to supporting resources

Objects

Foliated mirror with felines and birds
Middle Tang dynasty, 8th century,
China
Bronze, Diam x D: 19.3 × 1.4 cm,
Purchase, Freer Gallery of Art,
F1944.4

Events
sales, gifts, transfers
auctions, exhibitions

People
individuals, institutions

Media
documents, catalogues,
images

Mrs. Christian Ramus Holmes
(née Bettie Fleischmann)
Life dates: 1871-1941
Collector and philanthropist
Photo: Getty images

TON·YING & Co.
EARLY CHINESE ART
441 FIFTH AVENUE
NEW YORK CITY

PARIS   SHANGHAI   LONDON

Figure 13.1 For more information about the Asian Art Provenance Connections Project, http://www.freersackler.si.edu/collections/provenance-research/

New Partnerships and Big Data

Recently, to move to the next step, the federated searches of various databases, the Freer|Sackler began investigating provenance information expressed as LOD. In Chapter 4, Smith discusses the Smithsonian's collaboration with the Carnegie Museum of Art (CMOA) and the Yale Center for British Art, funded by a grant from the National Endowment for the Humanities. This collaboration uses the CMOA's Art Tracks project to develop a program to convert provenance information expressed as narrative text into structured data, as a first step to LOD. Smith's section articulates these recent developments, which herald the enhanced ability of art museums to develop and share provenance data and results.

In 2016, when SPRI learned of the University of Maryland's Digital Curation Innovation Center's (DCIC's) efforts to enhance federated search of the NARA Portal and to develop visualization tools for data representation, SPRI partnered with DCIC to help them test the effectiveness of their prototyping. The following section of this chapter, by Michael Kurtz, author of the 2006 book *America and the Return of Nazi Contraband: The Recovery of Europe's Cultural Treasures*, outlines a project employing students working with a professional software developer to map metadata for each of the 18 museums, libraries, and archives that are part of the Portal and to enhance its linking ability. Kurtz provides a case study of how big data and federated search capabilities are yielding exciting results and—Maxwell

Anderson would approve—are bringing students into the learning and producing process.*

The Enhanced "International Research Portal for Records Related to Nazi-Era Cultural Property" Project (IRP2): A Continuing Case Study

In February 2015, the DCIC at the University of Maryland's College of Information Studies (iSchool) initiated the "International Research Portal for Records Related to Nazi-Era Cultural Property" project (IRP2), a research project to enhance information search and retrieval capabilities for archival, library, and museum collections maintained online on The International Research Portal for Records related to Nazi-Era Cultural Property (Portal). Dr. Michael Kurtz, associate DCIC director, is the project director, assisted by DCIC software developer Gregory Jansen and a team of iSchool students. The students are enrolled in three of the iSchool's degree programs: Master of Library and Information Science (MLIS), Master of Information Management (MIM), and Master in Human–Computer Interaction.[†]

The Portal, launched in May 2011 and currently hosted by the US NARA, is a collaboration of 18 national and other archival institutions, libraries, museums, and research centers, with the intent of enabling researcher access across the distributed collections of the participating institutions. The Portal was established to fulfill the objectives of the 1998 Washington Conference on Nazi-Confiscated Art, the 2000 Vilnius Declaration, and the 2009 Terezin Declaration to make all relevant records and information publicly available (Figure 13.2).

---

[*] The author would like to thank her colleagues from SPRI and Freer Gallery of Art and Arthur M. Sackler Gallery for their collaborative efforts that have greatly contributed to the ideas and project presented in this essay: Elizabeth Duley, head of collections, Freer|Sackler; Jeffrey Smith, assistant registrar, Freer|Sackler; and David Hogge, head of archives, Freer|Sackler, as well as SPRI project consultants (unless otherwise noted, currently working on projects): Lynn Nicholas, SPRI advisor; Laurie A. Stein, LLC, SPRI senior advisor; Dorota Chudzicka, Provenance research associate (2008–2013); Nick Pearce, Richmond Chair of Fine Art, University of Glasgow, UK and SPRI senior research fellow; Samantha Viksnins, project coordinator, Freer|Sackler (2015–2016); Andrea Hull, SPRI Communications and Grants Associate; Johanna Best, program manager/ACLS postdoc fellow; and Colleen Carroll, program assistant.

[†] Student volunteers included the following: Karishma Ghiya (MIM), Allison Gunn (MLIS), Torra Hausmann (MLIS), Weidong Li (MIM), Lisa Rogers (Master of Human–Computer Interaction), Sohini Sarkar (MIM), Sanjna Srivatsa (MIM), Jennifer Wachtel (MLIS), and Melissa Wertheimer (MLIS).

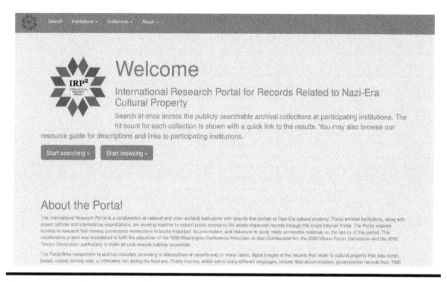

Figure 13.2   The Portal is designed to look right on mobile and desktop browsers.

Provenance and Technical Challenges

The Portal links researchers to archival materials consisting of descriptions of records and, in many cases, digital images of records that relate to cultural property that was stolen, looted, seized, forcibly sold, or otherwise lost during the Nazi era. These records, which are in many different languages, include Nazi documentation, governmental records from 1933 onward, and inventories of recovered artworks, postwar claims records, and auction house and art dealer records. Cultural property in these records covers a broad range of objects, from artworks to books and libraries, religious objects, antiquities, sculptures, musical instruments, and more (Figure 13.3).

Provenance issues abound. As is usually the case, archival information in the Portal collections is heterogeneous, the archival context ambiguous, and the original context difficult to reconstruct. Other problems hinder the effective use of the Portal. There is the problem of the sheer volume of information—hundreds of records series (complete and partial) and millions of discrete items of information, such as property cards of looted objects created by the Nazis and by the US Army during the postwar restitution program are siloed within the individual institutions, where it is not now possible to conduct searches and use search terms across the Portal.

Project Management

During the first phase of the IRP2 project, MLIS students, with the active involvement of the project director and software developer, mapped metadata for each

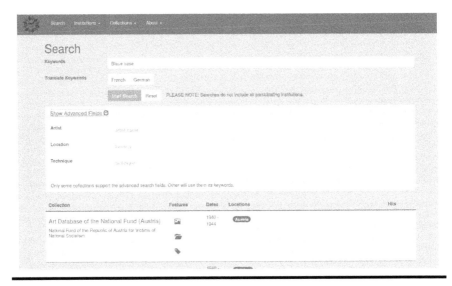

Figure 13.3   Portal searches may include advanced fields and translation of terms.

collection to identify relevant and comparable provenance data to the greatest extent feasible. To increase the expertise available to the project team, an international advisory board of experts provided content and technical guidance. In addition, art provenance research experts provided informal feedback when technical demos were presented at various stages of the project.*

On a parallel track, two MIM students, using the Portal as the basis for their required master's-level research projects, worked with the software developer to mock up a federation of catalogues to enable automated searches across the Portal's collections and to retrieve and consolidate information on individuals, organizations, and cultural objects related to Nazi-looted cultural assets. DCIC presented a proof of concept demonstrating a web-based federated search approach at an Advanced Art Provenance Research Workshop hosted by the Association of Art Museum Directors (AAMD) at the National Archives in Washington, DC, on November 3, 2015.

Building on the proof of concept, the project team has developed a federated search function for the Portal that provides tools for researchers with divergent needs, such as heirs and families of Holocaust victims searching for lost property,

---

* Advisory Board members include the following: Association of Art Museum Directors: Anita Difanis; EHRI Project: Conny Kristel; King's College London: Tobias Blanke and Michael Bryant; National Archives and Records Administration: Chris Naylor; National Gallery of Art: Nancy Yeide; Smithsonian Institution: Jane Milosch; US Holocaust Memorial Museum: Michael Levy and Michael Haley Goldman; Yad Vashem: Haim Gertner.

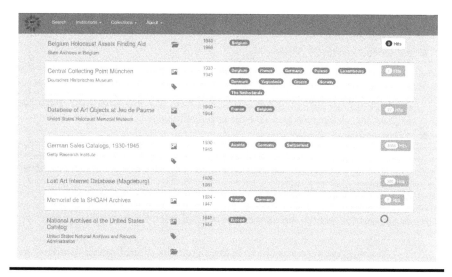

Figure 13.4   Search results are presented for various collections.

lawyers, investigators, provenance research experts, archivists, museum specialists, librarians, and interested members of the general public (Figure 13.4).

Technical Development

Since the proof of concept, the software has matured into a more stable, more modular codebase, which provides the basis for additional student developers to work on the project and for enhanced server operations. As a federated search site, the Portal must perform many search tasks at once for a single user. It also must interface with a variety of different institution search sites that have different technical implementations, including various data formats, search fields, query operators, and more. Over time, the software has been redesigned to address these issues more easily, and the ability to add new search sites has been enhanced.

Major development phases, much of it student led, has pushed the Portal to enhanced levels of function and usability. These include the following:

■ Federated search of participating institutions
  1. The ability to navigate, using a federated search strategy, across selected Portal collections with relevant keyword search terms to identify, consolidate, and present pertinent information.
  2. Local search implantation of a Belgian finding aid search, converted from the original PDF file into an XML-based search.
■ Translation of query terms
  1. Description language for each collection was catalogued.

2. Options were added for translation of English search terms into French and German.
- Advanced search fields were
    1. Added to the Portal site for artist name, location, and year.
    2. Mapped accordingly onto participating search sites.
    3. Enabled to reuse an advanced search term as a keyword when participating search sites do not have an applicable field.
- Autosuggestion of terms
    1. Authority lists were generated from the Getty Institutes' Union List of Artist Names, Cultural Objects Name Authority, and Thesaurus of Geographic Names.
    2. Authority lists were indexed with a Solr search engine.
    3. Advanced search fields were enhanced with "autosuggest as you type" terms.
    4. Autosuggest terms include hints that help disambiguate similar terms with relevant details, for instance, showing brief biographical information for an individual.
- Personalization for researchers, who can
    1. Sign up and log in to the Portal site.
    2. Save useful search queries for later use.
    3. Review and manage saved searches.
- Redesign of Portal web site
    1. A logo was designed and incorporated into the site.
    2. The site was migrated to the commonly used Bootstrap template system.
    3. The site was designed to adapt to mobile and desktop platforms.

Continued Development and Implementation

Students from the iSchool, other departments of the University of Maryland, and the Museum Studies program at Johns Hopkins University participated in testing and provided feedback for the federated search capability. Student feedback identified continuing challenges with linking search terms with relevant records. In response, the software developer redesigned the portal interface to emphasize the searching and the browsing of the extensive collection descriptions that make up the existing portal. The new design puts search and browse on equal footing and gives the user many more pathways into the browsing portion of the website (Figure 13.5).

The final phase of the project (begun in spring 2017) focuses on using structured data, drawn from the US Army property cards mentioned earlier to develop new research capabilities. Graph database and visualization technologies will be used to create linked relationships with people (looters, victims, and collectors), artists, works of art, dates, and locations of events. These relationships will help address the provenance issues that arise from heterogeneous collections with records and information melded from a variety of sources.

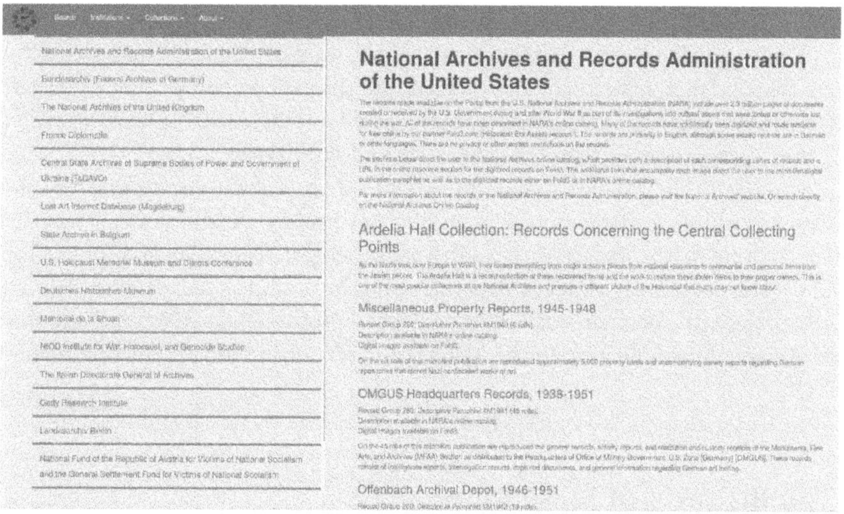

Figure 13.5 **Institution and collection descriptions presented with a table of contents.**

Software development will continue to focus on the design of visual and graph-based discovery features to enable lateral browsing across linked topics and facts. Based on the property card graph database feature, researchers will be able to reconstruct the journeys of looted assets across Europe and beyond. In this phase, the project director and the software developer will engage a visualization design expert to assist in graphically illustrating the linked relationships, which are often not possible to identify in traditional, hierarchical archival finding aids. They expect new relationships to be revealed, leading to fresh insights from a research perspective.

A significant issue in implementing the federated search capability for the Portal was the need for ongoing stewardship to ensure that the upgrades and maintenance required to keep the Portal vital and usable are properly managed. The IRP2 project team and the NARA officials responsible for the stewardship of the Portal decided that the European Holocaust Research Infrastructure (EHRI), which includes 16 of the 18 Portal contributing institutions in Europe, would be the best repository for and ongoing steward of the redesigned Portal. The goals of EHRI, a European Union-funded project, are to identify the approximately 1800 repositories (mostly in Europe) that have Holocaust-related documentation and to catalogue the records with the ultimate aim of providing the greatest digital access possible. The redesigned Portal is at http://irp2.ehri-project.eu

Student Learning

The combination of professional development support with student-led feature development is a strong model for interdisciplinary, collaborative student learning.

In the IRP2 project, students were free to experiment and prototype, receiving much-needed support from the professional software developer. Later, their efforts were consolidated, refactored, and merged into the evolving project. Project leaders carefully evaluated the abilities of team members so that all the students worked on features appropriate for their available time and skill levels.

Some features in any software development project will be beyond the skills of most graduate students outside computer science. In these cases, it is more efficient to draw on the expertise of a software developer. The balance of professional and student-led work ultimately depends upon the project's requirements. With the IRP2 project, the balance was 80/20 student to professional software development and metadata identification in the first year; in the second year, the breakdown was 60/40.

Conclusion and Next Steps

The provenance challenges reflected in the Portal will be much more manageable with the full implementation of the prototype described earlier. Major gains in researcher access can be appropriately anticipated. However, overall major provenance issues remain in the management and exploitation of big data in archives, special collections in libraries, and in museums. The DCIC and the SPRI, along with other national and international research collaborators, intend to explore archival and museum provenance issues with the goal of integrating archival research data and user-contributed data, at scale, with cyberinfrastructure to generate new forms of analysis and engagement.

Specifically, the DCIC and SPRI will use Dras-tic (Digital Repository at Scale that Invites Computation) to improve collections software currently used to research, record and securely share big data, including provenance data. Dras-tic is an open-source community software project that evolved from a $10.5 M National Science Foundation grant involving the University of Maryland and was developed in collaboration with Archival Analytics Solutions, Ltd., a software development firm in the United Kingdom.

The ability to accurately determine the provenance of archival and museum collections is at the heart of the Dras-tic enterprise: its goal is to build out a horizontally scalable archival framework to serve the academic, museum, archival, library, and scientific management communities as a credible solution for big data management in the cultural heritage community.

Reference

1. Anderson, M. L. 2011. The crisis in art history: Ten problems, ten solutions. *Visual Resources: An International Journal of Documentation*, 27, no. 4: 336.

Chapter 14

Mobile Technology to Contribute Operatively to the Safeguard of Cultural Heritage

Fabrizio Terenzio Gizzi, Beniamino Murgante, Marilisa Biscione, Maria Danese, Maria Sileo, Maria Rosaria Potenza, and Nicola Masini

Contents

Introduction

In recent times, several activities have been developed with the support of mass cooperation. This tendency, often adopted in public agencies and by local authorities, is based on an open government approach, as well as on a more participative method to government where citizen's ideas and activities have to be considered and collected in a sort of a continuous flow. Consequently, public involvement, getting ideas, suggestions, or simply data/information production, is a daily activity fundamental in decision-making process. Obama's administration has given a great impetus to this approach, implementing such a policy and enlarging the possibility to capture public imagination by means of social networks, blogs, and all possible solutions for directly interacting with citizens.

This new approach is often called Gov. 2.0. Open government without a 2.0 approach is still based on a direct action. "Providers" is a sort of Right to Information where the administration tries to inform people, but having interaction just with the main stakeholders. Gov. 2.0 is a more open approach, which "enables" citizens to have an important role in defining policies as well as in producing user-friendly, ubiquitous, and personalized services.

Social media and all 2.0 platforms are a key element in generating a direct contact with citizens. Extensions of 2.0 philosophy completely changed the relationship between citizens and administration. People directly subrogate services that public administration and private sectors consider uninteresting or unprofitable.

Web 2.0 tools, such as websites, blogs, WebGIS, and mobile applications for smartphone and tablet, represent a sort of transition from "one-way" to "two-way" information and interaction tools able to share ideas, compare opinions, and collect information (Conroy and Evans-Cowley, 2006; Murgante et al., 2011a).

This approach leads to "crowdsourcing" (Goodchild, 2009), where a lot of activities or decisions have been realized using a mass collaboration, or to "volunteered geographic information" (Goodchild, 2007), where distributed masses create, manage, and disseminate spatial data (Sui, 2008).

In the introduction to the book *Geocomputation and Urban Planning* (Murgante et al., 2009), the authors cited the famous paper by Franklin and Hane (1992), who, in 1992, quoted that 80% of all organizational information contain some references to geography.

After the publication of this book, a lot of discussions started on social networks and blogs on how was it possible that in 1992, 80% of information contained a spatial component. This book was published in 2009 and up to date; after only few years, the situation is completely changed: each mobile phone has a *Global Positioning System* and Google has transformed geographical information from a specialist interest to a mass phenomenon and probably 100% of data have a spatial relation.

In spatial information, the added value could be represented by "neogeography" (Turner, 2006; Hudson-Smith et al., 2009), where citizens produce data integrating maps with geo-tagged photos, videos, blogs, Wikipedia, etc. These actions directly derive from public administration in efficiency. One could say, "why do I pay taxes if citizens have to directly provide the services?" The reduction of funding, coupled with the increase in data availability, led governments to have huge data sets without having the possibility to check their quality and to update them. Consequently, these data have become old before they are published. In the geographical sector, it is very frequent that local authorities do not share data with the other actors involved in the production of similar data. The first attempt to solve this problem has been Executive Order 12906 (1994), "Coordinating Geographic Data Acquisition and Access: The National Spatial Data Infrastructure," imposed on American agencies, organizations, and local authorities, which led to a huge resource optimization. In Europe, the Infrastructure for Spatial Information (INSPIRE) Directive did not achieve the same results because of European bureaucracy and because of a sort of inertia from European countries in applying European directives. The other problem of the INSPIRE Directive is articulation based on a lot of detailed annexes, which are not easy to apply, which discourages many institutions in its application.

Obviously, there was a large increase in data sharing with the introduction of spatial data infrastructures, but this development is much lower than the growth of data production due to voluntary actions. Probably, in the future, spatial data infrastructures will be developed by big organizations, while local authorities will tend mostly toward cloud platform using Google or OpenStreetMap as base map. The great advantage of these solutions is the possibility to integrate Google data, Spatial Data Infrastructure (SDI) services (i.e., Open Geospatial Consortium Standards Web Map Service, Web Feature Service, etc.), OpenStreetMap data, and so on, with all data produced by administrations or volunteers. Another strength is the possibility to mash up spatial data with all possible information available on Internet (e.g., pictures, videos, descriptions, etc.).

In the last few years, terms such as "smart city" and "big data" became a sort of imperative. Despite that the two terms seem not connected, big data are mainly produced by intensive volunteer actions of citizens and by the shared data of national agencies and local authorities. These two aspects are strongly related to smart city.

Batty et al. (2012) identify seven points on which attention should be focused, analyzing key problems of cities, using information and communication technologies:

1. A new understanding of urban problems;
2. Effective and feasible ways to coordinate urban technologies;
3. Models and methods to use urban data across spatial and temporal scales;
4. Developing new technologies for communication and dissemination;
5. New forms of urban governance and organization;
6. Defining critical problems about cities, transport, and energy; and
7. Risk, uncertainty, and hazard in the smart city.

Murgante and Borruso (2015) defined the three main pillars of a smart city: connections, open data, and sensors, specifying that the third indicator has to be intended not only in terms of technology but also in terms of citizens able to actively participate in a bottom–up way in city activities and data production.

Murgante and Borruso (2013) defined a set of indicators able to identify the smartness level in cities:

1. Adoption of OpenData (Belisario et al. 2011) and Open Geospatial Consortium Standard;
2. Free wifi;
3. Projects implementation of augmented reality for tourism;
4. Crowdfunding initiatives;
5. Decisions taken by crowdsourcing;
6. Implementation of INSPIRE Directive; and
7. Quantity of public services achievable through apps.

Garau and Ilardi (2014) highlighted the importance of mobile technologies in managing and improving cultural heritage tourism. Murgante et al. (2011b) described a volunteered approach adopted in mapping all tourist services and related information. This mapping activity has been integrated with a neogeography approach linking all data with other information already existing on the web, such as movies, pictures, Wikipedia, historical documentation, etc., producing a sort of local miniportal for tourism development.

Considering the "citizens science" these two experiences can be located at the bottom part of the Haklay (2011) ladder, where crowdsourcing is the lowest level. The highest level is a sort of collaborative science, where citizens can have the responsibility in defining problems and in finding possible solutions. The application described in this paper (SaveHer App), developed in the framework of Pro_Cult project (Gizzi et al., 2015; Masini et al., 2016) can be located at the upper part of the Haklay ladder because citizens can support agencies and local authorities in cultural heritage safeguarding.

State of the Art

In recent years, many apps for cultural heritage promotion, disclosure, and enjoyment have been published. The content of apps embraces from the little known to well-known cultural heritage, with utilities such as localization, reporting points of interest, and associated digital assets. Among the most recent, we can mention Pompeii Sites, Cooltura TAG CLOUD, Beato Angelico, Cultural Heritage Administration, Smart Underground, Kulturarv, The Civil War Today, UNESCO

World Heritage, Patrimonio Mondiale Ticino-Svizzera, Florence heritage, and Appasseggio.*

The tourist can make use of several App guides in order to recognize and discover cultural heritage through the photos taken by the visitors and provide insights or comments suggesting sightseeing tours (see also Kenteris et al., 2006, 2009; Panda et al., 2012). From this point of view, some of the most popular apps are as follows:

- GetCOO (https://www.getcoo.com/, last accessed 2 February 2016), which recognizes major works of art and monuments of the world through their photos;
- ViviMondo (https://itunes.apple.com/it/app/vivimondo/id518122303?mt=8, last accessed 2 February 2016), which allows the user to explore his/her surroundings and to get information about the distance from important monuments.

In this case, detailed descriptions gleaned from Wikipedia, and the chance to see the environments through augmented reality are added. Other apps with the purpose of tourism multimedia content provide geolocation information to reach the preferred location (Discover Cape South, Calabria Grecanica).†

The civic involvement encouraged by apps is also useful for emergency management of cultural heritage. With this respect, we cite the ERS Emergency Response Services and the Library Floods apps. The first one outlines the critical stages of a disaster response such as stabilizing the environment and assessing the damage. It provides practical salvage tips for photographs, books and documents, paintings, electronic records, textiles, furniture, ceramics/stone/metal, organic materials, and natural history specimens. The second one, created by the US National Library of Medicine, provides information on how to recover collections after a flood emergency in libraries.

There are also apps for cultural heritage aimed at mobile learning (Dowling and Whalen, 2014) or applications that combine augmented reality and three-dimensional modeling techniques such as Jumieges 3D, MuseoSanGi, Art Glass,

---

* Appstore/Android market: https://play.google.com/store/apps/details?id=com.duva
.pompeiartem.en, https://itunes.apple.com/it/app/cooltura-tag-cloud/id1034307226?mt=8, https://
itunes.apple.com/it/app/fra-angelico-inside-painting/id982481167?ls=1&mt=8, https://
play.google.com/store/apps/developer?id=Cultural+Heritage+Administration, https://play
.google.com/store/apps/details?id=com.sinappsys.smartunderground, https://play.google
.com/store/apps/details?id=dk.codeunited.kulturarv, http://www.heritagemontgomery.org
/montgomery-county/civil-war-app, https://itunes.apple.com/it/app/unesco-world-heritage
/id412183802?mt=8, http://www.webatelier.net/mobile-app-for-two-world-heritage-sites
-in-ticino-switzerland-is-available-on-the-app-store, http://app.comune.fi.it/app/a0005.html,
http://www.creative-heritage.eu/internaz_and_localization.html, http://www.webatelier.net
/mobile-app-for-two-world-heritage-sites-in-ticino-switzerland-is-available-on-the-app-store.
† https://play.google.com/store/apps/details?id=com.map2app.CapoSudCalabriagrecanica

Liguria Heritage, CittàIdeale, and CittàIdeale AR* (Bonacini, 2014; Giloth and Tanant, 2014; Verykokou et al., 2014).

Also, the technologies typically used for diagnostic purposes (Masini and Soldovieri, 2017) such as x-ray fluorescence, infrared thermography, or reflectance transformation imaging (RTI) can make use of specific apps (Touch Van Gogh, Second Canvas, RTI Mobile App†).

High-quality content and sophisticated investigation technique make the users (not experts but attentive, curious, and demanding) confident with the cultural heritage. Artifact is instead a new app designed for diagnostic imaging presented at the Scientific Symposium of the International Council on Monuments and Sites (ICOMOS) (Vanoni et al., 2015).

The iTPC Carabinieri‡ app is an application developed by the Cultural Heritage Protection Unit of the Italian Police in collaboration with the Italian Ministry of Cultural Heritage and Activities and Tourism that targets the protection of cultural heritage. It helps citizens to fight theft and damage to cultural heritage and to support the activities of the police in search of works of art unlawfully removed.

From this overview, it emerges that SaveHer is an app that offers new dialogue perspective with the institutions responsible for the conservation of heritage properties: therefore, the user becomes a promoter and actor of the protection through the use of mobile technologies.

SaveHer Features

In order to make the application cross-platform and scalable to different operating systems, SaveHer was planned using the Cordova Phonegap by Apache Software Foundation by means of which it was possible to develop applications running on Apple iOS, Google Android, Microsoft Windows Phone 7/8, and RIM Blackberry.

The first release of the app was performed on PlayStore Google on February 2015 after having carried out several tests among different users and mobile devices both to bring to light technical problems and to improve the app graphical user interface (available in the Italian language at present).

As a matter of fact, it is well known that technological barriers can prevent the use of mobile devices with their content by users (Verkasalo et al., 2010).

---

* https://itunes.apple.com/it/app/jumieges-3d/id556799877?mt=8,http://t4all.it/portfolio -articoli/museo-civico-sangi/, http://www.liguriaheritage.it/heritage/it/home.do

† http://heritageinmotion.eu/project/touch-van-gogh-app-for-tablet/, www.secondcanvas.net https://itunes.apple.com/it/app/rti-mobile/id878658913?mt=8

‡ https://play.google.com/store/apps/details?id=it.reply.leonardo.mobile&hl=it, https://itunes .apple.com/it/app/itpc-carabinieri/id858588594?mt=8

Figure 14.1   Workflow of SaveHer app.

SaveHer works through eight main steps hierarchically arranged (Figure 14.1):

1. The citizen/user identifies the monument damaged or affected by problems.
2. The user starts SaveHer and performs the login through the App interface or using Facebook or LinkedIn social network login details (Figure 14.2a and b).
3. The user takes from one to three pictures of the considered monument, putting the attention to what he/she wants to be reported. The photos will be geotagged, including information about the latitude and longitude of the site (Figure 14.2c).
4. The user is asked to answer a simple questionnaire that consists of 10 questions aimed at identifying in a more detailed way the observed problems, such as vandalism, damage after extreme weather events, the effects of an earthquake or landslide, and so on (this phase is optional) (Table 14.1).

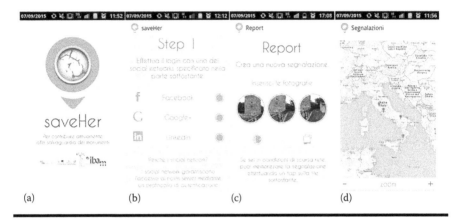

(a) (b) (c) (d)

Figure 14.2 **Screenshots of the four main steps of the use of SaveHer: the start of app (a); the login phase using the social networks Facebook, Google+, or Linkedin (b); the step for taking the photos of the affected monument so as to make a report (c); the georeferenced data sent by the user are reported on the map (d).**

5. All the data, including the georeferenced photos and the replies to the questionnaire, are sent to the remote cloud server and recorded in a database.
6. The website administrator will check the bearing, quality, and reliability of the information recorded on the database.
7. The data (with the user credits) will be published both on the dedicated web page (http://www.appsaveheritage.com/) and app: a map will show the location of the monument, the photos will explain the problems detected, and the replies to the questionnaire (if compiled) will add further information on the affected heritage (Figures 14.2d and 14.3).
8. The data will be sent to the institutions (e.g., municipality, monuments, and fine arts office) in charge of safeguarding the affected monument through an ad hoc e-mail form arranged in the administrator website page. In this way, the institution will be able to plan proper countermeasures to mitigate the risk affecting the heritage.

According to what was previously described, the user can draw up a questionnaire to better identify the problems affecting the monument. The survey is made up of 10 demands embracing both the type and cause/object of the damage affecting the heritage (monument or works of arts located inside it), starting from literature and the authors' personal experiences and skills (e.g., Marchetti et al., 2006; UNI 11182, 2006; Gizzi, 2008; Canuti et al., 2009; Papa and Di Pasquale, 2011; Gizzi et al., 2012, 2016).

Analyzing the questionnaire, it emerges that the first three demands refer to the damage brought about by natural events such as earthquakes, landslides, extreme weather events, and carelessness on heritage. We refer to collapses and cracks in the walls, floors, and roofs. Demands 4 and 5 deal with the damage caused by

Table 14.1 Questionnaire That Users of SaveHer Can Fill in to Identify Carefully the Nature of the Problems Affecting Heritage

Demand	Type of Damage	Cause of the Damage/ Object of Damage
1	✓ Collapses (walls, floors, roofs, etc.)	• Earthquake • Landslide • Carelessness • Weather event • Other • Unknown
2	✓ Cracks or deformations (walls, pillars, floors, etc.)	• Earthquake • Landslide • Carelessness • Weather event • Other • Unknown
3	✓ Disconnected roof	• Earthquake • Landslide • Carelessness • Weather event • Other • Unknown
4	✓ Decay and/or fall of material	• Plaster • Frescoes • Other
5	✓ Damage to water harvesting system	• Carelessness • Weather event • Other • Unknown
6	✓ Presence of water inside or near the building	• Flood • Water leak • Infiltration • Other • Unknown
7	✓ Building damage due to vandalism	• Graffito • Illegal billposting • Mechanical action • Fire • Explosion • Other

(Continued)

Table 14.1 (Continued)   Questionnaire That Users of SaveHer Can Fill in to Identify Carefully the Nature of the Problems Affecting Heritage

Demand	Type of Damage	Cause of the Damage/ Object of Damage
8	✓ Damage to works of arts (e.g., frescoes, mosaics, hangings)	• Graffito • Mechanical action • Fire • Explosion • Other
9	✓ Theft	• Sacred furniture • Works of arts • Other
10	✓ Other (to be filled in by the users)	...

carelessness such as the detachment of plasters or the rainwater picking system leakage.

Question 6 considers the effects as a consequence of natural events such as floods or water leak. Questions from 7 to 9 regard the consequences of vandalism actions on monuments or works of art. The last question was not predefined by the authors: in this way, the user can include another type of damage cause (and the causes of it) that was not considered in the previous nine questions.

The main focus of SaveHer is to involve citizens/users to supply a support to the institution to put into the field timely measures to safeguard cultural heritage. The aim can be reached if at least three main conditions are met: user-friendly features of the app, clearness of the questions proposed by the questionnaire, and awareness by people and institutions that a collaboration between them is desirable to ensure the posterity of heritage. The third point, which is taking up and will take up the authors in the next months, is crucial: massive information campaigns to awaken all the actors, both private citizens and institutions in charge of the heritage safeguard (e.g., monuments and fine art office, town council), which will be focused on the usefulness and the potentiality of SaveHer in

1. Making easier the relationship between the citizens and the institutions in charge of safeguarding the tangible cultural heritage;
2. Getting timely and suitable data about problems affecting monuments;
3. Identifying, on the basis of the statistical analysis of data produced by the users, the areas to monitor with regard to particular causes of damage (e.g., vandalism or theft); and
4. Spreading the knowledge of less known heritage (e.g., rural churches), of which the Italian heritage is rich.

Figure 14.3   Some typologies of problems affecting heritage: biological coloni-zation (upper, left); fractures and cracks (upper, right); graffiti/paintings (lower, left); and disaggregation and loss of 3D elements in columns (lower, right).

Summarizing, the philosophy on which SaveHer is based starts from the con-sideration that the heritage protection is a challenge that needs more and more efforts and synergies between all the actors. With this in mind, an information and communication technologies (ICT) tool such as SaveHer can contribute in this perspective, facilitating the profitable collaboration between people and authorities.

Conclusions

An important consideration can be done comparing the impacts of Executive Order 12906, "Coordinating Geographic Data Acquisition and Access: The National Spatial Data Infrastructure," after 23 years, Google Hearth after 12 years, and

OpenStreetMap after 13 years. Traditional approaches to geographical information system require a high expertise level of users, while Google Earth and OpenStreetMap are wider communities without a great knowledge in the field of cartography, spatial database, computer science, image processing, etc. Consequently, the main advantage is the possibility to have a mass of disseminated volunteers, very motivated, able to populate databases. Another important advantage is resource optimization. Local authorities or agencies are not obliged to continuously produce new maps, but they can use Google or OpenStreetMap data as official cartography. These public administrations can build new information at the local scale also using part of volunteered data modifying them according to administration needs. When great part of data are ready, it is important to publish and share them on a cloud service using citizens' collaboration in checking and updating them. Cloud services are fundamental in saving resources; in fact, their use can avoid the costs and management of servers.

This approach has been adopted in the SaveHer app experience, where mass cooperation through the use of ICT such as mobile applications can be a cost-effective and pervasive way of contributing to uphold cultural heritage safeguard, particularly in a period in which national funds are diminishing more and more and no prospect of turnabout can be expected.

With this in mind, this paper has considered the main technical features of free-of-charge SaveHer mobile app designed for tablets and smartphones. According to the participative philosophy of citizens, the community is called to assume an active role consisting in putting at institution's disposal information about problems affecting both the built heritage and works of art.

In keeping with the Open Government, the use of SaveHer App can contribute to the raising of awareness that mutual cooperation among all actors, such as institutions, the local community to which the monuments belong, and tourists, is crucial to preserve cultural heritage.

There is a widespread belief that the realization of a Smart City is based on extreme use of applications for smart phones and tablets. Very often, attention has been focused exclusively on device applications, forgetting that there is a city. Whenever automation through mobile applications is proposed, it is important to consider its effects on the city. When someone proposes a complex technological system, it is important to ask "is it really useful for the city?" The SaveHer application is a case where technologies have a central role in preserving cultural heritage, avoiding the typical situation of technologies developed without a specific purpose, solutions looking for a problem, or technologies for technologies (Murgante and Borruso, 2014).

Acknowledgments

This work has been developed in the context of Project PRO CULT ("Advanced Methodological Approaches and Technologies for Protection and Security of Cultural Heritage") funded by Basilicata Region ERDF 2007-13 and "Smart Cities and

Communities and Social Innovation" Project (Call MIUR n.84/Ric2012, PON 2007–2013 del 2 March 2012) Measure IV.1, IV.2,2013–2015.

References

Batty, M., Axhausen, K.W., Giannotti, F., Pozdnoukhov, A., Bazzani, A., Wachowicz, M., Ouzounis, G., Portugali, Y. 2012. Smart cities of the future. *The European Physical Journal Special Topics* 214(1), 481–518.

Belisario, E., Cogo, G., Epifani, S., Forghieri, C. 2011. Come si fa Open Data? Istruzioni per Enti e AmministrazioniPubbliche. Santarcangelo di Romagna, MaggioliEditore.

Bonacini, E. 2014. Augmented reality and cultural apps in Italy: Stories from a marriage in mobility. Il Capitale Cultural. *Studies on the Value of Cultural Heritage* 9, 89–12.

Canuti, P., Margottini, C., Fanti, R., Bromhead, E.N. 2009. Cultural heritage and landslides: Research for risk prevention and conservation. In: Sassa, K., Canuti, P. (eds.), *Landslides—disaster risk reduction*. Springer, Berlin. pp. 401–433.

Conroy, M.M., Evans-Cowley, J. 2006. E-participation in planning: An analysis of cities adopting on-line citizen participation tools. *Environment and Planning C: Government and Policy* 24, 371–384.

Dowling, C., Whalen, M. 2014. ARCH-APP: the city as classroom builder. Proceedings of INTED 2014 Conference, March 10–12, 2014, Valencia, Spain. ISBN: 978-84-616-8412-0, 3729-3739 (http://www.mimiwhalen.net/wp-content/uploads/2013/12/Inted-2014-Paper.pdf, accessed September 7, 2015).

Evans-Cowley, J., Conroy, M.M. 2006. The growth of e-government in municipal planning. *Journal of Urban Technology* 13(1), 81–107.

Franklin, C., Hane, P. 1992. An introduction to geographic information systems: Linking maps to databases. *Database* 15, 13–21.

Garau, C., Ilardi, E. 2014. The non-places meet the places: Virtual tours on smartphones for the enhancement of cultural heritage, *Journal of Urban Technology* 21(1), 79–91.

Giloth, C.F., Tanant, J. 2014. Reconstitution of the Labyrinthe of Versailles as a Mobile App. 18th International Conference on Information Visualisation (IV), 269–274.

Gizzi, F.T. 2008. Identifying geological and geo-technical influences that threaten historical sites: A method to evaluate the usefulness of data already available. *Journal of Cultural Heritage* IX(3), 302–310.

Gizzi, F.T., Masini, N., Murgante, B., Saulino, N., Biscione, M., Danese, M., Sileo, M., Zotta, C., Potenza, M.R. 2015. SaveHer: Un'applicazione (App) per contribuire attivamente alla salvaguardia del Patrimonio Culturale. Masini, N., Gizzi F.T. (eds.), In *Salvaguardia, Conservazione e Sicurezza del Patrimonio Culturale. Nuove metodologie e tecnologie operative*. Lagonegro (PZ). pp. 201–214. ISBN 978-88-995-2000-7 (in Italian).

Gizzi, F.T., Potenza M.R., Zotta C. 2012. 23 November 1980 Irpinia–Basilicata earthquake (Southern Italy): Towards a full knowledge of the seismic effects. Bulletin of Earthquake Engineering, 10(4), 1109-1131, DOI: 10.1007/s10518-012-9353-z.

Gizzi, F.T., Sileo, M., Biscione, M., Danese, M., Alvarez de Buergo, M. 2016. The conservation state of the Sassi of Matera site (Southern Italy) and its correlation with the environmental conditions analysed through spatial analysis techniques. *Journal of Cultural Heritage* 17, 61–74.

Goodchild, M.F. 2007. Citizens as voluntary sensors: Spatial data infrastructure in the World of Web 2.0. *International Journal of Spatial Data Infrastructures Research* 2, 24–32.

Goodchild, M.F. 2009. NeoGeography and the nature of geographic expertise. *Journal of Location Based Services* 3, 82–96.

Haklay, M. 2011. Citizen Science as Participatory Science, Retrieved November 27, 2011, from http://povesham.wordpress.com/2011/11/27/citizen-science-as-participatory-science/.

Hudson-Smith, A., Milton, R., Dearden, J., Batty, M. 2009. The neogeography of virtual cities: Digital mirrors into a recursive world. In: Foth, M. (ed.), *Handbook of Research on Urban Informatics: The Practice and Promise of the Real-Time City, Information Science Reference.* Hershey: IGI Global.

Kenteris, M., Gavalas, D., Economou, D. 2006. A novel method for the development of personalized mobile tourist applications. In: 5th IASTED International Conference on Communication Systems and Networks, WMSF, CSN Palma de Mallorca, 208–212.

Kenteris, M., Gavalas, D., Economou, D. 2009. An innovative mobile electronic tourist guide application. *Personal and Ubiquitous Computing* 13(2), 103–118.

Marchetti, L., Carapezza, G.F., Mazzini, G., Di Gennaro, M., Galanti, E., D'Annibale, A. 2006. *Scheda per il rilievo del danno ai beni culturali—Chiese. Gruppo di lavoro per la salvaguardia e la prevenzione dei Beni Culturali dai rischi naturali. Dipartimento della Protezione Civile Nazionale.* Modello A-DC. Prima sezione (in Italian).

Masini, N., Gizzi, F.T., Biscione, M., Danese, M., Pecci, A., Potenza, M.R., Scavone, M., and Sileo, M. 2016. *Sensing the Risk: New Approaches and Technologies for Protection and Security of Cultural Heritage. The "PRO_CULT" Project.* Springer International Publishing AG. Ioannides, M. Fink, E., Moropoulou, A., Hagedorn-Saupe, M., Fresa, A., Liestøl, G., Rajcic, V., Grussenmeyer, P. (eds.). pp. 99–106. EuroMed 2016, Part II, LNCS 10059. DOI: 10.1007/978-3-319-48974-2_12.

Masini, N., Soldovieri F. (eds.). 2017. *Sensing the Past. From artifact to historical site.* Series: Geotechnologies and the Environment, vol. 16. Springer International Publishing. DOI: 10.1007/978-3-319-50518-3.

Murgante, B., Borruso, G. 2013. Cities and smartness: A critical analysis of opportunities and risks. *Lecture Notes in Computer Science* 7973, 630–642. ISSN: 0302-9743, DOI: 10.1007/978-3-642-39646-5_46.

Murgante, B., Borruso, G. 2014. Smart city or Smurfs city. *Lecture Notes in Computer Science* 8580, 738–749. DOI: 10.1007/978-3-319-09129-7_53.

Murgante, B., Borruso, G. 2015. Smart cities in a smart world. In: Rassia, S., Pardalos, P. (eds.), *Future City Architecture for Optimal Living.* Berlin: Springer Verlag, pp. 13–35 DOI: 10.1007/978-3-319-15030-7_2 ISBN: 978-3-319-15029-1.

Murgante, B., Borruso, G., Lapucci, A. 2009. Geocomputation and urban planning. In: Murgante, B., Borruso, G., Lapucci, A. (eds.), *Geocomputation and Urban Planning.* SCI, vol. 176. Berlin: Springer, pp. 1–18.

Murgante, B., Tilio, L., Lanza, V., Scorza, F. 2011a. Using participative GIS and e-tools for involving citizens of MarmoPlatano–Melandro area in European programming activities. *Journal of Balkans and Near Eastern Studies* 13(1), 97–115. DOI: 10.1080/19448953.2011.550809.

Murgante, B., Tilio, L., Scorza, F., Lanza, V. 2011b. Crowd-cloud tourism, new approaches to territorial marketing. *Lecture Notes in Computer Science* 6783, 265–276. ISSN: 0302-9743, DOI: 10.1007/978-3-642-21887-3_21.

Panda, J., Sharma, S., Jawahar, C.V. 2012. Heritage app: Annotating images on mobile phones. 8th Indian Conference on Computer Vision, Graphics and Image Processing, edited by ISRO, IUSSTF (ICVGIP Mumbai).

Papa, S., Di Pasquale, G. 2011. *Manuale per la compilazione della scheda per il rilievo del danno ai beni culturali, Chiese.* Modello A-DC. Dipartimento della Protezione Civile.

Sui, D.S. 2008. The wikification of GIS and its consequences: Or Angelina Jolie's new tattoo and the future of GIS. *Computers, Environment and Urban Systems* 32(1), 1–5.

Turner, A. 2006. *Introduction to Neogeography.* Sebastopol: O'Reilly Media.

UNI 11182. 2006. *Beni culturali, Materiali lapidei naturali ed artificiali. Descrizione della forma di alterazione—Termini e definizioni.*

Vanoni, D., Stout, S., Cosentino, A., Kuester, F. 2015. Artifact Conservation: Representation and Analysis of Spectroscopic and Multispectral Imaging Data Using Augmented Reality. Scientific Symposium at the General Assembly of the International Council on Monuments and Sites (ICOMOS).

Verkasalo, H., López-Nicolás, C., Molina-Castillo, J., Bouwman, H. 2010. Analysis of users and non-users of smartphone applications. *Telematics and Informatics* 27, 242–255.

Verykokou, S., Charalabos, I., Georgia, K. 2014. 3D Visualization via augmented reality: the case of the middle stoa in the ancient agora of Athens. In: Ioannides, M., Thalmann, N., Fink, E., Žarnić, R., Yen, A., Quak, E. (eds.). *Digital Heritage. Progress in Cultural Heritage: Documentation, Preservation, and Protection.* Volume 8740 of the series Lecture Notes in Computer Science (LNCS). pp. 279–289.

Chapter 15

Artists, Data, and Agency in Smart Cities

Roz Stewart-Hall and Martha King

Contents

Introduction

This chapter describes work happening at Knowle West Media Centre (KWMC*) in Bristol, to ensure that local people have greater agency in determining both the data gathered for "The City" and the ways in which this data are used. Since 1996, KWMC has been commissioning socially engaged artists to work with data in various ways. Most recently, working with Ideas for Change,† supported by the Bristol City Council (BCC) and with input from the University of Bristol, KWMC has developed "The Bristol Approach to Citizen Sensing" (TBA).

---

* See kwmc.org.uk
† See ideasforchange.com/en/

The apparent dominance of information technology (IT) companies, within many current "Smart City" developments, leaves little space for community agency. This leads to a significant divide:

> The current ecosystem around Big Data creates a new kind of digital divide: the Big Data rich and the Big Data poor. (Boyd and Crawford, 2012)

In our contemporary cultural and social ecosystem, this is highly significant because big data can be understood as an "archive" of our day-to-day experiences, which is continually updating and expanding.

Derrida (1996) wrote that "Effective democratization can always be measured by this essential criterion: the participation in and the access to the archive, its constitution, and its interpretation."

There is a significant danger that an overreliance on an archive comprised solely of big data will lead to decision-making processes becoming increasingly undemocratic, as they will be removed from most people's influence or agency. There is a danger in disregarding the significance of who is influencing and accessing the big data archive, for the type of data that are collected into big data sets is usually determined without the conscious agency of those who supply it. Most people will not be involved in deciding what data are collected, how they are interpreted, or what decisions are made on the basis of those data. Instead, these decisions will be dominated by the priorities, perceptions, and interests of those who have power and control over big data.

This chapter articulates KWMC's work with artists, data, and people, from data visualization projects to The Bristol Approach, as alternatives that challenge dominant Smart City narratives.

Why Participation Is Key in a Smart City

There are clearly strong links between traditional social exclusion and digital exclusion (Helsper and Reisdorf, 2016). Furthermore, continuing digital exclusion threatens to amplify existing patterns of social exclusion:

> Digital exclusion is seen as a dual threat, with access to ICT and the ability to use it potentially creating a new form of exclusion as well as reinforcing existing patterns of exclusion from society. (Selwyn, 2002)

Digital exclusion is likely to lead to exclusion from online services, further extending the gap between those thriving and those struggling. This is important across all Smart Cities, and although Bristol, which has been identified alongside London as the only other leading UK smart city (Woods et al., 2016), has a high percentage of Internet users among its population (91.3% compared to the England average of 86.2%; BCC/NHS, 2015), there are still areas of the city where digital and social exclusion persists.

There are significant differences between the experiences of people living in the wealthier areas of Bristol and those in wards that rank among the highest in the country in the Government's Multiple Deprivation Indices. For example, "In Bristol as a whole…17% of the population suffer from income deprivation. The proportion varies across the city" (BCC/NHS, 2015). Furthermore, the percentage of people living in areas of deprivation in Bristol is increasing, with 16% of Bristol's population living in the 10% most deprived areas in England in 2015 compared to 14% in 2010 (BCC/NHS, 2015). The differences between "those who have" and "those who have not" are stark, for example:

> the gap in healthy life expectancy between the most deprived 10% and the least deprived 10% within Bristol…for males is 16.3 years and for females it is 16.7 years. (BCC/NHS, 2015)

In areas of the city where social exclusion persists, which includes KWMC's location of Knowle West,* where 35% of the population is "income deprived" (BCC/NHS, 2015), digital exclusion is also more likely to persist, as

> People who are disadvantaged in areas of economic, social, and personal wellbeing also tend to be the ones least likely to engage with ICTs. This has caused concern among policymakers (European Commission, 2010), since the socio-economically disadvantaged could benefit most from services offered online and are the heaviest users of services offline. (Helsper and Reisdorf, 2016)

In order to ensure that Smart City developments don't increase and amplify existing patterns of social exclusion, approaches need to be developed with local people, rather than technology being developed in isolation of the needs of communities by big IT companies or people in control of big data. KWMC has developed such an approach, which promises an alternative process for developing Smart Cities that have smart citizens at their heart and that help to decrease and diminish existing patterns of digital and social exclusion.

---

* Knowle West is the ward of Filwood.

How KWMC Has Developed Work with Artists, Data, and People

Since 1996, KWMC has been working with artists to generate new ways of thinking about decision-making, inclusion, and empowerment. Since 2008, KWMC has been working with data, initially working with the Government's Multiple Deprivation Indices and more recently commissioning artists through programs like "Whose Data?" where artists have had key roles in visualizing data, making "real-life" objects to gather data and using visual tools to represent data in ways that enable people to make more informed choices and decisions.

One early example of this was work by artist Dane Watkins, in devising visualizations to help people monitor their energy use, during the 3e Houses project. Partners Toshiba Labs developed relevant energy monitoring software, for which Dane Watkins produced visualizations. This monitoring tool was then installed on tablets that were given to 100 Bristol homes to reduce energy consumption. KWMC also explored the potential of using artist-led design to engage people with data. Workshops supported local people to use the tablets and devise additional apps and widgets on the basis of their priorities. By nurturing enthusiasm for using the tablet, the work supported people to understand and be control of their energy use, for example:

> The main thing has been finding out how much electricity my sons use in their rooms… and how much it costs. It has made them cut back and they don't leave things on standby now. (Stephen, participant, quoted at kwmc.org.uk/projects/3ehouses)

This type of finding is reflected in the data visualized in Figure 15.1.

The project addressed digital inclusion as participants engaged in the development of apps and widgets, motivating them to use their tablet computer regularly.* In addition, 3e Houses informed other work using data visualization for renewable and efficient energy in Knowle West. (For example, see SoLa and its outcomes: https://vimeo.com/163389485)

Throughout its 20-year history, KWMC has supported local people to voice their opinions and influence decision-making processes in their community. KWMC also develops relevant tools to heighten awareness of current issues, such as during the 2012 election to decide whether Bristol would have an elected mayor. "Mayor for the Day" was developed by Dane Watkins as an interactive way for people to consider which issues were important and to encourage people to cast their vote in the election.† The app presents a series of questions, about local issues,

---

* A guide is available at kwmc.org.uk/wp-content/uploads/2013/05/3E-Houses-Best-Practice -Guide.pdf
† Mayor for the Day is available at http://iconikit.com/mayor/index.html?id=122

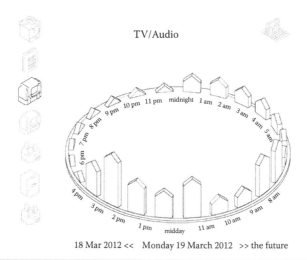

Figure 15.1   Data visualization for 3e Houses tablets by Dane Watkins.

through illustrations. A unique coat of arms is generated by the app, based on the answers given to the questions, such as the example in Figure 15.2.

"Mayor for the Day" is an example of early work at KWMC that brought together artists, data, and people to nurture greater interest in having influence within and on behalf of their community. Citizen-generated data are all very well, but what is more important is the need for people to understand and be able to interpret that data.

Artists like Dane Watkins have used visual tools to create a relationship between the data and the user, based on understanding. They have done this by creating visualizations that provoke an emotional response from a user and lead them to think more deeply about an issue or situation, supporting them to reach their own conclusions through reflection. For example, Mayor for the Day offered more than the "yes" or "no" offered by many "democratic" processes so people could think about how being offered just two options denies the opportunity to engage in a more nuanced debate or set of choices. In the future, this could help to develop a greater understanding of the shortcomings of binary electoral processes that deny people the opportunity to have wider influence.

For further example, Citizens' Dashboard was a pilot project to explore how data could enable citizens to see how Bristol is performing, by viewing, interacting with, and contributing to visual representations of data gathered across the city. A prototype of the "dashboard" was used during the 2014 "Data Patchwork" project to develop an online resource that focused on community priorities in Knowle West. KWMC also developed a range of accessible offline opportunities to contribute data through an installation entitled "The Cardboard Living Room."

A group of eight apprentices, KWMC's Junior Digital Producers, developed the Cardboard Living Room as a new way of gathering data; each piece of interactive

Figure 15.2   Mayor for the Day coat of arms, Dane Watkins.

cardboard furniture contained sensors that collected responses to generate data (Figure 15.3). For example, a cardboard window featured a set of photos representing issues that local community members highlighted as significant, such as drug-related litter, graffiti, and dog waste. Visitors were given three cardboard bricks to throw at those windows that represented the main issues for them. On impact, the brick caused the windows to make the sound of breaking glass and the sensors registered the "votes."

The Cardboard Living Room appeared across six community venues in Knowle West.*

Artists and creatives working with KWMC have challenged what we mean by "data" and the meaning and interpretation of specific data, by supporting people to question data and to expose the "stories" behind it.

Artists have been well placed in these roles as they have an understanding of what it means to have the right to contribute and control data because of copyright, owner-ship, and intellectual property rights. Furthermore, artists who work with KWMC are aware of the significance of their role in "demystifying" data and technology for others, by bringing data to life through visualizations or interactive objects:

---

* The Living Room launch can be seen at http://kwmc.org.uk/projects/datapatchwork/

Figure 15.3 KWMC's 2013 junior digital producers and the Cardboard Living Room.

> Technology can be a chilly business, and we need to avoid it being so.
> (Caleb Parkin, artist in TBA)

Making sure that technology and data are less "chilly" is important, in order that more people can make sense and use of data and technology. Artists who work with KWMC are committed to supporting people to realize their own power through arts interventions by creating space in which exchange and change can take place. This exchange is essential in order to expose and explore issues and problems that people face in any community:

> If you're trying to make things better for the people who live in a community the first thing you need to understand is what it's like to live in that community—what the issues and problems are. (Local trader participating in TBA)

Artists working with KWMC are able to acknowledge and appreciate the things they don't know or understand:

> We can't pretend to know what the issues are. (Paul Hurley, Artist in TBA)

This is essential, because:

> Anything that's going to create change needs to be built on what people actually need and it's only by getting to know them and understanding what it's like to live in their shoes that you can say 'ok, well actually this is what we really need to do.' (Workshop participant in TBA)

Artists' approaches to uncovering issues and working creatively with people and data, combined with KWMC's approach, informed the development of TBA.

The Bristol Approach to Citizen Sensing

KWMC's approach is aligned with participatory action research approaches, whereby all involved are "finding out together" as co-researchers, to bring about change:

> Action research… seeks to bring together action and reflection, theory and practice, in participation with others, in the pursuit of practical solutions to issues of pressing concern to people… (Bradbury, 2000)

The starting point for The Bristol Approach is the belief that citizens should have a leading role in imagining, designing and building their future. In this way, The Bristol Approach acts to:

> …challenge and unsettle existing structures of power and privilege, to provide opportunities for those least often heard to share their knowledge and wisdom, and for people to work together to bring about positive social change… (Brydon-Miller et al., 2011)

The Bristol Approach "'provides opportunities for those least often heard to share their knowledge and wisdom," as it has people and their everyday experiences and knowledge at its heart. It is driven by people and the issues they care about and pulls in relevant data, know-how, and resources (including technology) to address issues and facilitate meaningful action. "Citizen Sensing" is a process where citizens build, use, identify, and/or gather data to tackle an issue that's important to them. KWMC continued to work with artists in order to open inclusive dialogic spaces around data, bridge gaps between partners from different backgrounds, and make sense of data in meaningful ways, during the development of The Bristol Approach.

Following research and development drawing on learning from other international Smart City citizen initiatives, Ideas for Change and KWMC developed the six-step Bristol Approach framework, which supports the deployment of new or adapted sensing technologies into everyday environments:

1. *Identification:* identifying issues people care about, mapping communities, organizations, businesses, and others affected by the issues who might be interested in working together toward a solution.
2. *Framing:* exploring issues in detail and framing it as a shared goal. Identifying if and how technology and data could be utilized, uncovering resources that are available and identifying gaps in resources or knowledge.

3. *Design:* working with people to cocreate tools, governance, and data infrastructure to help tackle issues.
4. *Deployment:* taking the tools created into the community to be tested.
5. *Orchestration:* drawing attention to what has been made, encouraging others to use tools created and data collected, celebrating what has been cocreated.
6. *Outcome:* assessing if and how goals have been achieved, finding out what has been learned, sharing insights gained, creating new solutions to issues, identifying opportunities for new business, and making changes to available infrastructure.

This is visualized in Figure 15.4.

The framework aims to enable citizen-generated data to be used for the common good and for the service of its citizens. The framework was structured to ensure that programs are driven by issues that are relevant to local needs and take

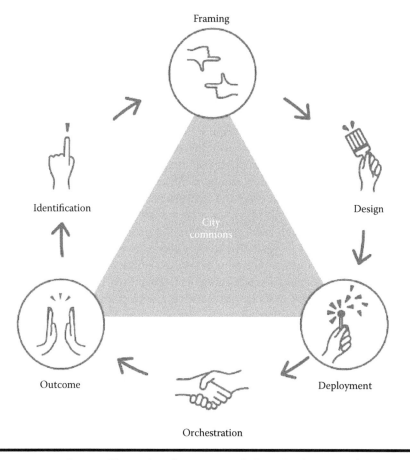

Figure 15.4 Diagram illustrating the process of The Bristol Approach.

place at community level, with local people actively involved in designing, testing, and evaluating.

A pilot project took place in 2016 to test how the framework works in real communities, with real issues. The purpose was to learn from this process, to improve the framework as a guide for citizens and cities and help inform the design and development of Smart City programs. The pilot project was organized through two strands of activity:

1. A focus on damp in homes emerged through a series of participatory workshops. This evolved into the Damp Busters action group.
2. A group of eight 18–25-year-olds from Bristol took part in a creative leadership program. This "Change Creators" group developed two projects: diversifying mental health support and reducing food waste.

The pilot project aimed to undertake a complete iteration of the Bristol Approach framework through its six stages, working on live issues that communities care about and building tools that explore how to integrate new and existing technologies to address these issues. All activities were creative, hands-on, and participative and mixed up people with different backgrounds and skills to build a "commons community" to tackle the issues people cared about.

Three sets of prototype citizen sensing tools were devised, designed, deployed, and tested through the pilot project. "Damp Busters" led to the design and deployment of Frogbox damp sensors (see Figure 15.5) in homes in east Bristol, the design of an online citizen reporting tool and the creation of a community "damp busting" team of people trained to support their neighbors.

One Change Creators group created a "SMART bin" named "Food Boy," to collect household data about types and amounts of food waste. The second Change Creators group created "It's Okay," a project that included a "Sensing Booth" designed to sense, through facial expressions, how people feel about mental health issues and whether people agree that services needed to be diversified.

The project demonstrated the value of taking a citizen sensing approach to tackling city issues. The focus on motivating and integrating different types of contributions then combining them with existing resources and knowledge was key. Contributions from across Bristol proved diverse, talented, and generous:

> I enjoyed working with people from different backgrounds. There were designers, there were people who work in housing, there were artists, there were students. That was an interesting experience because we all brought something different to the discussion, different skill sets and expertise… (Workshop participant, TBA)

A wide range of people gave their time, skills, and ideas to the project and a large community of interest grew around the project. Over 717 participants aged 13–80

Figure 15.5   Frogbox casing for damp sensors manufactured at KWMC: The Factory.*

contributed over 45 events, including neighborhood events, codesign workshops, data jams, maker days, and tech building skills days.

Maintaining momentum and coordinating activity was a challenge throughout. The team had to use a mix of social media tools, online tools, e-mail, texting, and telephoning to coordinate and share activity and decision-making among participants. This highlighted the need for an effective shared "commons" communications and organization tool at city level.[†]

The pilot showed that a citizen sensing project requires a wide range of expertise beyond data and programming skills. These include knowledge about neighborhoods and networks, people and communications skills, data infrastructure and governance, coding, interface and user experience design, product design, behavior economics, anthropology, visualization, sensor hardware, workshop facilitation, documentation, and sharing skills.

---

* KWMC: The factory is KWMC's Digital manufacturing space. kwmc.org.uk/projects/thefactory

[†] While "the commons," alongside ideas of "the collaborative city," were influential in developing TBA, this is a significant area for debate demanding further interrogation (especially concerning rules of engagement and responsibilities).

The development of The Bristol Approach has exposed that technology is only a small part of citizen sensing work. A wider set of tools and resources are needed, including combining community know-how and drawing on existing resources and assets. It is also essential that findings from data gathered can be reflected on to identify solutions. To this end, a "Solutions Workshop" was organized, which demonstrated the potential to inform the development of city services, infrastructure, and new models of community action and business development.

Securing the solutions identified marks a clear agenda for the development and deployment of The Bristol Approach.

Difference Made

The TBA pilot project has made a difference for people engaged. For example, it has nurtured a greater sense of people's own potential to bring about change:

> I've realised how much power I have to effect change and how much power we have working within a team. (Yelena, Change Creator participant)

It has achieved this through its holistic approach, which involved people reflecting on issues and gathering and using relevant data in order to devise solutions to address those issues:

> The Bristol Approach is interesting because it is not just a matter of getting the technology right—it's taking a much more holistic approach to gathering data and using it. (Nigel Legg, TBA workshop participant)

Solutions were identified by first identifying the most pressing issues for people living in challenging circumstances, then gathering and using relevant data to help evidence and address those issues. In many instances, the differences that this process has made have been more far-reaching and effective than could have been anticipated. For example, the following story, recorded during the deployment of the Damp Buster Frogbox sensors, shows how people developed a heightened awareness of the ways in which they can use data to ensure justice:

> In the case of one family, living on a low income and suffering from health conditions, their energy bill forms a significant part of their household expenditure...Their most recent bill was higher than usual, yet initially they believed this to be due to the colder than average spring weather...taking meter readings and discussing energy measures prompted Brian to check his utility bill and compare readings...the energy company had made an error...the family had been charged for

an additional 100 units of gas. Empowered with the recordings taken by the project, Brian had the confidence to contact the energy company and file a complaint. The energy company…agreed to refund the difference accordingly. (Joe Firth, Easton Energy Group)

The Bristol Approach enables identification of solutions to issues that are apparent, but also, because of its integrated and holistic approach, it ensures that people become familiar with how data are and can be used to tackle issues. People are therefore better equipped to tackle unforeseen issues that they may encounter beyond the project remit. TBA has made a difference not only for participants, including local residents, but also for professionals who have roles that relate to the issues and solutions identified.

The pilot project aimed to make a positive difference to people's lives, but on a larger scale, it aimed to show how it is possible to establish citizen-generated evidence sets that can be used to understand the issues that people face and identify solutions to those issues. The Damp Busters program fulfilled this aim as it illustrated how a key issue in a city can be identified and then tackled through working together. Sharing and collaboration are key in this era of increased funding cuts, not for councils or others in positions of power to absolve responsibility, but to establish an equality of input in determining the issues that need to be addressed and the best ways to address them.

Partners and experts have highlighted the contemporary significance of The Bristol Approach, in a society where the sands are shifting considerably in terms of the resources available. For example, during the solutions workshop, a member of BCC's environmental health team explained that they have to use a severity index, regarding damp, whereby they have to be sure of the severity of a situation before being able to investigate it:

> I'm a senior environmental health officer in the private housing service and am really interested in this project. We can investigate problems with damp and mould growth in privately rented houses and flats, and if it's severe enough we do have legal powers… In the past we'd try to help informally by giving advice and guidance to tenants and landlords but recent cutbacks mean we just don't have the resources to do this anymore. Therefore your project might go a long way to help plug this gap. (Senior environmental health officer at BCC)

Citizen-generated data sets, such as those nurtured through The Bristol Approach, which can make the case for the issues that demand interrogation and action, are increasingly becoming important. It is therefore important that relevant academics and policy makers learn from these findings and endeavor to employ The Bristol Approach to identify, interrogate, and find solutions to address issues through Citizen Sensing.

Conclusions

KWMC's work with communities and data has supported people to have greater autonomy in understanding and using data as a useful asset for bringing about positive social change:

> It's a big step to make local people feel like they've got the power, explaining data, taking the fear out of that space, and then getting them in an empowered space where they can actually be involved. (Workshop participant, TBA)

A report published by the UK charity Nesta* identified seven factors that have prevented Smart City initiatives from delivering real value to the cities where they were deployed:

  i. Not taking human behavior as seriously as technology;
  ii. Lack of use, generation and sharing of evidence, leading to little evidence of return on investment;
  iii. Lack of focus on data skills;
  iv. Lack of integration with other work in cities;
  v. Over reliance on hardware and technology;
  vi. No role for the citizen; and
  vii. Closed and proprietary projects (Saunders and Baeck, 2015).

This chapter highlights how initiatives such as The Bristol Approach are needed to offer alternative processes, resources, and ways of thinking about data and their role in order to develop Smart Cities, where

  ■ Human behavior is taken more seriously than technology
  ■ There is plenty of use, generation, and sharing of evidence
  ■ There is a focus on developing data skills
  ■ Work is integrated with other activities happening in cities
  ■ Hardware and technology are used as and when there are useful
  ■ Citizens' roles are central
  ■ Projects are open and shared

Data projects like The Bristol Approach show the potential of such alternative processes while also raising important challenges and thereby contributing to the development of future work. For example, Open Standards and transparent data contracts are issues that have not been fully resolved in many Smart City projects.

---

* Nesta is the National Endowment for Science, Technology, and Art. www.nesta.org.uk

KWMC's work highlights the importance of testing and exploring ideas with people and cocreating new technologies that can be applied to real life scenarios.

It is essential that aspiring Smart Cities, whether followers, challengers, contenders, or leaders (Woods et al., 2016) replicate the processes developed in The Bristol Approach, using iterative, reflective processes and creative approaches, to ensure that "Smart Citizens" are central to the Smart City vision and that, in our emerging cultural and social ecosystems, people are central to decision making, not only big data in isolation. This restructuring of processes to ensure that citizen agency is at the center of decision-making offers opportunities to combat the threat that people could be completely left behind.

References

Boyd, D. and Crawford, K. 2012. Critical questions for big data. *Information, Communication & Society*. 15:5, pp. 662–679. http://www.tandfonline.com/loi/rics20

Bradbury, H. 2000. Learning with the Natural Step: Action research to promote conversations for sustainable development. In: *Handbook of Action Research: Participative Inquiry and Practice*. Ed. Reason, P., and Bradbury, H., pp. 307–314. London: Sage Publications.

Bristol City Council and NHS Bristol Clinical Commissioning Group. 2015. *Joint Strategic Needs Assessment Report 2015: Data Profile of Health and Wellbeing in Bristol*. www.bristol.gov.uk/jsna (Accessed April 24, 2017).

Brydon-Miller, M., Kral, M., Maguire, P., Noffke, S., and Sabhlok, A. 2011. Jazz and the Banyan Tree: Roots and riffs on participatory action research. In: *The SAGE Handbook of Qualitative Research* (4th edition). Ed. Denzin, N., and Lincoln, Y. pp. 387–400. California: Sage Publications.

Derrida, J. 1996. *Archive Fever: A Freudian Impression*. Chicago: University of Chicago Press.

Helsper, E.J. and Reisdorf, B.C. 2016. The emergence of a "digital underclass" in Great Britain and Sweden: Changing reasons for digital exclusion. *New Media and Society*. 19:8, pp. 1253–1270. ISSN 1461-4448.

Saunders, T., Baeck, P. 2015. *Rethinking Smart Cities from the Ground Up*. Nesta. www.nesta.org.uk/sites/default/files/rethinking_smart_cities_from_the_ground_up_2015.pdf (Accessed November 20, 2016).

Selwyn, N. 2002. E-stablishing an inclusive society? Technology, social exclusion and UK government policy making. *Journal of Social Policy*. 31:1, pp. 1–20.

Woods, E., Alexander, D., Labastida, R.R., Watson, R. 2016. UK Smart Cities Index. Assessment of Strategy and Execution of the UK's Leading Smart Cities. Commissioned by Huawei. http://www-file.huawei.com/-/media/CORPORATE/PDF/News/Huawei_Smart_Cities_Report_FINAL.pdf?la=en (Accessed April 24, 2017).

Index

Page numbers followed by f and t indicate figures and tables, respectively.

For Product Safety Concerns and Information please contact our EU
representative GPSR@taylorandfrancis.com
Taylor & Francis Verlag GmbH, Kaufingerstraße 24, 80331 München, Germany